Parental Involvement in the Education of Mentally Handicapped Children

Parental Involvement in the Education of Mentally Handicapped Children

P.S. Sukumaran
Department of Education
University of Kerala
Thiruvananthapuram

DISCOVERY PUBLISHING HOUSE
NEW DELHI—110 002

First Published - 2000

Reprinted - 2015

ISBN: 978-81-7141-520-5

Parental Involvement in the Education of Mentally Handicapped Children

Published by:

DISCOVERY PUBLISHING HOUSE PVT. LTD.

4383/4B, Ansari Road, Darya Ganj

New Delhi-110 002 (India)

Phone: +91-11-23279245, 43596064-65

Fax: +91-11-23253475

E-mail: discoverypublishinghouse@gmail.com

sales@discoverypublishinggroup.com

web: www.discoverypublishinggroup.com

Printed at:

Infinity Imaging Systems

Delhi

Acknowledgement

The author wishes to place on record his deep gratitude to all those who have helped in the successful completion of this study.

Words fail to express the author's profound indebtedness to his supervising teacher Dr. R. Sujatha Rani, Senior Lecturer, Department of Education, University of Kerala, for her constructive guidance, infinite patience and constant encouragement to complete the work successfully.

Dr. Vasantha Ramkumar, Professor and Head, Department of Education, University of Kerala, is also gratefully remembered and thanked for her untiring support and encouragement throughout the research work. Sincere thanks are also due to Dr. K.R. Sivadasan, Professor (Rtd.), Department of Education, University of Kerala, for his ingenious suggestions for the statistical analysis of the data.

The author acknowledges with gratitude the valuable help rendered by the principals, special teachers and social workers of the special schools for mentally retarded children in collecting the data. The parents of these retarded children deserve a special thanks for their whole-hearted cooperation and selfless help.

The invaluable suggestions, consistent support and timely help offered by all the members of the teaching faculty in the Department of Education, University of Kerala, and the Director and faculty members of the School of Behavioural Sciences, Mahatma Gandhi University, Kottayam, are gratefully acknowledged and deeply appreciated by the author. Above all, Dr. P.N. Gopalakrishnan Nair, former Principal of S.N.M. Training College, Moothakunnam is most kindly remembered and thanked for his immense inspiration as a mentor and guiding light in the author's professional life.

It is only fitting to add a word of thanks herein to the Librarians and office staff of the Department of Education and to the Librarians of the Kerala University Library, Thiruvananthapuram, NCERT Library, New Delhi and NIMH Library, Secunderabad, for providing necessary facilities for literature collection. The research scholars and M.Phil. students of the Department of Education are also thanked for their inspiration and encouragement.

Special thanks are also due to Dr. Verghese Leena, Senior Lecturer, Department of English, Baselius College, Kottayam for helping with the editing and proof reading of the manuscripts and to M/s. Copy Write, Ettumanoor, for word processing and photocopying of the manuscript on time.

Personal debts are the most difficult to express in formal terms. Yet the author wishes to take this opportunity to thank his family members for their support and prayers throughout this endeavour.

P.S. Sukumaran

PREFACE

"Parental Involvement in the Education of Mentally Handicapped Children" is a unique book. Parental involvement in any type of education is very important, especially when it is in the field of special education of mentally handicapped children.

The book includes five chapters. The introductory chapter provides a brief account of the evolution of education of mentally handicapped children with emphasis on the Indian scenario. It also includes the need and significance of the study and a summary of the research design. The second chapter deals with the literature review and relevant details on Family of the Mentally Handicapped, Socio economic status and Mental Retardation, Education of the Mentally Retarded, Parental involvement in the Education of Mentally Handicapped, etc.

The third chapter explains the research method adopted for the study. The fourth chapter presents the details of the statistical analysis, results and discussion. The fifth chapter includes the major findings, conclusions and suggestions.

Author

Contents

1 Introduction

Context of the Study

Mental retardation is a condition characterised by significant impairment in intellectual functions associated with or accompanied by deficits in adaptive behaviour during the development period. As compared to children of same age, the child with mental retardation has significant developmental delay and lags behind in cognitive, language, social, and occasionally motor functions as well.

The World Health Organisation has classified the mental retardation into four groups, namely, mild, moderate, severe, and profound. Mental retardation is observed to be prevalent in all societies and cultures. Throughout the world, the prevalence of the mental retardation is estimated to be 30 per thousand. As per the 1991 survey report of National Sample Survey Organisation, India has about nine million mentally retarded children under 14 years of age (RCI, 1996, p. 6). Nearly 75 per cent of the people diagnosed to have mental retardation fall in the category of milk mental retardation, while the remaining 25 per cent having IQ 50 or below are classified as moderately, severely or profoundly retarded (NIMH, 1994, p. 1).

The history of the care, treatment, and education of the mentally retarded has been cyclical, alternating between compassionate concern and neglect and ridicule. Society's early treatment of the retarded was rooted in superstition rather than scientific knowledge. Prior to the nineteenth century, the mentally retarded were treated as fools, monsters, individuals possessed by the devil, or special children of God. During the nineteenth century, a more rational and more scientific attitude started to prevail. Itard, a French doctor greatly influenced the field of special education through his work with a 12 year old wild boy in the year 1799. Itard's training programme is generally considered as the first scientifically documented report of the treatment of a retarded person by means of planned education and stimulation.

Two significant trends occurred during the first half of the twentieth century. First, special classes for the retarded were established within the public school systems. Second, although residential institutions for the retarded were conceived for the purpose of treatment and education, this goal was for the most part abrogated, and a custodial care orientation emerged.

During the 1950s and 1960s a growing concern for the mentally retarded and an awareness that "not enough was being done for this population" developed. Parents of the retarded started to organise. Concurrent with this type of development, public enlightenment and awareness about retardation increased. In the early 1970s, a number of laws were designed to protect the rights of the handicapped. As Tse (1991) states, the trends in the 1990s are: (a) protecting human rights, (b) arousing public concern, putting normalisation into practice, (c) bridging the gap between research and practice, (d) developing more employment opportunities, (e) searching for a better curriculum, (f) caring for older people with mental retardation, (g) providing more quality education, and (h) improving the quality of life.

In India, formal efforts towards education of mentally retarded children were initiated in 1939 through the establishment of the first school for these children at Bombay (Narayan, 1994). Since then, the movement of special education has gained strength. The integrated education programme was conceived by the Government of India in the year 1976. The National Institute for the Mentally Handicapped was established in 1984 to organise and promote training, research, teaching and management services in the field of mental handicap. Normalisation or integrated education of disabled children began to gain importance and the separate section on disabled children in the National Policy on Education of 1986 (Ministry of Education, 1986) saw the emergence of University courses offering Bachelor's and Master's degrees in Special Education in India. The first part of the

1990s witnessed the professionals focussing on the vocational rehabilitation of the retarded individuals. Most importantly, "The Persons with Disabilities (Equal Opportunities, Protection of Rights and Full Participation) Act, 1995 received the assent of the President of India on the 1st January, 1996 (NIMH. 1995). Its provisions range from prevention, early detection to education, vocational training and employment, preferential treatment to people with disabilities and protection from negative discrimination. This comprehensive act covers all kinds of disabilities including mental retardation.

Every child has the right to education and if for reasons of either sensory, motor, or intellectual impairment he is unable to cope with the regular syllabus then he deserves the benefit of special education which is tailored to suit his special needs. The aim of special education is for teaching them independent living skills that are necessary to live in society with confidence.

In the case of mentally handicapped individuals, their intellectual ability is below average and the degree of impairment varies from person to person. This is reflected in their adaptive behaviour, necessitating an individualised instructional programme. The current trend in planning the programme is not to depend on IQ scores but to make a functional assessment for grouping, programing and implementation. For mentally retarded children a function oriented special curriculum is required. Ecology based curriculum and activity based Individualized Educational Programme are the current trends in the special education of mentally handicapped children (Narayan, 1994, pp. 1-7).

There is increasing recognition within developmental, educational, and sociological theories that both school and home are important institutions and socialise and educate children. While theorists have identified inherent conflicts and lack of complementarity between these two institutions, most current theories stress the need for connections between families and schools (e.g., Epstein, 1990). Within the framework of home-school connections, much of the specific debate and hope for change focuses on parent's involvement in their children's schooling. Several studies have demonstrated the positive effect of parent involvement in children's schooling across a wide range of populations and ages (Epstein, 1983; Fehrmann *et al.*, 1987; Reynolds, 1989; Anderson, 1994).

Professionals working in the field of mental retardation are increasingly realising the necessity to involve families having children with mental retardation early enough in the habilitation programmes. This is precisely for the reason that such an involvement not only helps in strengthening the families but also ensures meaningfulness to the services. In a developing country like India the responsibility for caring and bringing up a child throughout his life falls on the parents and families (NIMH, 1994, p. 31).

There are many examples nowadays of parental participation in educational programmes, wherein parents have amply demonstrated their competence as 'teachers' and 'tutors'. As Adams (1986, p. 142) states, "parents are, first of all, home teachers,...parents teach their children the skills of daily living, they serve as models for appropriate behaviour and by listening to and talking with their children they make the most of the environment around them." From the early days of the America Headstart Programme, in the 1960s, introduction of Portage in America in the late 1960s, its advent in the UK in 1976, and its widespread application by the end of the 1980s, all attest to the powerful influence parents can exert in their own children's development.

Many facets have been explored with reference to specific special needs and curriculum areas; for example, involvement of parents in developing reading skills in children with Down's syndrome have been studied extensively by Buckley (1985) and Buckley *et al.* (1986). Carr (1980) and Newson and Hipgrave (1982) who have provided blue prints for parents along the lines of helping the handicapped children which include teaching and behaviour management strategies.

Westmacott and Cameron (1981) and Herbert (1985) in their books written specifically for parents, dealing with 'problem behaviour', suggested a number of management and coping strategies.

Turnbull and Turnbull (1978) have listed certain reasons for the enhancement of the parental role in educational programmes for the handicapped : (a) The experimental evidence that parents can influence positively the development of their children through teaching them at home. (b) The encouraging results of early intervention in ameliorating some of the developmental deficits associated with moderate and severe handicaps. (c) The success of parents in bringing litigation to establish the educational rights of their children. (d) Federal legislation, notably Public Law 94-142, that sets forth clear standards for parental involvement in the educational process.

Similarly, Reddi (1994) too has stated the advantages of family's involvement in special education programmes as, (a) effective results in achievement of objectives for child with mental handicap, (b) easier generalization occurs, because of uniformity of goals within institution and home, (c) reducation in confusion, in learning new concepts due to uniformity of teaching strategies adopted in institution and home, and (d) evolves a complementary relationship between staff and family in order to develop appropriate support for child, both at the institution and home.

All these evidences point towards a considerable potential for a greater amount of cooperative work between school and home, in devising and carrying out learning and behaviour management programmes.

Need and Significance of the Present Study

Parenting is a complex, dynamic process that affects both parent and child. A parent develops and uses the knowledge and skills required to plan for children, give birth to them, and/or rear and care for them (Morrison, 1978). Parenting is the most essential and enduring profession acknowledged by society, but it is one for which most participants are inadequately prepared.

Psychologists, educators, and sociologists all agree that the family is the most significant single influence on the development of the child. The role of parents in the structure and product of education is child centred now, and also to think of education in terms of parentless child is a meaningless speculation. It necessarily follows that education of the child is determined to a large extent by the varied and dynamic role of parents. Before a child can be expected to make adequate school and community adjustments, he must have learned to make reasonable home adjustments.

The home, or some proper substitute situation provided through the home, has the responsibility for the physical care and health maintenance of the mentally retarded child. As far as he is able to do so, the child should be taught to care for his own physical and health needs. It is in the home that the child must learn to walk and talk. The home has the responsibility for the child's all important early language learnings. It is the responsibility of the parent; or parent substitute, to provide the mentally retarded child with experiences which acquaint him with his environment. It is the responsibility of the home to provide opportunities for constructive play, and to provide contacts with recreational outlets in terms of the child's needs and interests. Another important responsibility of the home is to inculcate in its mentally retarded member a body of socially acceptable habits and attitudes.

Home and school have cooperative duties toward the retarded child. The home has the responsibility of preparing the child for school entrance, and if school facilities are available for him in terms of the needs, to admit him in school. The home has the responsibility of abetting the efforts of the school in every reasonable manner It should augment the teachings of the school by continuing as the child's teacher in his out of the school hours, nor primarily academically, but rather in terms of the child's social and emotional development.

The parents of retarded children need a great deal of information about such subjects as diagnosis, treatment, management, and support services. Successful relationship between parents and professionals depend on mutual trust and understanding. Parents can assist in the identification, assessment, and programing of their children and in the implementation and evaluation of their children's programmes.

Hence, the involvement of parents in the education of mentally handicapped children is taken up for the present study. The investigator intends to study the extent of parents' involvement in developing basic living skills in the mentally retarded children, their existing and expected levels of involvement in the educational decision-making, efforts taken by school authorities and teachers for enhancing parental involvement, and the perception of parents and teachers with regard to parental guidance and counselling.

In India, especially in Kerala not much research has been done in this area to-day. Identification of the existing and expected levels of parental involvement in the education of mentally handicapped children and studying the role of teachers in enhancing parental involvement remains highly significant in this context.

Statement of the Problem

The problem under investigation is the involvement of parents in the education of their mentally handicapped children. The study is entitled : "*A Study of the Parental Involvement in the Education of Mentally Handicapped Children*".

Definition of Terms

Operational definitions of the important terms used in the present study are given below for the sake of clarity.

Parental Involvement

Parental involvement is described in the child development literature as the degree to which a parent is "committed to his or her role as a parent and to the fostering of optimal child development" (Maccoby and Martin, 1983). It typically concerns the amount of effort put into child oriented versus other activity (Pulkkinen, 1982).

In this study, 'parental involvement' means the active role of parents at all stages of the education of their mentally retarded children.

Education

Here, it means the special education programmes for the mentally retarded children, which is provided primarily in special schools with special curriculum. This includes developing the basic living skills such as self care skills, motor skills, language skills, numerical ability, health and safety skills, social skills, vocational skills, and leisure time skills.

Mentally Handicapped Children

Mentally handicapped or mentally retarded children are those who are characterised by the phenomenon of mental retardation. There are many definitions of mental retardation. The latest definition of mental retardation adopted by the American Association on Mental Retardation (1992, p. 5) has evolved through a number of revisions and it states:

> Mental retardation refers to substantial limitations in present functioning. It is characterised by significantly subaverage intellectual functioning, existing concurrently with related limitations in two or more of the following applicable adaptive skill areas: communication, self-care, home-living, social skills, community use, self-direction, health and safety, functional academics, leisure and work. Mental retardation manifests before age eighteen.

The following four assumptions are essential to the application of the definition:

1. Valid assessment considers cultural and linguistic diversity as well as differences in communication and behavioural factors,
2. The existence of limitations in adaptive skills occurs within the context of community environments typical of the individual's

age, peers and is indexed to the person's individualised needs for supports,

3. Specific adaptive limitations often co-exist with strengths in other adaptive skills or other personal capabilities, and
4. With appropriate supports over a sustained period, the life functioning of the person with mental retardation will generally improve.

Objectives of the Study

The major objectivity of the study are:

1. To study the involvement of parents in developing the basic living skills (self-care, motor, language, numerical, health and safety, social, vocational, leisure) in mentally retarded children.
2. To investigate the existing the expected levels of parental involvement in the education decision-making,
3. To examine the efforts taken by the teachers and school authorities for enhancing parental involvement.
4. To study the parental perceptions with regard to the effect of associated problems in the education of retarded children and the services available for their education.
5. To study the extent of parental satisfaction in the method of training provided to the mentally retarded children.
6. To study the perceptions of parents and teachers with regard to parental guidance and counselling.

Methodology in Brief

This study is conducted on a sample of parents of 170 mentally retarded children studying in various special schools of Ernakulam and Kottayam districts of Kerala state and 85 special teachers teaching in these schools. The tools used for the collection of data are: (a) General Data Sheet, (b) Parent-Involvement Interview Schedule, (c) Parent-Involvement Questionnaire, and (d) Interview Schedule for Teachers. All the tools are developed by the investigator and administered on the sample. The data collected are analysed using 't' test, analysis of variance, least significant difference test, coefficient of correlation, chi-square test, and 'z' test of double proportion. The results obtained are interpreted accordingly.

Scope of the Study

This study is expected to throw light on the various aspects of one of the most important issues in modern special education, that is, parental involvement. The advantages of examining the different aspects of parental involvement in the education of mentally retarded children are many. Firstly, being an exploratory study it is expected to reveal many interesting findings and thereby increase the knowledge base regarding parental involvement. Secondly, concrete recommendations can be made to schools and families on different phases of parental involvement that can be targeted in interventions. Thirdly, the boundaries of parental involvement can be broadened from traditional practice of providing material supports and helping with homework. It is also hoped that, the findings of the study will help administrators and special educators to create an awareness among themselves about their own roles in enhancing parental involvement. Lastly, the findings of the study may give directions for further research in this area. In short, the investigator expects that the results of the study would be of immense use to all, concerned with the education and welfare of the mentally retarded children.

Limitations of the Study

Even though the investigator was cautious enough to make the present study as scientific as possible, certain limitations could not be avoided, which are inevitable in survey studies of this type. The following limitations should be taken care of, while generalizing of results.

1. Sample: The size of the sample (parents) studied was only 170 and also it was taken from only two districts of Kerala. A larger sample selected from all districts of the state could have given scope for wider generalization to the findings. Practical difficulties to contact the parents of mentally retarded children, which is a scattered population, did not permit the investigator to increase the sample size.

2. Participant observation as a data collecting technique, if employed, could have given more objective data.

3. While collecting data, the opinion of fathers and mothers were not recorded separately as it was not intended to do so. But the recording of the joint expression of the parental feelings prevented the investigator from elucidating the level of involvement of fathers and mothers separately.

4. Classification of the retarded children into mild, moderate and severe categories was done only on the basis of school records. The classification could have been made more scientific, if a standardised intelligence test was administered.

Despite all these limitations, it is hoped that the results of the study would be of much practical utility.

Format of the Report

The report consists of five chapters, namely :

Chapter 1 is the introduction which contains all the necessary parts of an introductory chapter.

Chapter 2 consists of the relevant background literature and abstracts of related research findings.

Chapter 3 present the details of the method of study, description of the sample and the sampling procedure, the tools used, the data collection procedures adopted, the details of the classification of sample, and the statistical techniques used for the analysis of data.

Chapter 4 deals with the analysis of data and the interpretation of results.

Chapter 5 provides a summary of the study, implications of the results and suggestions.

2

Review of Related Literature

The review of related literature is as important as any other component of the research process. It involves the systematic identification, location, and analysis of documents containing information related to the research problem. The major purpose of reviewing the literature is to determine what has already been done that relates to one's problem. Another important function of review is that it points out research strategies and specific procedures and measuring instruments that have and have not been found to be productive, in investigating one's problem. Being familiar with previous research also facilitates interpretation of the results of the study. Finally, these reviews give information which can either support or challenge the conclusions of the investigator's research and therefore provide clues for later research.

In India, research in the field of mental retardation is of recent origin. Consequently, research publications in this field is very limited. As can be seen in this chapter only a few reviews of Indian studies are included and most of the reviews reported are of studies conducted abroad. An abstract of relevant materials is presented here under appropriate heads.

Family of the Mentally Handicapped

The process of bringing up a child is rarely entirely pleasant, although in most families the rewards far more than compensate for the discomforts. Patience, understanding, ingenuity and strength are required in large measure from the parents of even a bright and healthy youngster. For the family of a retarded child, the situation is more complicated and more hazardous. The particular handicap of the child, the slowness of this development, the necessity of special arrangements for his physical care, training, and companionship, and the adjustments which must be made in the family's expectations for the future, combine to create pressure on the parents which tends to disrupt the normal family equilibrium. Added to this pressure may be tensions created by child's difficulties in interpersonal relationships, his slowness to learn, his immature self-control, and his handicap in communication. At the same time, the parent-child relationship is intensified by the child's prolonged immaturity and isolation from a peer group. In some instances, the child will remain emotionally and economically dependent upon his family throughout his life.

Thus the relationship between a retarded child and his family is not only more complex and ambivalent than the ordinary one, but also intense and prolonged.

1. Parental Reactions

A wide range of parental reactions have been documented on the discovery of the child's disability: shock, denial, despair, depression, and marital disintegration (Blacher, 1984); shock, anger, denial and rejection, blame and guilt, over protection and cognitive versus emotional acceptance (Hall and Richmond, 1984). Cunningham and Davis (1985) report that, they may feel inadequacy as parents and fear for the future, also they may experience feelings of bereavement and embarrassment. Kisanji's (1993) literature survey clearly indicates negative family and community actions towards the handicapped ranging from hiding, rejection, over protection, and even denying formal education to children with mental disability.

No two sets of parents or for that matter, any two parents themselves go through these stages in the same style, at the same level of involvement, or necessarily in the same order.

Some investigators have postulated that parental responses and adaptations to a child with handicaps may be an extension of the coping and adapting skills that they use in dealing with other family stressors (Fortier and Wanlass, 1984; Schneider, 1983).

2. Impact on Family

The birth of a mentally handicapped child has a profound effect on the structure, functioning, and development of a family. A child's severe symptoms can make even healthy, stable families anxious and defensive. Even the most mature parents worry about how to handle a mentally retarded child with behavioural problems without harming him further.

For decades, researchers have investigated the impact of a child with retardation on the members of his or her family. Among the outcomes that have been examined are the well being of the parents as individuals, the quality of their marital relationship, and the adjustment of the other children in the family. It is interestingly recognised that overall family adaptation in families with a child with mental retardation is quite varied, with some families coping well and others manifesting more serious problems (Bristol and Schopler, 1984).

Farber (1975), one of the first investigators in this area has pointed out that the presence of a handicapped child often represents a developmental delay in family evolution as well. He has defined the character of the crisis faced by families with mentally retarded children as an arrest in the family life cycle.

Hammer (1972, p. 10) recognised six periods of stress in the lives of families with exceptional children: (1) at birth or upon suspicion of the handicap, (2) at time of diagnosis and treatment of the handicapping condition, (3) as the child nears age of school placement, (4) as the child nears puberty, (5) as the child nears the age of vocational planning, (6) as parents age and the child may outlive them.

The family situation has been studied by several researchers along the following dimensions: (a) *The time dimension*: impacts are described as either temporary and time bound, or as chronic, the latter demonstrating an arrest in the life cycle of the family (Wikler, 1981; Wikler *et al.*, 1981), (b) *The range dimension*: impacts are either related to limited and specific areas of functioning; or are generalised (Chess *et al.*, 1980), and (c) *The psychological dimension:* impacts are related to family climate in terms of marital satisfaction, social support and psychological well-being (Friedrich and Friedrich, 1981).

An exhaustive review of research reports reveal a wide range of impacts: radical changes in household tasks over time, changing relationships with friends and relatives, diminution of social activities, excessive time commitments, neglects of needs of family members who are not handicapped, difficulties in maintaining stable marital relationships, and limited independence (Lefley, 1987); social isolation, role overload, depression, chronic fatigue (Jennings, 1987; Lefley, 1987); chronic sorrow, continuing feelings of guilt, advocacy when no time exists, permanency planning, and the desire to completely reject the care giving role (Jenings, 1987); psychological distress that is associated with problems of daily living (Schilling *et al.*, 1984); anxiety and depression (Breslau and Davis, 1986); high levels of anxiety that restrict decision-making skills (Janis, 1982); additional financial costs, stigma, considerable amounts of time given to personal care of the child, interruptions of family sleep, social isolation, limitations in recreational activities, difficulty in handling behavioural problems, difficulty in shopping and other normal household routines, and pessimistic feelings about the future (Moroney, 1981); more frequent spousal interchanges with regard to the child (Levy-Shiff, 1986); impact on the direct interactions of family members with the retarded child, the functional integration of the family unit and its relation to the outside world, and the feelings and attitudes of family members (Stanhope and Bell, 1981, p. 689); parental concern about the impact on siblings and peers in the neighbourhood (Powell and Ogle, 1985); drain on the family finances, difficulty in travelling, and the attendance at the hospital appointments, excessive demand of time, attention, and energy (Mittler *et al.*, 1986; Dupont, 1980); marital dissatisfaction (Crnic *et al.*,1983); financial burden (Rees and Emerson, 1983; Chetwynd, 1985;. Gunn and Berry, 1990; Preetha Rajam, 1987; Kurtz, 1983, p. 234; Kibria, 1994); and burdensome, stressful, frustrating, and alienating for parents (Farzanch, 1985); increased demand of time, mental and physical ill health (Kropf, 1990); and negative functioning during marital and parent-child interactions (Floyd and Zmich, 1991).

Problems in accessing social support for families of handicapped children (Friedrich and Friedrich, 1981), and acute problem for single parent mothers have been reported. Kazak and Marvin (1984) found that the social support network of the parents of handicapped children were smaller than those of the comparison group.

It is commonly accepted that both mothers and fathers are deeply affected by the presence of retarded child in the family. Mothers, however, have been found to be more vulnerable (Margalit and Raviv, 1983).

While some families do experience increased stress when there is a disabled member, it is also true that many report no such effect.

Farber (1975) reports that many studies treat the family with a retarded child as if the presence of the child were the only problematic element in its existence. But families with retarded children also consist of parents and siblings who must face the same predicaments and dilemmas faced by other people. The retarded child is just one of the several potentially problematic elements in a family. Farber (1975, 1976) further observes that not all families find living with a severely or profoundly retarded child equally difficult. There are broad variations in the sense of stigma, in the amount of time and energy demanded, in the amount of family resources, and in prior loyalties and commitments.

Tymchuk (1983) states that although the birth of a mentally retarded child usually requires some adjustment on the part of the parents, the reactions attributed to parents may be exaggerated and are still not well understood.

Turnbull and her colleagues (Turnbull and Behr, 1986; Turnbull and Turnbull, 1985) have documented, both descriptively and quantitatively, the joys, the rewards, and the personal growth that can result from the experience of being the parents of a child with mental retardation.

Townsend *et al.* (1989) in research on care-giving by adult (non retarded) children for their aged parents, unexpectedly found that overtime adult children adapted to the care-giving role and some improved in psychological functioning, rather than manifesting the deterioration that the researchers had originally expected. Some preliminary support for this adaptational hypothesis is suggested by the research conducted by Seltzer and Krauss (1989a) an older mothers who provided long term care for their adult sons and daughters with retardation.

Similarly, the sample of older mothers with retarded adult children reported substantially higher life satisfaction than did a sample of care-givers for the elderly and slightly less care giving stress and feelings of burden than other samples of care-givers (Friedrich *et al.*, 1983; Gallagher *et al.*, 1985; Zarit *et al.*, 1980). The study conducted by Glidden *et al.* (1988) on the positive family impact of adopted children with mental retardation showed that 62 per cent of the mothers responded that they had become better people as a result of the adoption, citing changes such as greater tolerance, less selfishness, more sympathetic attitudes, and increased compassion. Similarly, 69 per cent of the mothers believed that they had become more flexible since their child's placement, and 54 per cent of the mothers with other children thought that their children had also become more flexible. Overall, mothers perceived that the impact of the placement was quite positive for their other children, with 67 per cent reporting no discernible negative effects, 54 per cent responding that other children were happier and 52 per cent that other children were better people as a result of the placement.

The study conducted by Anderson (1993) showed that there is no significant difference between the depression and anxiety levels of parents with and without children having mental retardation. Similarly, Leary and Verth (1995) examined the functioning of 22 families of extreme Third World poverty in which there was a child with severe mental handicap and found that despite a very restricted cash income, the family units endured, and 79 per cent of the marriages were stable.

3. Impact on Siblings

Many studies have been reported on the impact of retarded children on their normal siblings. Vadasy *et al.* (1984) found increased vulnerability of the siblings to stress and other problems, while Simeonsson and Mc Hale (1981) observed that siblings are supplanted in their role by the slower-developing retarded child.

Hattersley *et al.* (1987, p. 40) report that brothers and sisters are almost inevitably required to be tolerant, to keep quiet, let mothers devote much time to feeding, or reluctantly share toys to keep the peace. Games and toys may be spoilt, or homework interrupted. Children can still experience deeply hurtful teasing at school about their sibling's condition. The problems may become worse in adolescence when the behaviour of the disabled child in the home may intrude on the social life of a teenage brother or sister.

It appears that siblings play different roles in the family depending upon their age and sex. A study by Breslau *et al.* (1981) revealed that older sisters were under more stress than older brothers. Vadasy *et al.* (1984) in their review suggest that the "sister of a handicapped child appears to be most vulnerable".

While in most families, parents function as the primary care-givers for persons with mental retardation throughout their lives, in some families siblings assume this responsibility after the parents are no longer there to provide care. Research on siblings of persons with mental retardation, like research on families in general, has tended to emphasise relationships among siblings in childhood (Simeonsson and Bailey, 1986; Siltzer, 1985; Simeonsson and Mc Hale, 1981). While most of this body of research describes the negative impacts on siblings of a brother or sister with retardation, some research has provided evidence of positive adaptation.

In some of the few studies that included a wide age range (12 to 69 years of age), Bugn (1989) reported numerous age-related and birth order differences in the relationships between siblings. For example, siblings who were several years older than the sibling with retardation were more satisfied with the sibling relationship than those several years younger than the sibling with retardation.

Similarly, Zetlin (1986) described the heterogeneity of sibling relationships between adults with mild mental retardation and their brothers and sisters. She noted that these relationships differed at various points in the family life span, with middle-aged siblings perceived by their sisters and brothers with retardation to be the closest and most supportive, while young adult siblings were perceived as being less dependable.

Seltzer *et al.* (1991) found that mothers between the ages of 55 and 85 reported feeling less stressed and less burdened by care-giving when there was more social interaction between the non-handicapped sibling and those with retardation. Further, the majority of mothers (62%) expected a sibling to assume the responsibility for their son or daughter with retardation after they are no longer able to provide care or supervision.

Studies point out that the assumption that siblings are inevitably affected negatively by the presence of a handicapped child is incorrect. When siblings were given direct responsibility for the care of the handicapped child, they tended to express satisfaction (Chintz, 1981; Schreibman *et al.*, 1983), particularly when the results of their efforts helped the handicapped child.

Sukumaran (1986) found that most of the normal brothers and sisters of mentally retarded children as sympathetic, helpful and understanding and did not seem to have been adversely affected. In their study, Auletta and DeRosa (1991) found that siblings of mentally retarded children have no special difficulties in psycho-social adjustment when compared with the siblings of normal children. Similarly, the study conducted by Weinger (1992) revealed higher feelings of self worth among siblings of mentally retarded children.

From the above discussion it can be concluded that a retarded member has an impact on the parents and siblings. The impact need not necessarily be adverse, but some modification in roles, communication networks, norms, power structure, decision-making patterns and the relationships of the family to the community is inevitable. The decisive factors identified are age and gender of child, sibling and parent, social class, birth order, family size, degree of retardation, presence of behavioural problems in the retarded child and the educational status of parents and siblings.

4. Parental Need for Guidance and Counselling

All parents wish for a healthy and a normal child. However, when a disabled child is born all hopes of the parents are shattered. This calls for a life long adjustment. In order to assist the parents in dealing effectively with the situation counselling is essential, as a part of the whole management plan. It aims at helping parents understand and accept the child's problems. This also helps them in making plans appropriate to the capability of the mentally retarded person.

The literature is full of countless testimonials that when a child is born with marked impairment, the parents are all too often left in ignorance or, worse, yet, with inappropriate information, injurious to them as much as to the child. So a proper system should be established, which will assure that the family is enabled, right from the start, to develop its own resources in meeting the needs of the new arrival.

Families with moderately to severely handicapped children have many problems in common, regardless of the specific nature of the handicapping condition. Five problems that appear to weaken the family's solidarity, and that require special attention from the researcher and the service provider (Gallagher, 1983) are that : (1) the child has lesser ability to form reciprocal and mutual reinforcing transactions with parents, (2) the handicapped child's greater dependency needs force the caretakers within the family to spend more time and effort coping with the child's needs. (3) there is the danger of a lessening of mutually reinforcing social interactions with other adults and children within the extended family, friends and neighbours, (4) families must cope with the symbolic death of their aspirations and hopes, (5) many varied family structures must cope with these problems. These increased needs call upon modified behaviour on the part of family members.

According to Peshawaria (1994, p. 41), parent counselling if given early and effectively, can help parents to come to terms with their child's disability, develop right understanding about the condition of the child and positive attitudes towards the child, help involve parents in training their child, promote healthy interactions within the family and with the community thus promote positive development of both child and family members.

From the experience on developing services for pre-school mentally handicapped children in New Delhi, Balasundaram (1989, p. 57) emphasises the need for early counselling of parents for their active involvement in the training of their mentally handicapped child.

Family therapy for families of mentally handicapped children, which aims to increase acceptance of the child and to identifying family roles, gives practice to the family in relating to the child's problems, etc. (Turner, 1980). Typically the whole family, including the deviant member, is involved in therapy sessions and it is suggested that the mentally handicapped child should participate through the use of drawing, music, clay modelling and so on in place of verbal communication (Gomersall, 1981).

Black (1982) advocates family therapy at times of crisis and gives examples of successful interventions, some of which combine family therapy with behavioural methods, resulting in a highly appropriate model of help for parents who wish for this type of approach. Preetha Rajam (1987) found that the parents are not having apt guidance to give a proper environment and proper behaviour to the mentally retarded children.

According to Turnbull and Turnbull (1982), one belief inherent in the parent involvement policies is that all parents should be both counselled and trained to be the child's teacher. This belief is based on the following assumptions: (a) all parents need and want counselling, (b) all parents can and should be teachers of their children, (c) all parents are interested and willing to receive counselling and training to fulfil this role, and (d) all handicapped children will benefit from receiving instruction at home.

But parents are not homogeneous; predictably, they have different reactions to being counselled. What is beneficial for one parent is not necessarily beneficial for another. Just as children have individual styles of learning, so parents have individual preferences for counselling, support, and other involvement.

Parent counselling can generally be divided into two major strategies. The first attempts to deal with the emotions and attitudes of the parents and their feelings about the parent-child relationship while the second focuses on preparing the parents to change child behaviours and parent-child interactions (Gallagher and Bristol, 1989).

In short, parent counselling is an essential scientific step towards helping the family and the retarded child.

Socio-Economic Status and Mental Retardation

It is uniformly accepted today that poverty and lack of a stimulating environment in childhood causes retardation, usually of a milder variety, but children so affected will not be able to complete regular schooling.

It has been found in the western countries that poverty and cultural deprivation are interrelated to a very large extent. Cultural deprivation consists of a complex set of conditions like lack of stimulating environment, lack of verbal communications with adults, poor sensory experience, and other deleterious environmental factors usually associated with poverty. Scientific evidence indicates that cultural deprivation induces intellectual subnormality among children (Prabhu, 1977).

Low socio-economic status is one of the most consistently found correlates of poor academic achievement and mild mental retardation. One of the explanations of the processes underlying these relationships is that, home environments influence learner characteristics as early childhood environments have an impact on learner's readiness for and response to the educational setting; cognitive style vary according to socialisation patterns; and self-concepts, aspirations, and motivation are influenced by the parental values and student identification patterns and are further shaped by school climate variables (Brantlinger and Guskin, 1987; p. 7).

It has long been documented that low income and minority students' IQ and achievement scores are lower than those of high income and majority children. Mare (1981) projected an increasing dependence of educational attainment on social origins. Proportionately more black and other minority children are placed in special classes (Anderson and

Anderson, 1983; Argulewicz, 1983; Educational Testing Service, 1980; Ford *et al.*, 1982; Pink, 1982; Rolloway and Smith, 1983; Ysseldyke *et al.*, 1982).

Low social class status and poverty conditions have important effects on human growth and development. According to Prabhu (1977) malnutrition is one of the major problems in India as it is widespread in the country. Malnourished children are known to show noticeable deficiencies in the intellectual area and the degree of intellectual deficiency in many ways is directly related to the degree of malnutrition.

Using a dynamic model for preventing mental retardation in the population McDermott and Altekruse (1994) found that prevention of mild mental retardation can most effectively be accomplished through lowering the rate of poverty and its resultant deprivation.

The above review clearly reveals the relationship between poverty, cultural deprivation, lower socio-economic status and mental retardation.

Education of the Mentally Handicapped

Education and training of the mentally retarded person has been a challenge for centuries. There has been tremendous advances in the past few decades with an increase in the number of qualified special teachers, special schools, special teacher training programmes and special teaching methods throughout the world. Special classes do not serve as a mere respite for parents any more, but specific individualised educational programmes are tailored for each of the children based on the current level of performance of the child and carried out. The progress is monitored periodically and fresh programmes are developed. As long as the right to education exists and as long as there are disabled individuals there will be a continuous need for special education. With the U.N. Declaration of "Education for all by AD 2000", the special education of mentally retarded children has gained further importance.

1. Objectives

The objectives of special education for the mentally handicapped are no different from general educational aims of all children, namely, through the provision of opportunities to acquire skills and knowledge, to lead the child towards the fullest realisation of his potential. For the wide range of the retarded, a similarly wide range of provision is needed, ranging from short term remedial teaching of the basically normal child who is retarded because of minor health or environmental factors to permanent institutional care of the most severely mentally handicapped. The goals for each individual need to be set. For many of the more severely retarded the goals may best be formulated in terms of self-confidence, social competence and the acquisition of a range of skills rather than in terms of "educational" objectives, although these latter should not be underestimated. Such an approach is more likely to lead to a successful transfer to adult life and acceptance by the community than is concentration on an academic syllabus presented in a manner which can only reinforce failure.

Mentally retarded persons can lead successful adult life by becoming independent in personal, social, and occupational spheres if proper training programme can be imparted from the beginning. For the achievement of this goal, carefully planned training programme has to be carried out at different levels such as pre-primary, primary, secondary, pre-vocational and vocational with appropriate emphasis on the curricular goals at different levels.

Outlining the steps for ensuring equal educational opportunity for the handicapped, the National Policy on Education states that the objective should be "to integrate the physically and mentally handicapped with the general community as equal partners, to prepare them for normal growth and to enable them to face life with courage and confidence" (NCERT, 1987, p. 3).

Objectives of education of mentally retarded children differ from the education of the normal in the lack of emphasis on academic achievement, and the emphasis on development of personality and adequacy in occupational and social areas. The educational programme should enable the retarded child to develop: (a) social competency, (b) occupational competency, (c) emotional security and independence, (d) habits of health and sanitation, (e) the minimum essentials of the tool subjects, (f) leisure time activities, (g) necessary skills to become adequate member of a family, and (h) necessary skills to become adequate member of a community.

2. Service Delivery System

A wide variety of educational service delivery options is available for the mentally handicapped pupils. The figure given by Berdine and Meyer (1987, p. 221) illustrates a continuum of special education services.

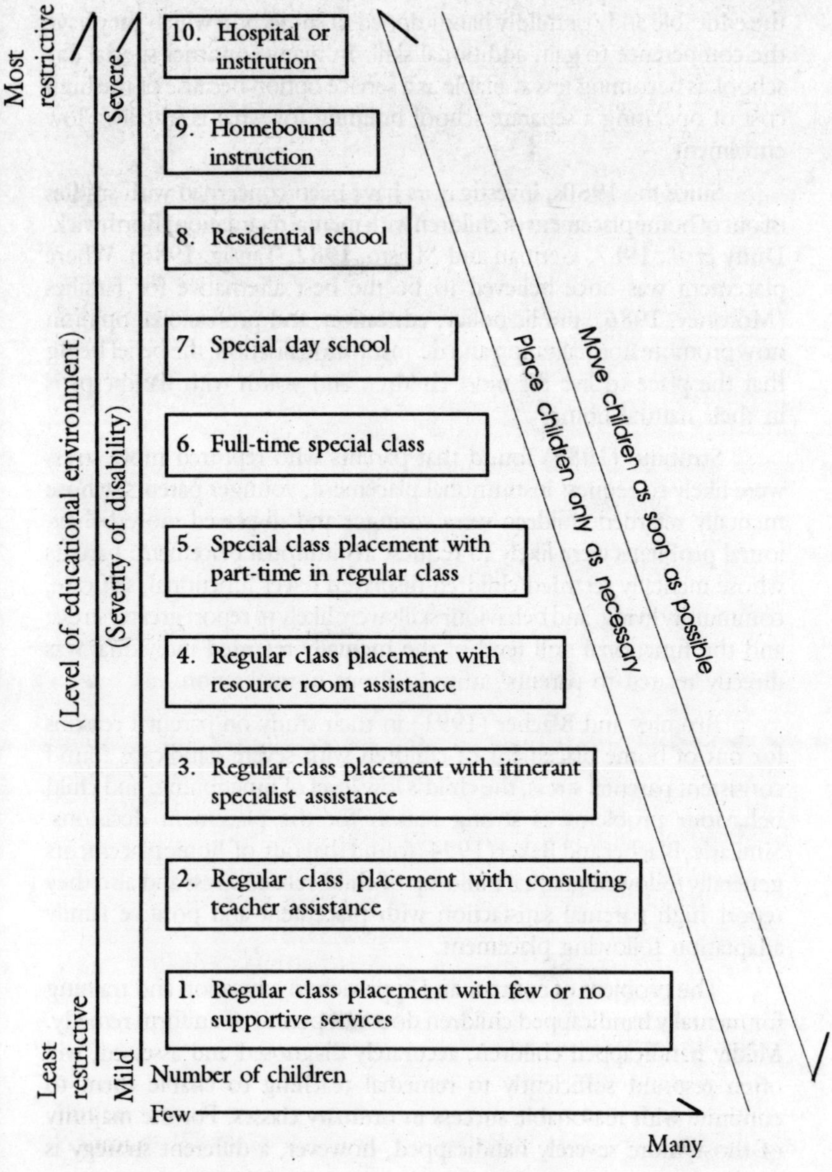

Fig. 2.1 : Continuum of Special Education Services

In schools that have a comprehensive array of services, trainable mentally handicapped pupils may be mainstreamed into classrooms for the educable and/or mildly handicapped in subjects in which they have the competence to gain additional skill. In many countries special day school, is becoming less available as a service option because of the high cost of operating a separate school building for what is usually a low enrolment.

Since the 1950s, investigators have been concerned with studies of out of home placement of children with mental retardation (Borthwick-Duffy *et al.*, 1987, German and Maisto, 1982; Tausig, 1985). Where placement was once believed to be the best alternative for families (Moroney, 1986), public policy, education, and professional opinion now promote normalisation and de-institutionalisation, the belief being that the place to live for most children and youth with handicaps is in their natural home.

Strobino (1984) found that parents who reported more stress were likely to request institutional placement; younger parents, whose mentally retarded children were younger and displayed more behavioural problems were likely to request institutional placement; parents whose mentally retarded children displayed fewer functional, self care, community living, and behaviour skills were likely to report greater stress; and the functional skill level of the mentally retarded individual was directly related to parents' attitude about normalisation.

Bromley and Blacher (1991) in their study on parental reasons for out-of-home placement of children with severe handicaps found consistent parental stress, the child's low level of functioning, and child behaviour problems as strong reason for the placement decisions. Similarly, Blacher and Baker (1994) found that out-of-home placements generally followed gradual build-up of child-related stress and also they report high parental satisfaction with placement and positive family adaptation following placement.

The problem of content and approach to education and training for mentally handicapped children does not permit of uniform remedy. Mildly handicapped children, accurately diagnosed and assessed, will often respond sufficiently to remedial teaching to enable them to continue with reasonable success in ordinary classes. For the majority of those more severely handicapped, however, a different strategy is required.

So there exists many models of service delivery and it is the duty of the professionals and parents to decide which specific model is more suited to the unique needs of any single retarded child.

5. *Curriculum*

Historically, educational services for the mentally retarded children were designed to be provided in segregated settings. With the efficacy research done in recent years, the idea of providing services in as close to the normal environment as possible became the trend. While developing such a programme, the varied needs of mentally retarded children, with different age and severity levels, belonging to different socio-economic groups, and having various cultural practice should be taken into consideration which makes it difficult to develop curriculum and plan programme uniformly (Narayan, 1994).

A good function-oriented curriculum should include: activities that are age appropriate, community referenced, comprehensive, future referenced, efficient, and integrated. According to Baine (1986), the curriculum should incorporate the instructions of motor, sensory, communications, social, personal and self-help skills into activities that are functional in the learner's natural environments, including his home, school, recreational and vocational settings.

The inclusion of academic skills in the curriculum such as reading, writing, and arithmetic must be absolutely function-oriented and that the mentally retarded person is able to use what is learnt in his daily living. In addition to academic, self care and communication skills, the curriculum should provide for recreational skills, home management skills, health and safety and community oriented skills which contribute to social competence. The curriculum should take into consideration, the economic, social, cultural and such environmental characteristics of the society in which the mentally retarded child lives. This should be emphasised especially in the vocational training aspects (Narayan, 1994).

As per the reseaıch reports and literature, the following are the specific areas to be included in the curriculum.

Language : Language deficiencies in the form of speech defects occur in retarded children. Instruction in reading and other language arts skill areas has been given considerable attention in most curricula for mildly and moderately retarded students. Professionals have felt that mildly retarded students could learn to read that would fall behind in achievement levels, possibly attaining third or fourth grade reading skills. Moderately retarded learners have been thought to be capable of reading cautionary words, with little need for moving beyond that level. Written expression has been generally overlooked in curricula for the moderately retarded, while mildly retarded learners have been expected to master the spelling of basic words and construct basic sentences (Langone, 1986; p. 237). According to Kaczmarek (1985), speech, language, and communication skills must be an important programme component for all retarded learners as it is a prime determinant of their successful community integration.

Arithmetic: Teaching retarded students arithmetic skills has long been a priority of special educators. Traditionally, mildly retarded learners were expected to learn by rote arithmetic skills at about the third grade level. Moderately retarded learners were thought to be able to count basic groups of objects and add and subtract simple numbers. Severely retarded learners were not expected to learn arithmetic skills. Research findings have provided evidence that these students can learn more advanced arithmetic skills. For example, Lancioni (1982) used non-handicapped peer tutors to teach abstract problem solving to retarded elementary school students. Smeenge *et al.* (1980) in an applied behaviour analysis study, demonstrated the effectiveness of using a task analysis for teaching measurement skills to moderately retarded students.

Self-help Skills: One of the most critical problems confronting educators who work with the severely and profoundly retarded is that of incontinence. Incontinence refers to the involuntary passing of urine or faeces outside an appropriate toileting area. So it is very essential that toilet training is given priority early in life.

Severely and profoundly retarded persons frequently do not feed themselves, dress themselves or perform basic personal hygiene tasks such as bathing, tooth-brushing, and hair care. For the acquisition of these skills, a mentally retarded child needs special training. The mentally retarded persons, even with profound retardation can learn some of these skills with systematic training.

Independent living skills: The domain of independent living is potentially so large, it is generally narrowly defined in terms of the "general domestic" and "general community living" roles and related skills commonly identified as essential for handicapped students. Relevant research on programme development and instructional technology has been concentrated in the areas of home-living (cooking, cleaning, telephone use); use of community facilities (restaurants, grocery stores); mobility in the community (bus riding, street crossing); personal appearance (dressing, laundry, grooming); use of money (coin summation, change computation, banking); and health care (medication, first aid) (Cuvo and Davis, 1983).

Independent living in our society also requires skills in such areas as obtaining and maintaining employment, providing for one's own health care, participating in leisure functions, and interacting with other persons in a socially acceptable manner. The development of adaptive skills by the severely and profoundly retarded in these areas has recently received a considerable amount of attention from behaviour modifiers. A common problem area for severely and profoundly retarded persons is deficient gross motor skills. Frequently, these deficiencies are exemplified by serious delays in the development of basic motor skills such as walking and running, and the absence of the more advanced skills such as swimming and climbing. These gross motor deficiencies present a serious handicap to these children in a number of respects. Hence, special training in these areas is very essential (Whitman, *et al.*, 1983, p. 173).

Recreational skills: Leisure service for children and adults with mental retardation historically have, unfortunately, han relatively low priority. These individuals currently may lack the skills needed to participate in traditional recreation activities (Wehman and Schleien, 1981). In addition, they may have extensive amounts of free time that is not a source of enjoyment, pleasure, or satisfaction and, thus, may be viewed as negative and undesirable (Rynders and Schleien, 1991). This shortage of appropriate leisure services for those with mental retardation is particularly unfortunate because leisure participation is an important aspect of successful community adjustment (Rynders and Schleien, 1988).

An examination of the leisure services typically available to children and adults with mental retardation reveals a substantial gap between the services needed and those currently offered (Dattilo, 1991a).

Hutchison and Lord (1979) described the process of integrating individuals with disabilities and recreational activities as one that (a) provides opportunities for them to experience participation and enjoyment similar to that of their peers without disabilities, (b) allows them to develop their skills and confidence, (c) permits their participation in community activities of their choice, and (d) encourages them to develop self-confidence and dignity.

An example of a systematic approach to leisure education was presented by Dattilo and St. Peter (1991) via their model designed to facilitate independent leisure participation for young adults with mental retardation. The model involves development and implementation of a leisure education course supplemented with community support by a leisure coach and active participation of the person's family and friends.

According to Dattilo and Murphy (1991), professionals should not only include instruction in leisure skills in services for individual with mental retardation, but also adopt a more comprehensive strategy geared toward promoting an awareness of self, an appreciation of leisure, self-determination and decision-making relating to leisure, knowledge and utilisation of leisure resources, as well as development of skills in the areas of social interaction and recreational activities.

Individuals with mental retardation need to develop a repertoire of leisure skills that (a) is appropriate to their chronological age, (b) is based in their community, and (c) will facilitate successful integration into the community (Schleien *et al.*, 1985).

To meet the needs of individuals with mental retardation, leisure professionals, educators, and families must work together to improve and expand leisure services.

Vocational Skills: According to Thressiakutty (1994), vocational training plays an important role in the overall plan of the education for the mentally retarded persons. In order to maximise this potential, the handicapped must be educated and trained for the world of work and this training must begin at an early age and continue until successful employment.

Majority of the special schools in India limit their education to children up to 14 to 15 years. Instead of this, the special schools should extend their education programme to vocational training and placement, and should view their objective as total rehabilitation of mentally retarded or should coordinate with agencies providing such facilities (Myreddi, 1992).

Vocational competence may be viewed as the product of three interacting factors: (1) job responsibility, (2) task production competence, and (3) social-vocational competence. Job responsibility refers to behaviours that suggest a commitment to the job, such as being punctual, low absenteeism, and working continuously at job tasks

(Rusch and Mithaug, 1980; Sowers *et al.*, 1980; Wehman, 1981). The second factor, task-production competence, refers to the production of work tasks to company standards for accuracy and for expected rates. Social-vocational competence, a third factor that contributes to vocational competence (Schutz and Rusch, 1982), refers to the adequacy of an individual's interactions with coworkers or supervisors. These interactions may be directly related to an individual's ability to get along with other workers.

Chronic unemployment has been a bane to handicapped people in general and mentally retarded individuals in particular. Moreover, underemployment and low wages further exacerbate the employment problems experienced by mentally retarded individuals (Mithuag *et al.*, 1985). Although employment problems have plagued mentally retarded persons, the recent development of sophisticated competitive employment training and placement models (Brickey and Campbell, 1981; Krauss and Mac Eachron, 1982; Walls *et al.*, 1981; Wehman and Hill, 1981) demonstrate that with systematic support, some mentally retarded persons can succeed at work. Brickey and Campbell (1981) examined the outcome of mildly and moderately mentally retarded workers in a model programme. A retention rate of 59 per cent was reported in the first year of this project. In the second year the retention rate increased to 100 per cent.

Job retention data available on a limited sample of mentally retarded workers compares favourably with that on non-handicapped entry-level workers. Wehman *et al.* (1982) followed-up 63 moderately and mildly mentally retarded individuals that had been placed in entry-level jobs. After one year, 67 per cent of the mentally retarded subjects had retained their jobs. Likewise, Brickey *et al.* (1982) reported on 73 former sheltered workshop employees (mean age of 26.9 years) who were placed in competitive jobs. The majority of those workers were mildly or moderately retarded. Only two had IQs exceeding 70. A follow-up investigation revealed that 60 per cent of these workers were still employed.

Studies that identified causes for termination of mentally retarded employees (Brickey *et al.*, 1982; Ford *et al.*, 1984; Greenspan and Shoultz, 1981; Wehman *et al.*, 1982) cite one or more behaviours relating to job responsibility. Apart from poor attendance and punctuality, stealing was a frequently noted job responsibility problem. In addition, some employees failed to consistently attend to required tasks.

Studies (Brickey *et al.*, 1982; Ford *et al.*, 1984; Wehman *et al.*, 1982) have noted that problems in interacting with co-workers and/or supervisors contributed to job termination. Generation task-related social behaviour problems frequently cited included not following directions, not listening to others, back-talk to supervisors, blaming others (Greenspan and Shoultz, 1981), and failure to cooperate (O'Reilly and Weitz, 1980). Many unsuccessful mentally retarded workers also had critical personal social behaviour problems.

In addition, bizarre emotional behaviour has often been noted (Greenspan and Shoultz, 1981; Wehman *et al.*, 1982). Hygiene problem has also frequently cited (Ford *et al.*, 1984), as were personal appearance problems (Brickey *et al.*, 1982; O'Reilly and Weitz, 1980), general health (Ford *et al.*, 1984) and general unspecified inappropriate behaviour (Brickey *et al.*, 1982). Most important is the consistency replicated finding that a large proportion (greater than 40%) of mentally retarded workers who had failed to retain jobs did so for reasons related to social and life skills rather than for reasons directly related to performance of job tasks (Ford *et al.*, 1984; Greenspan and Shoultz, 1981).

The changing technology in the field of special education makes it possible to train to the optimum even severely and profoundly retarded. Over the last two decades intensive research in training methodology has shown the positive work potentials in mentally retarded adults and has opened further avenues for a contributive role.

It can be said that teaching social skills in the context of productivity will probably enhance mentally retarded workers' chances for employment.

In short, a good function oriented curriculum should include areas like self-help skills, basic language skills, numerical skills, independent living skills including social skills, recreational skills, and vocational skills.

Parental Involvement

Parents of handicapped children, who had long been in the background of special education, began in the 1940s and 1950s to organise themselves to represent the needs of handicapped children and wherever necessary, to provide educational services for those handicapped children not being served by the public schools. Now there is a great deal of emphasis in all fields of special education, but especially in the area of mental handicap, on parental involvement. The movement produced a great deal of activity, in which researchers established parent workshops or parent training programmes and evaluated their effects. The results were usually extremely positive.

The concept of parent participation pervades the requirements of the Education for All Handicapped Children Act of 1975 (PL 94-142) in USA. As a result of the enactment of this law, parental involvement and participation must begin at referral and continue through evaluation, placement, and individualised educational planning.

In UK, the Warnock Committee included references to parental involvement throughout their report and concluded: "we have insisted throughout this report that the successful education of children with special needs is dependent on the full involvement on their parents, indeed, unless parents are seen as equal partners in the educative process the purpose of our report will be frustrated" (DES, 1978).

A review of the research on families with mentally retarded offspring indicates that each historical era presents its own unique concerns about the role of the family in relation to mental retardation (Farber, 1986).

Report of an international study conducted by UNESCO (1995, p. 22) revealed that "most of the 63 countries studied, acknowledged the importance of parents in matters relating to special educational provision and some gave them a central role in the assessment and decision-making procedures, requiring their involvement in the process and seeking their assent to placement decisions."

The literature in special education regularly cities the need for parent involvement (e.g., Epstein, 1987; Turnbull, 1983). It points to the need for providing parents with some understanding of the nature of their children's problems and indicates the importance of sharing educational and treatment methods and goals.

Parental involvement through membership of school committees and parent teacher associations is important from the perspective of the political rights of parents to be represented in the running of institutions at which their children attend. However, such participation involves only a very few parents and typically is not concerned with the solving of individual children's learning difficulties. Parent involvement usually means parental contribution of money or time to achieve material benefits for the school in general.

More extensive parental involvement and input in the daily activities of school are viewed by many educators as essential (Lynch and Stein, 1982; Paul and Warnock, 1980). The research base which has demonstrated the significant impact of parental behaviour on the development of a child's motor, language, academic, and social skills serves as an additional impetus to expanding parental involvement in the child's education (D'Alonzo, 1982; Goldstein *et al.*, 1980).

From his experience with community based rehabilitation (CBR) in Guyana, O'Toole (1990b) reports, that "mothers expressed less feelings of sadness and anxiety, more confidence in themselves and more support from community members as a result of their involvement with CBR". In Philippines, Lagerkvist (1992) reports that 78 per cent of parents experienced some degree of improvement in their abilities as a result of CBR.

Evidence from several investigations suggests that parental participation in the development and monitoring of their child's special education programme is quite limited (Scanlon *et al.*, 1981; Lynch and Stein, 1982; Mc Kinney and Hocutt, 1982).

According to Turnbull and Turnbull (1982), parent involvement in their retarded child's educational programme may be a benefit to some parents and a detriment to others. Because not all parents are suited to be advocates, the Turnbulls pointed out the need to individualise programmes for parents as well as their exceptional children.

In short, erstwhile demarcations between teaching in the school and caring in the home are breaking down, with the advent of shared ventures, and complementary expertise.

1. Parent-Teacher Partnership

Parent-teacher partnership is now seen as the hallmark of a good service for retarded children. Starting at the time when the retardation is identified, continuing through pre-school and into the period of formal schooling, partnership between parents and professionals is seen as making a major contribution to meeting the needs of children, parents and professionals alike.

The roles of parent and professional in the field of disability are more than usually interactive and complementary. Parents have knowledge, skills, and experience in bringing up their child which they can offer to the professional and to other parents. Similarly, the knowledge and experience which professionals have accumulated in working with disabled children need to be passed on as skills to parents, to enable them to minimise the child's handicap by continuing teaching at home (Mittler *et al.*, 1986, p. 12).

Partnership involves sharing, not only of skills and information, but also of feelings. The notion of collective responsibility towards meeting children's special needs has been expounded elsewhere (Wolfendale, 1987c), in which key parts are played by designated personnel, including, parents. In this model, support is given to teachers by parents for the specialised, responsible jobs that they do. Reciprocally, teachers manifest their concern for parents of handicapped children, and their awareness of the stress and awesome responsibilities placed upon them (Millard, 1984; Russell, 1986).

Partnership between parents and professionals can take many forms, but certain elements can be clearly distinguished at the time of school leaving. Parents should be fully involved in the process of assessment of strengths and needs and should be seen as full members of the multi-disciplinary team, participating in detail in contributing their unique knowledge of their child's abilities and needs and in making decisions on how these can most appropriately be met locally (Centre for Educational Research and Innovation, 1983; p. 146).

Findings from diverse studies over the past two decades have revealed that an active parent-school partnership can contribute not only to the enhancement of the educational performance of students, but also to the improvement of parenting skills and family life (Cone *et al.*, 1985).

Although collaboration between parents and professionals has made considerable gains, it is good to recognise the serious obstacles which stand in the way of further progress in this direction. Those relevant to professionals include: (a) lack of discussion and preparation for parental participation in their basic training, (b) resistance and anxiety at the prospect of parental involvement in schools and programmes, problems in coming to terms with parents as partners, (c) a tendency to display their expertise and to adopt a didactic and sometimes authoritarian approach to parents, (d) difficulty in sharing their own limitation in knowledge and skill with parents, (e) tendency to make excessive demands on parents, and (f) failure to take account of the variety of needs and the range of variation from one family to another. Similarly, those relevant to parents include: (a) difficulty in coping with the demands that are made on them by professionals: they may be too busy, too exhausted or too pre-occupied with day to day problems presented by the handicapped person or by problems concerned with poverty, poor housing, unemployment or chronic ill health, (b) problems in reconciling demands made by the handicapped person with the needs of other members of the family, (c) tendency to attribute too much expertise to professionals, thereby resulting in the assumption that the staff will accept full responsibility for training a young person, (d) underestimation of the abilities and potential of their child to respond to independence training, possibly due to a history of earlier failure, and (e) where parents do succeed in collaborating with professionals in achieving goals for the handicapped person, they may tend to undermine 'professional expertise' by displaying competence in the use of the techniques and terminology traditionally regarded as the exclusive preserve of professionals (Mittler, 1979b).

It may not be easy to form a perfect partnership between parents and teachers, but it is essential for the harmonious development of the retarded children.

2. *Perception of Parents and Teachers*

To assess parents' perspectives concerning their own involvement in their children's educational programme, Winton and Turnbull (1981) conducted a two-phase interview with thirty–two mothers of pre-school handicapped children. When discussing factors important to them in their selection and evaluation of pre-schools, 65 per cent of the respondents said they needed consistent professional involvement with their child so that they could take a break from a full-time educational responsibility. When asked to rank the characteristics of an ideal pre-school, the respondents identified parent involvement as the least important characteristic.

According to Scott and Carran (1989), the issues and concerns of the parents of a handicapped child are generally the last thought on the minds of researchers, educationists, and practitioners. Parents complain of poor communication and a lack of dissemination of information, while practitioners, educationists, and researchers forge ahead looking for answers to alleviate the problems the handicapped child presents.

In their comparative study of parental participation in regular and special education programmes Yanok and Derubertis (1989) found that only a small proportion of each group reportedly had been contacted by either a teacher or school administrator to request their participation in a school related activity; substantial majorities of both groups nonetheless agreed that sufficient opportunities for involvement were available to them; most respondents expressed satisfaction with their present levels of participation in educational decision-making; more parents perceived education to be a mutual obligation of home and school.

In a study of forty educationally subnormal mentally, retarded children, all the parents whose children were in or moving into special education were interviewed to elucidate their views on the assessment process, and their involvement. The majority of parents felt that rather than being consulted about their children's possible learning and behavioural difficulties, they had been 'sent for and told' by the heads of the referring schools (Tomlinson, 1981).

Results of a qualitative analysis of the effects of the parent-teacher relationship on parent education behaviour (Melton, 1985) confirm that parents are interested in active participation in the education of their children and that they work with their children at home often without suggestions from teachers. They use strategies they experienced in school.

Results of the research conducted by Austin (1984) revealed that an overwhelming majority of the parents perceive themselves to possess significant role within their child's pre-school centre.

Another study carried out by Cleveland (1984) showed that parents who do not participate in school activities do not perceive opportunities to participate, do not perceive actual parental participation, and have greater feelings of alienation.

Stone (1987) highlights an uneasy relationship between professionals and parents going through the assessing and stating process, documenting, in so many instances, a story tale of misunderstanding and inadequate communication, despite best intentions. Parents in her study confessed to uncertainty about what kind of information professionals wanted to elicit from them, and how best to convey it.

Blacher and Turnbull (1982) report that teachers indicated the role of parents as "class room volunteers", was important for successful mainstreaming, although parents clearly did not see this as important.

Both parents and teachers did, however, seem to agree on the relative importance of home follow-up activities.

Results of the study conducted by Robinson (1994) showed that according to the perception of special education teachers parents are not active and equal participation at the IEP conference and do not participate in the decision making and writing of the IEP.

A study conducted by Minikutty (1993) on the perception of teachers on involvement of parents in the education and training of mildly and moderately mentally retarded children revealed that: (a) the existing level of parental involvement in developing self help skills, number concept, time concept, domestic skills, recreational skills, and vocational skills in mildly mentally retarded children and the level of involvement as decision-makers, advocates and supporters is very low; whereas teachers perceived a higher existing level of parental involvement in developing communication skills and social skills, (b) for mildly mentally retarded children, teachers expect a higher level of parental involvement in developing most of the skills as advocates and supporters; however, they expect only a lower level of parental involvement in the role as decision-makers.

In a study of 145 special teachers, Gerber *et al.* (1986) found that 71 per cent of the teachers believed that parents should be given the option to waive the requirement of parent participation and place decision-making solely in the hands of professionals. Further, 31 per cent indicated that parents do not make a significant contribution to the IEP process. This information, coupled with the fact that IEPs appear in some cases to be completed even before the meeting with the parents (White and Calhoun, 1987), indicates that professional attitudes toward parent participation may be as much an obstacle to the achievement of this goal as family characteristics.

3. Nature of Parental Involvement

The roles of parents of handicapped children have been outlined as that of advocates, resources, teachers, and counsellors by Knoblock (1983), Heyward and Orlansky (1984), and Brown and Moersch (1982).

In US Public Law 90-538, the Handicapped Children's Early Education Act, four types of parental activity were noted: (a) planning, development, operation and evaluation of project; (b) parent training; (c) participation in the educational and therapeutic components of the project; and (d) dissemination of information about the project (Gallagher and Bristol, 1989, p. 307).

Parents may feel that it is entirely the school's responsibility to plan their child's education. They may wonder how they can even help. However, they are valuable members of the Individualised Educational Programme (IEP) team. Downs *et al.* (1981, p. 18) give a list of the things that parents can offer educators:

A unique perspective: Since parents have been with the child all his or her life, they have a wealth of information to offer the school about the child's growth and development, behaviour, habits, feelings and responses. Parents have many insights about their children that educators never can have.

The parent as teacher: Most of the learning that children bring with them to school comes from their parents. Even without lesson plans, teacher's guides, and formal training, many parents have successfully taught their children valuable skills.

An extended classroom: Even after schooling begins, much of a child's interesting and meaningful learning takes place on trips and family outings, during talks, and as a result of other experiences offered by the parents.

A class room volunteer: Since the parent was the child's first teacher, the parent is naturally suited for the job of class room volunteer.

A consultant: Few teachers know as much about a specific handicapping condition, such as cerebral palsy, as the parent of a child with the condition. Teachers can benefit from the parents' experience with the child and his/her condition as they attempt to provide the best possible programme for the child.

A means for reinforcement of learning: The home that "backs up" the work of the school goes a long way of ensure good learning. Parents can provide opportunities for reinforcement of learning at home if they are aware of what is happening at school.

A handicapping condition places not only the child but also the entire family at risk. A model of parent involvement is needed that responds to the needs and preferences of families as well as of handicapped children. Parents are a heterogeneous rather than a homogeneous group. They have different degree of capability, time, energy, and interest in being educational decision-makers (Turnbull and Turnbull, 1982).

Losen and Losen (1985, p. 87) report that prior to the passage of PL 94-142 in 1975, few state statutes required any sort of the special education identification procedures, special education team meetings or consistent efforts to involve parents in decision-making processes. According to Losen and Losen (1985, p. 108), cooperative parent participation is critical for the following reasons, among others: (a) parents have more time to spend helping children, and are more motivated to do so, than anyone else, (b) parental cooperation is mandatory to ease any familial problems that may be contributing to children's educational difficulties, (c) parents have a long term relationship with, and impact on their children.

Mittler *et al.* (1983, p. 141) report that parents frequently complain that they are not involved in the process of decision-making about their son or daughter. For example, when there are case conferences to discuss future placement after leaving school, parents may be left to wait outside while the discussion is proceeding among professionals and are only invited in to comment on a decision that has already been formulated.

In USA, PL 94-142 extends the right and arguably the duty of parents to handicapped children on their assumption of the role of educational decision-makers. In this role, they are expected to receive and act up on information, consent or withhold consent to proposed educational evaluations and placements, collaborate in making instructional and other service provision decisions, and contest educator's decisions. The belief that parents should share the rights and responsibilities of decision-makers and be an integral part of the educational process is based on the following assumptions: (a) parents want to be involved in education decision-making and when given the opportunity, will take advantage of it, and (b) attending the meeting to plan their child's IEP will enable parents be decision-makers (Turnbull and Turnbull, 1982).

Studies of parent involvement in IEP meetings have revealed consistently that, while parent attendance is fairly high, parent participation in actual decision making is very limited (Goldstein *et al.*, 1980; National committee for Citizens in Education, 1979). For example, the National Committee for Citizens in Education (1979) surveyed approximately 2,300 parents. A slight majority (52%) of the respondents indicated that their children's IEPs had been completed before the IEP meetings. In a follow-up study, Goldstein and Turnbull (1982) found that the majority of parent contributions in the IEP meetings were on the topic of personal/family issues, not on such educational issues as evaluation, curriculum, and placement.

Lusthaus and Lusthaus (1982) conducted a survey on a sample of 200 parents on the parental involvement in decision-making. The results of the study indicated that most parents were involved in educational decision-making at a level of giving and receiving information about decisions, rather than actually having control in making the decisions (or having no involvement at all). For no decision did parents believe they had decisional control, and in only a few school-related issues did some parents say that they had no involvement. Thus the great majority of parents felt that they were involved in decision-making in the sense that they discussed information regarding the decisions with the school professionals, but not in the sense that they had any real control over what the decisional outcome would be.

Furthermore, the results of the study also indicated that virtually all parents wanted to be more involved in the educational process of their children. In some of the issues that related to their own children, the majority of parents said they wanted more than merely an increased give-and-take in discussing decisions; rather, they wanted decisional control. This was true of decisions about the school transferring their children to other schools, providing medical services and keeping information on their children. Slightly less than a majority of parents also said they wanted control in decisions about their children's placement within the school. Studies conducted by Darga (1993) and Clark (1994) also revealed the parental desire for more active involvement in decision-making.

Strickland and Turnbull (1990, p. 193) report that the nature of parental participation in educational decision-making may take many forms, including the provision of consent for evaluation, input at the IEP conference, opportunity to review records, initiation of due process proceedings, membership on advisory boards, and notification and consent before release of any personally identifiable information on the student.

Winer (1982) studies six families who have children with special needs ranging from mild learning disabilities to profound retardation examined how the parents of these children became involved in various aspects of the decision-making process. Findings reveal that the least potential for conflict between parents and professionals occurred in interactions relating to identification of special needs. In decisions relating to the evaluation of handicapped children there was greater potential for conflict, while the most likely source of conflict was found to be in issues relating to the relative success of the children's educational placements.

Brooks (1984) found that both parents and educationists recognised the function of parents as decision-maker.

It is now regarded as good professional practice to develop an Individualised Educational Plan (IEP) for each child. The Education of All Handicapped Children Act (1975) in the United States and Education Acts in Britain (1981) are two examples of national legislation which specifically provides rights for parents to participate fully in the process of assessment and decision-making.

The IEP requirement was intended to provide several potential benefits to parents, including an opportunity to participate in the development of their child's special education programme, to obtain a written definition of the specially designed educational programme provided to their child, and to have at their disposal a mechanism for ensuring that the services specified in the IEP are, in fact, provided. Without question, many parents have taken full advantage of the intended benefits of the IEP. Despite the requirements of PL 94-142, however, the expectation that all parents of students with disabilities should and would be equal participants along with school personnel in developing, reviewing, and revising the students, IEP has not materialised (Singer and Butler, 1987; Turnbull and Hughes, 1987; US Department of Education, 1987; Vaughan *et al.*, 1988).

Morgan (1982) provided the following guidelines for parental involvement in the IEP process: (a) parents should participate in the process as much as they want to and are able to, (b) schools should deal with parents on a programme level rather than on a legal level, (c) professionals should not view parent participation as an intrusion but as a help in controlling arbitrary evaluation, placement, and instruction.

Polifka (1981) found that the greatest degree of parental satisfaction occurred when parents were involved in the development of their child's IEP; were comfortable about their child's placement, and were informed of their rights.

The evidence gathered in the study conducted by Leyser and Cole

(1984) demonstrates the low level of parent involvement in IEP meetings, and a lack of knowledge of what an IEP constitutes. Similar results have been reported in other investigations (Goldstein *et al.*, 1980; McKinney and Hocutt, 1982). A sizable number of these parents (between 40 and 60%) indicated that they preferred not to be actively involved in working with the teacher in developing their child's educational programme. Low levels of parental involvement and participation in other activities such as conferences and parent group meetings were also acknowledged.

Results of the study conducted by O'Connell (1992) indicated that the parents view the child's IEP as not being the product of the entire team's input, and they did not participate in the development of the document. On the other hand, a study conducted by Shellady (1994) revealed the parental desire for active role in the IEP process.

A study conducted by Moulin (1984) to ascertain the effect of parent participation in the IEP development on student achievement indicated a positive impact on their children and their school programme. The results also showed that the more actively parents participate, the more satisfied they tend to be with IEP. Parents with more formal education and more experience with IEP meetings tend to participate more actively than parents with less normal education and less experience with IEP meetings.

Brooks (1984) found that both parents and educationists recognised the parent's role as provider and receiver of information. Both groups recognised that parents have valuable information to contribute in the areas of problems, interests, and future goals. Both groups indicated that the IEP process has had a positive impact on children's educational programmes and on their parents' involvement in them. Also, both groups indicated a desire for more parent involvement.

The foregoing discussion reveals that parental participation in the educational decision-making process may be a benefit to some parents and detriment to others and many parents apparently prefer a role of receiving and confirming information at the IEP meeting, and not one of active and assertive contribution.

One of the major developments in mental handicap has concerned the inclusion of parents in the teaching and training of their children. Some workers have aimed at increasing the rate of developmental progress of the children through the teaching of their mothers. In a number of studies mothers attended a centre for training (Connolly *et al.*, 1980; Piper and Pless, 1980), in others they were visited and trained at home (Cuningham *et al.*, 1982; Sandow *et al.*, 1981). In each case mothers worked daily with their children on developmental objectives, putting into practice the methods they had learnt, while progress was assessed at intervals, and usually, compared with that of a similar, non-trained group of children.

In other studies the aim was to enable mothers to teach variety of skills and to manage or eliminate behavioural problems in their children. Mother were visited individually at home by therapists who discussed objectives and demonstrated methods, and the mothers were asked to carry out training sessions with their children and to keep records of progress until the therapists' next visit (Burden, 1978).

In a review of the effectiveness of a home-visiting service the parents' success was found not to be affected by social class; behavioural problems were better dealt with where marital relationships were satisfactory and the family a small one; learning skills were more successfully taught to brighter children (IQ 36-51) but IQ did not affect success with behavioural problems; parents receiving more home visits were more successful than those visited less (Callias and Carr, 1975).

An important question concerns the extent to which parents can maintain and extend the changes they have brought about in their children once training sessions are ended. Doleys *et al.* (1976) at 30 week follow-up found parents' teaching skills significantly above baseline though somewhat lower than immediate post-training levels. Baker *et al.* (1980) report a follow-up of four groups of mothers trained by different methods, all of whom had done significantly better than a control group. Fourteen months later initial gains, in both mothers and children, were maintained and 86 per cent of mother reported the continuation of "some scorable teaching efforts", but most of this was incidental teaching rather than carried out in regular sessions.

In the ever-developing area of parental involvement in reading, the bulk of the work has taken place in mainstream schools, and effectiveness has been demonstrated with children learning to read, with those who are maintaining and extending their reading skills, and others who have reached plateaux in performance (Topping and Wolfendale, 1985). While there remain some fundamental issues to be explored and resolved, such as the desirability of and limitations upon power-sharing (Beattie, 1985), there is nevertheless a broader acceptance of parents-as-educators (Topping, 1986) and commensurate acknowledgement of the prime part played by parents in their children's development, socialisation and education.

Many parents of handicapped children have achieved impressive success as teachers of their own children (Boyd, 1980; Karnes and Teska, 1980). But being an effective teacher of one's own child is a formidable undertaking. For example, Karnes and Teska (1980, p. 99) list, those competencies desirable for parents to be teachers for their children. No less is required of every master's level special education teacher. Below is an excerpt that includes less than half of the skills they identify as important for parents:

> The parental competencies required for direct teaching of the handicapped child at home involve interacting with the child in ways that promote positive behaviour; reinforcing desired behaviour; establishing an environment that is conducive to learning; setting up and maintaining a routine for direct teaching; using procedures appropriate for teaching concepts and skills; adapting lesson plans to the child's interests and needs; determining whether the child has mastered knowledge and skills, keeping meaningful records, including notes on child's progress; participating in a staffing of the child; communicating effectively with others; and addressing the child's stage of development.

It is now well documented that parents can be trained as effective teachers of their retarded children. After 14 months of a 20-week behavioural training programmes for parents of retarded children, Baker *et al.* (1980) assessed maintenance of child gains and parents' knowledge of programming principles, as well as the extent and quality of continued and new programming, and perceived obstacles to home-teaching and noted the effects of the training programme. The results reveal that parents had retained their knowledge of programming principles, and the children had retained their original skills gains. Many families had initiated some teaching of new skills, although few parents carried out regular formal training sessions. The main perceived obstacles to home-teaching were limitations in time, in the child's learning ability, in the parents' teaching ability, and in professional support.

Azad (1986) and Dutta (1986) studied the adaptation and effectiveness of the Portage home based training programme for cognitive and motor development of young children. Both studies report improvement in mentally retarded children on different measures accompanied by improvement in parents' attitude. Pandit (1987) carried out an experiment of training parents of mentally retarded children for educating and managing them. Only 67 per cent of the parents accepted the programme, but they were reluctant to assume that role of a teacher.

From the above investigation, we can infer that parents differ in their response to their handicapped children and in their willingness or ability to participate in intervention programmes. Yet, it is widely recognised today that parents play the central role as educators as well as nurtures of their own children. As Love and Biervliet (1984) state, by teaching parents to be effective home-based remedial tutors, many more children can be provided with the individualised instruction they need and the generalisation and the maintenance of school taught skills may be enhanced.

Advocacy for handicapped people has become a multifaceted reality in today's world of concern about the legal rights of those with disabilities. In its essence, advocacy refers to attempts by an individual handicapped person, by another person, or by a group of guarantee that all rights due to a handicapped person are realised. Roos (1983) traces the origins of the advocacy movement to the 1930s. When parents of mentally retarded children begain to react against neglectful or inappropriate actions by professionals who claimed to be helping these children and their families. Frustrated with the professionals' response, parents turned to each other for help.

As Kirk *et al.* (1993) state, history of legislation concerning disabled children in the developed countries indicate that parent organisations have successfully stimulated public attention to their needs and demands.

Parents serve as advocates not only for their child and for themselves but also for other parents and exceptional children. They know their child's legal rights and their rights as their child's principal advocate. Armed with a thorough knowledge of their rights, parents must then know when to negotiate and compromise in planning and implementing services (Shea and Bauer, 1985, pp. 67-68).

Wolfensberger (1978) identified three criteria for effective advocacy. First, advocates possess a special commitment to advance the cause of another person. Second, advocates spend their own time, effort, and other resources. Finally, advocates are free from conflicts of interest and independent of the outcomes they seek.

Brooks (1984) found that both parents and educationists recognised the functions of parents as advocate. A study of three special education parent teacher associations (Herstek, 1985) revealed that parents grouped together as a result of their frustrating efforts in attempting to ensure proper placement, and/or programmes for their handicapped children. The study concluded that parent groups which advocate for the handicapped have proven through their efforts that they can access the schools, and effectively apply the necessary pressure to guarantee appropriate educational programmes for their children.

Wilgosh (1990) found that many parents of children with a disability believe that educational opportunities are a direct result of advocacy for their child. A study conducted by Clear and Mank (1990) found that parents and families play a significant role as advocates.

As Myreddi (1992) states, it has been proved in developed and developing countries that parents have tremendous strength, will power and decisiveness, which lead them to form pressure groups in fighting for the rights of their children, establishment of good schools and effective training of their own handicapped children by themselves.

However, advocacy can exclude parents of handicapped children from the opportunity of having mainstreamed experiences with parents of non-handicapped children. If they function as advocates, parents of handicapped children frequently must choose between the conflicting demands of spending time with their child or going to one meeting after another to act as advocate for the child's needs.

In short, many parents are highly interested and successful in being advocates for their handicapped child. But the assumption cannot be made that all parents are suited to be advocates and will function as such, thereby ensuring their children's rights and school's accountability.

4. Role of Teachers and School in Enhancing Parental Involvement

It is imperative for the school staff to view parents not as enemies but as important, helpful allies with an active, major role to play in the schooling of their children. It is equally important for the school staff to help parents to see their own role in this light. Unfortunately, however, parents are still too frequently not accorded equal status in special education identification and planning matters affecting their children.

A child's parents must feel themselves as a part of the team in order to work with the team, and to communicate with ease within that team for effective problem-solving. The team staff members, individually and as a group must convey the message that the parents are welcome, that they will be respected for what they have to contribute, and that they are considered capable of joining in a process where everyone's views will be heard (Losen and Losen, 1985, pp. 58-59).

The preparation of parents for team meetings should be given high priority. It is important to overcome anxiety and negativism prior to team meetings, if possible, through pre-conference consultation designed to identify and overcome parental resistance. Once identified, parents' concerns should be dealt with respectfully, sensitively, and honestly. During the meeting, parents should not be overwhelmed with statistics or unfamiliar technical terms or intimidated by professional jargon or unexpected negative diagnoses of their children's difficulties. Parents should be fully informed about available services and programme options (Losen and Losen, 1985, p. 109).

Most families of handicapped children need strong support systems to handle the additional stress the handicap imposes. The early childhood special educator should be sensitive to the needs of the parents. He or she should listen to them and in many cases should serve as their advocate and help them learn to advocate for themselves.

According to Wikler and Keenan (1987) parents of students with disabilities are faced with needs not apparent to parents of students without identifiable disabilities. They are no longer passive recipients of services but assume a strong advocacy role on behalf of their children. Specifically, skills to be developed include learning to reduce stress, being involved in the individualised education plan, following through on home programming, helping the child to interact with friends and siblings, and managing behaviour.

Determining the support needs of parents requires interacting with them in a sensitive, observant fashion to determine their individual needs (Berdine and Meyer, 1987, pp. 136-37).

As Peshwaria and Venkatesan (1992, pp.203-04) state, the role of teachers is gradually expanding as more and more teachers are beginning to realise the advantages of involving parents and other family members in the training programme for children with mental handicap. Teachers may have to work with parents/families in order to : (a) impart information about the child's condition, (b) explain the nature, causes and managment techniques for children with mental handicap, (c) help them develop right attitudes towards their child with mental handicap, (d) elaborate the role of parents in the training and habilitation of these children, and (e) make plans and programmes for training appropriate behaviours to the child at home.

According to Baker and Bovair (1989, p. 90), if the special school is being encouraged to be a resource, it has an exciting opportunity to develop a network for parents of children with special needs. It can build up a library of practical information. It can establish an additional base for all the voluntary agencies who work for the individual child to meet with the parents. It can act as an advocate for parents, to ensure they are receiving appropriate services for their child. It can provide the context in which parents can meet to support each other or organise speakers who can give parents the feeling of a better status than victims of circumstances manipulated by professionals.

Yanok and Derubertis (1989) in their comparative study of parental participation in regular and special education programmes conclude that teachers and administrators will need to redouble their efforts to increase the involvement of parents in school planning and decision-making. Parents of the handicapped and non-handicapped alike must be persuaded to become active participants rather than passive observers of their children's education. Realisation of this outcome will require that school officials successfully communicate to parents that meaningful opportunities for educational collaboration truly exist.

To strengthen the linkage between school and family, Fuqua *et al.* (1985) have recommended that special educators organise parent support groups and home-based training programmes. These researchers concluded that direct, informal, and personal interactions between home and school not only facilitated dual directional communication, but also enhanced teacher appreciation of parent involvement.

As Mittler and Serpell (1985) point out, it is the task of the professionals not only to recognise the distinctive and unique characteristics of each family, but also to approach the task of building a working relationship with the family in flexible and individually appropriate ways.

During the initial contact visit, teachers of handicapped children are frequently confronted with difficult questions and other responses from parents. This initial session is of great importance as it sets the stage for the parents' participation during assessment, programme planning, implementation, and evaluation services (Barlett and Smith, 1978). During the session, the teacher gathers data and, in addition, must deal with the concerns of the parent and establish a positive relationship for future involvement (Mattson, 1977).

According to Wright (1976), parents need someone to talk to, to share their problems with, and to understand them without blaming them or rejecting them. Teacher's tasks is to "actively" listen. Parents need to know that teachers want to understand them, that teachers respect their ability to come to grips with their problems. Teachers should be especially, careful to avoid moralizsing, advising unnecessarily, blaming, analysing, pitying or consoling. Be sure parents are aware of community and regional services that are available for them and their child, such as clinics, special day schools, and parent groups, and aware of behavioural management techniques for use in the home. Encourage them to join a parents' group and be sure they are involved in developing a realistic educational plan for their child.

In order to assume the role of parent trainers, teachers must become knowledgeable in several areas. A few of the specific competencies needed by teachers to be effective in parent or parent-surrogate training as suggested by Stainback *et al.* (1976) are given below: (a) explaining student abilities and progress to help parents overcome the problems of under or over protection and inappropriate expectations, (b) training parents to deal with explosive, stereotype, self-stimulative behaviours as well as appropriate motor responding and verbalisation behaviours, (c) being a source of information concerning community resources that can provide health care, social interaction, recreation, etc., (d) providing parents with knowledge of sources of special clothing and equipment that can aid in easing home-care problems and encourage greater independence and self-care, (e) training parents in lifting, carrying, and positioning the non-ambulatory, (f) training parents in techniques for fostering sensory awareness, motor development, communication, eating, toileting, bathing, and dressing, etc.; and (g) explaining the importance of having the non-ambulatory child sit up and correctly positioned for part of each day in a chair, even if strapped in, rather than flat on his back in a crib or bed.

Robinson (1994) found that special education teachers perceive a need for teacher training in all skills relevant to working and communicating with parents, and skills pertaining to the special education teachers' role as conference facilitator.

According to Schafler (1980), school social workers can play a crucial role in preparing and supporting parents to participate in relevant school tasks such as an IEP conference. Steinberg (1983) found that intervention in the form of either formal training or ongoing experience can assist parent to be effective participants in programme planning for their handicapped children. Vema *et al.* (1992) conducted a study to evaluate a home-care programme for the mentally retarded children through training of the mother and found a significant improvement in the behaviour of the children and and in the marital adjustment score, parental attitude and social burden felt by the mothers.

Levenson (1994) found that the parent education course for the parents of children with disabilities as helpful in increasing their parenting skills and decreasing their parental stress. Similarly, the results of the study conducted by Wells (1994) indicated a significant relationship between parent involvement and parent knowledge of special education.

Simpson (1982) suggested that just as mainstream teachers must learn new skills to deal with exceptional children, teachers of exceptional children must expand their skills to work with parents. According to Shea and Bauer (1985, p. 175), a home visit helps the teachers get to know the child's family, environment, and culture better in order to serve both child and parents more effectively.

In terms of facilitating active parental participation, Yamilkoski (1983) found that professionals often appear to ask parents for their preferences concerning placement, and encourage them to develop IEP objectives. They less often involve parents in teaching academic skills, assessing their child's behaviour, and accomplishing IEP objectives.

It should not be assumed that all parents desire or need to be involved to the same degree (Allen and Hudd, 1987; Singer and Butler, 1987; Turnbull and Turnbull, 1982). The school's responsibility, however, is to encourage and to enable the active and meaningful involvement of parents in decisions regarding their children.

PL 94-142 provides the procedural mechanism for doing so by ensuring that parents have the following opportunities: (a) be informed about all actions proposed regarding their child, (b) request meetings and attend all meetings at which decisions regarding their child are discussed or made, (c) participate in long range programme planning, policy development, and serve on advisory panels regarding programmes for students with disabilities (Strickland and Turnbull, 1990, p.26).

The above analysis clearly indicates the important role of teachers and school authorities in enhancing the involvement of parents in the education of their mentally retarded children, also the review throws light into various aspects of the role of teachers.

5. *Factors that Influence Parental Involvement*

Historically, both general and special educators have held a number of beliefs and attitudes about families of children with handicapping conditions. The most predominant beliefs have been (a) parents are not willing or able to work with their handicapped children, (b) parents have unrealistic expectations regarding their handicapped children, (c) parents do not know how to teach their handicapped children, (d) parents need professionals to help them, and (e) parents contribute to the problems of their handicapped children (Vincent *et al.*, 1981). These negative assumptions or beliefs have been particularly destructive—not only because they are mostly erroneous, but also because they have tended to foster a hostile parent-teacher relationship in which both parties have perceived their efforts to be at cross purpose (Donnellan and Mirenda, 1984).

Research conducted by Minikutty (1993) revealed that, according to teachers, the absence of father or mother, poor health condition of the parents, poor relation between parents and teaches, mental tension of parents, feeling that the child is of no use, non-availability of professional service, and feeling of shame due to the presence of the child are the factors which unfavourably affect the parental involvement of mentally retarded children. On the other hand, the guilty conscience of parents, over protection of the child, sympathetic attitude towards the child and other deformities of the child are found to be the factors which favourably affect the parental involvement.

O'Toole (1990a, 1990b) found that parents' desires to help their children were the best predictors of effective parental involvement. Other variables such as family size, income level, mothers' educational background, and severity of the child's disability did not prove to be reliable predictors of parental involvement. Dorgu (1993) noticed a significant relationship between knowledge of the programme, and overall parental involvement.

According to Turnbull and Turnbull (1982), many parents do believe that their child needs to be protected from the special education system. According to them, it is also not surprising that parents express a lack of self-confidence and skills in improving their child's education. Their concern is that, if it requires a master's degree in special education to qualify a person in assessment, curriculum planning, methods and materials, and behaviour management, it is questionable how parents without specialised training ever could be equal participants in developing an IEP, much less advocate for more appropriate IEPs, programmes, related services, placements, or teachers.

Ballmer (1978) identified a number of factors that directly related to the participation of parents in pre-school special education programmes. Programmes in the high involvement category exhibited the following characteristics; a real commitment to the importance of parent participation; parent contacts occurred both in the home and at the programme site; one staff member was assigned for every family; programme personnel had to be extremely flexible in their roles; many options were offered for parent participation, however, working with the handicapped youngster was of primary importance; a systematic and frequent review of short and long-term goals; specific appointment times were arranged; contacts with parents were very frequent; parents were involved in the initial diagnostic and planning stages.

Some programme factors appear to be related to levels of parental involvement. The smallest programmes have a highe· percentage of parents involved (Weigerink and Hocutt, 1979). Behaviourally oriented programmes have higher levels of involvement than other types (Reisinger *et al.*, 1970); and programmes with transportation facilities have greater participation (Schaefer, 1976) than those that do not. School-based programmes may have lower levels of parent involvement because a bureaucratic or hierarchical system may have no meaningful role for parents (Ora, 1973).

Study conducted by Robert (1994) revealed a higher level of parental involvement if the programmes are family-centred. To ensure continued parental involvement intervention programmes must focus on goals that are important to the family. Research studies indicate that parents who are committed to programme goals are more likely to carry out suggested activities, will become more skilled as teachers, and are more likely to have children who show measurable progress (Roseenberg, 1977). Grizzle (1993) identified home-school contact as the best single predictor of parental involvement.

As Tomlison (1982, p. 118) states, middle-class professional people do not geneally involve or consult as 'equals', parents whom they associate with incompetency, and since the majority of parents in special education are likely to be working class, and likely to be associated with incompetence, this may be one of the crucial difficulties in developing adequate involvement of, and consultation with, all parents whose children may be considered to be in need of special education.

Haigh (1977) reports that working class parents find difficulty in communicating their concern relating to their children's education. This view is also supported by Tizard (1977) who, in a survey on parental involvement in nursery education, referred to a number of parents who stated that they would like to help their children with their education, but did not do so because they did not know how to, or because they were afraid of interfering.

According to Beveridge and Jerrams (1981), it would appear that the resentment which many teachers feel for these parents stems from ignorance on both sides. The teachers think the parents don't care, while the parents remain uninvolved because of a total unawareness of what the teachers require of them.

Leyser and Cole (1984) conducted a study and concluded that the reasons for the lack of more active participation and involvement are found to be timing of school meetings, transportation, the feeling of parents that they did not gain any better understanding of their child's problems from attending school meetings, and the confusion experienced by parents following conferences.

A study conducted by Countryman (1994) on the parental involvement in at-risk pre-school programme revealed that, the stresses of parents' lives such as poverty, unemployment, separation, single parenthood, homelessness, lack of transportation, and lack of affordable child-care are creating enormous obstacles for parents to participate in school-based parental activities.

Lee (1980) cited several failings of parent-teacher programmes that many parents see as insurmountable barriers to their participation in conferences, workshops, meetings, and other activities: (a) inconvenient meeting times and locations, (b) inadequate paents input during programme planning, (c) unwarranted assumptions about parents' skills, (d) inadequate feedback and follow-up services for parents, (e) parental feelings of inadequacy, (f) inability to implement suggestions,

(g) parent-teacher competition, (h) parental exhaustion, and (i) unresponsiveness.

According to Losen and Losen (1985, p. 108), parental involvement in collective decision-making tends to be less than optimal as a result of the following factors: parents' passivity, anxiety, feelings of dependency, guilt feelings, mistrust of school staff, fear that their child will be labelled, lack of full awareness of the child's difficulty, and negative expectations about the school staff or the school's competence.

Karnes *et al.* (1977) report that two basic factors seem to be associated with the lack of success of efforts to involve parents, namely, attitudes of professional personnel and their lack of skills in working with parents. The attitude that the professional person is an 'expert' and must impart knowledge, as reflected in parent-teacher conferences and to a large extent in Parent Teacher Association meetings, prevents his listening to parents which is an essential ingredient for working with them.

Parents give many reasons for their lack of involvement: (a) past bad experiences in the school system, (b) ineffective teachers, (c) belief that the school has total responsibility for educating their children, (d) belief that the teachers want parents to do their jobs for them, (e) personal, marital, and social problems of parents, (f) for some parents the school day is their only respite so they seek to stay uninvolved from it, (g) family factors such as one parent family, the availability of family support, whether both parents work, and the availability of child care (Shea and Bauer, 1985, p. 44).

The last section of this review of related literature deals with the stress of parental involvement.

It has become apparent that some services intended to help have themselves brought stress to families. This may come about because of the number of interventionists involved: "there are frequently five or more professionals in daily contact" (Lacoste, 1978). Involving the mother as "therapist, teacher, trainer or, at the least, transporter" (Doernberg, 1978), so that she has her work cut out to keep up with the child's treatment, let alone function as wife, mother to her other children or as a human being in her own right. "If she even considers some time for herself she suffers such guilt that it is not worth it to her" (Doernberg, 1978). The result may be to damage the whole family (Zigler, 1981).

These alarms by professionals are echoed by parents' comments that they felt looked down up by professionals (Berry *et al.*, 1981) who undervalued parents' achievement: "they always tell us how well we are doing but then go on to say, but if you do this it will be more helpful" (Black, 1978) and rushed them on: "no sonner is one skill mastered than another skill is presented (clouding) the simple sweetness of success" (Fulwood, 1981). These complaints seem to be voiced by a majority of parents and the majority welcome the help which enables them to help their own children (Baker *et al.*, 1980; Holland, 1981). Interventionists, however, should be alert to the potentially stressful effects of their efforts and aim, always, at the benefit of the whole family as the ultimate goal, warns Carrr (1985).

This section of the review has covered the aspects such as concept and nature of parental involvement, parent-teacher partnership, perception of parents and teachers, role of teachers and school in enhancing parental involvement, factors that influence parental involvement, and stress of parental involvement. Recent research reports and observations of researchers were reviewed and discussed in detail.

Summary

An exhaustive review of the literature and research studies pertaining to various aspects of this research problem has been made. Topics such as family of the mentally handicapped, socio-economic status and mental retardation, education of the mentally handicapped and parental involvement in the education are discussed in detail.

The review presents a clear picture of the complex structure and characteristics of a family with a retarded child. The literature which was surveyed helped to identify a number of parental reactions to the discovery of the child's retardation. The nature of the impact of retardation of the child on the parents and siblings as well as the factors that decide the intensity of the impact were also discussed. Further, the survey points out the necessity of parent counselling and also brings out the relationship between poverty, cultural deprivation, lower socio-economic status and mental retardation.

The review gives a comprehensive account of the aims and objectives of education of the mentally retarded, different models of special education services and the important factors in an ideal function-oriented curriculum. Moreover, the abstracts of research studies were also included.

The concept and need of parental involvement in the education of the mentally retarded as well as the evolution of parental organisations were also discussed. An analysis of the importance of parent-teacher partnership and different forms and potential problems of healthy parent-teacher collaboration were also incorporated. The abstracts of studies regarding the perception of parents and teachers on the parental involvement in education were also included in this chapter.

The review gives an outline of the different roles of parents in the education of their retarded children. The review throws light on the various roles of teachers and school authorities in promoting parental involvement. The last part of the review deals with aspects such as factors that influence parental involvement and the stress caused by parental involvement.

The studies and literature surveyed herein have helped the investigator throughout his research work, especially in the designing of the study and in the preparation of the tools and the interpretation of the results. A detailed description of the research methodology followed is given in the following chapter.

3

Methodology

This chapter gives details about the methodology followed in this study. The method of research adopted, the description of tools and techniques used, the sample, the procedure of data collection and the outline of statistical techniques utilised in the analysis of data are described under appropriate heads and presented below.

Method Adopted

In order to achieve the objectives of the study the investigator selected the descriptive method. Because, "descriptive research involves collecting data in order to test hypotheses or to answer questions concerning the current status of the subject of the study" (Gay, 1990, p. 189). A descriptive study determines and reports the way things are. As expressed by Best and Kahn (1992, p. 76), "it is concerned with conditions or relationships that exist, opinions that are held, processes that are going on, effects that are evident, or trends that are developing."

Among the different approaches that may be used in descriptive research, the survey method was selected for the present study. A survey is an attempt to collect data from members of a population in order to determine the current status of that population with respect to one or more variables.

Description of Tools

The following tools were used to collect the necessary data for the study.

1. General data sheet
2. Parent-involvement interview schedule
3. Parent-involvement questionnaire
4. Interview schedule for teachers

All the four tools were prepared in Malayalam language. The details regarding each of the tools is given below.

1. General Data Sheet

The general data sheet was prepared to collect general information about the retarded child and his/her family from the parents. This include information such as the child's name, sex, age, birth order, severity of retardation and religion, total number of children in the family, name and type of school in which the mentally retarded child is attending, number of years of schooling, and locality of residence. In addition, details of parents such as age, educational status, occupation, and monthly income were also collected using the general data sheet. These particulars are required for categorization of the subjects into the respective sub-samples.

2. Parent Involvement Interview Schedule

Parent involvement interview schedule was prepared to collect necessary data for the realisation of the first and the most important objective of the present investigation. This deals with involvement of parents in developing the basic living skills in their mentally retarded children. There are altogether 88 items in this structured interview schedule which are grouped under eight different sections. The schedule seeks information from parents on how much they involve in developing basic living skills such as self care, motor, reading and writing, numerical, health and safety, social, occupational, and leisure time skills. All the items were provided with four alternative answers, viz., 'high', 'average', 'low', and 'nil'. Either father, or mother, or both of them together was expected to respond to the schedule. The details of each section of the schedule is given below.

Section I includes ten items based on toileting, brushing, bathing, dressing, and eating skills. Section II has six items based on motor skills; Section III has eight items which are concerned with reading, writing, and communication skills; Section IV has 14 items and these deal with numerical ability and basic skills of measurements, usage of money, calender and time; Section V includes seven items on skills related to health and safety; Section VI has nine items on social skills; Section VII has 24 items of which the first nine are common items and the remaining 15 are given as different vocational alternatives, and finally, Section VIII consists of 10 items, which deal with leisure time skills.

The investigator made an extensive review of all the related literature available and discussed with a few parents of the retarded children and special teachers for the preparation of the schedule. The investigator also visited reputed research centres and discussed with researchers and experts in the field of education of the mentally retarded. After completing the initial form, it was field tested by administering on a small sample of parents. This was helpful in restructuring, modifying and reducing the size of the schedule.

3. Parent Involvement Questionnaire

The questionnaire was constructed to gather information regarding perception of parents on (a) the existing expected levels of parental involvement in the educational decision-making, (b) the effect of associated problems in the education of retarded children and services available for their education, (c) the extent of satisfaction in the method of training provided to the mentally retarded children, and (d) the parental guidance and counselling. It is a structured questionnaire having five different sections. Altogether there are 65 items in the questionnaire. Either father, or mother, or both of them together was expected to respond to the questionnaire. The details of each section of the questionnaire is given below.

First three items in the questionnaire seek the name of the child, name of the school, and name of the father. Section I has three parts, in the first part there are 10 items, which are meant to collect information on the nature of the existing and expected involvement of parents in the educational decision-making. Two sets of alternative responses were given to each of these 10 items. First set is meant for existing involvement and the second set stands for expected involvement. Each of these has four responses, namely, 'high involvement', 'only giving information to the authorities', 'only receiving information from authorities', and 'no involvement'. The responder was expected to record his or her response in each of these two sets of responses.

The second part of the first section contains four questions on certain general aspects of educational decision-making such as satisfaction of parents in their existing role, existing rights to participate in the educational decision-making meetings, need for further training and information on decision-making and their role in the selection of teachers. All these four questions were provided with four alternative responses, viz., 'certainly', 'somewhat', 'little', and 'not at all'. The third part of this section contains 10 items which deal with different factors that can be potential barriers restraining parents from attending the educational decision-making meetings.

Section II has three different parts. The first part has six items on the associated problems of the retarded children such as reduced ability to learn, reduced ability in daily living skills, health problems, lack of discipline, behavioural problems and language problems. All the items were provided with four alternative responses, namely, 'high,' 'somewhat' 'low', and 'not at all'. Parents have to record how much these problems affect their retarded children's education. The second part has nine items based on parental satisfaction with regard to the general educational services available in the school. This includes ability of teachers, appropriateness of curriculum, individual attention from teachers, scientific methods of assessment, medical care, transportation facilities, counselling programmes, day care facilities, and parent education programmes. All the items were provided with four alternative responses, namely, 'certainly', 'somewhat', 'little' and 'not at all'. Parents have to record their degree of satisfaction with the availability of these facilities in the school.

The third part of this section contains six items on necessity of certain facilities such as parent education programmes, parent groups, sibling's counselling, services of doctors, psychologists, and social service agencies. These items also were provided with the four alternative responses as mentioned above. Parents are expected to record whether these facilities were needed for the progress of their retarded children.

Section III has 10 items relating to parental satisfaction with regard to the method of education and training provided to the mentally retarded children in the school for developing different skills such as skills of daily living, language, numerical, health and safety, social, vocational, communication, and discipline. All the items have been given the same four alternative responses. Parents were expected to indicate their level of satisfaction in the method followed in schools.

Section IV consists of seven questions to elicit the parental perceptions with regard to the efforts that have been taken by the teachers and school authorities for enhancing parental involvement. The items help to ascertain whether the teachers encourage parents to attend the educational decision-making meetings, involve parents in the formation of curriculum, educate parents for training their retarded children at home, approach parents for discussing matters related to the children, encourage parents for contacting school regularly, get satisfactory help from school authorities in child-related matters, and involve the representative of parents in the committee for selecting teachers. All the questions were provided with two alterative responses, 'yes' and 'no'.

In Section V, five question were included which were concerned with parental perception with regard to their need for guidance and counselling. Questions were based on whether they need guidance and counselling for the existence and progress of the family, for leading normal social life, and avoiding emotional problems in the family, for normal growth and development of siblings, and alleviating anxieties regarding the retarded child's future. All the questions were followed by two alternative responses, 'yes' and 'no'.

As in the case of interview schedule, questionnaire also was prepared after a thorough review of related literature and discussion with parents, special teachers, and researchers in the field. The questionnaire was also field tested and certain modifications were made in the structure and content before printing out the final format.

4. *Interview Schedule for Teachers*

To realise two of the objectives of the present investigation it was needed to collect certain information from teachers of the mentally retarded children. Therefore a structured interview schedule was prepared, which has altogether 34 items. Most of the questions were followed by two alternative responses, 'yes' and 'no'. First three items were included to gather general information regarding personal details of teachers such as their name, teaching experience, and educational qualifications. Fourth item seeks to find out whether the teacher had special training, and the fifth tries to elicit information as to whether the teacher received special training from India or abroad. The question number six to twelve were added to find out whether teachers have included parents in different aspects of the education of the retarded children such as inclusion of parents in the school's policy decision-making committees, considering parental opinions while formulating the curriculum, inclusion of parents in the assessment of child's abilities and progress, in deciding the class placement, including parents in the disciplinary action taking committees; financial committees; and other administrative decisions. Item number 13 attempts to know whether teachers recognise the importance of parents as home teachers. Item number 14 details with providing help to parents for teaching and training their retarded children at home. Item number 15 seeks to know the teacher's perception of the role of parents in the education of their retarded children. It was followed by three alternative responses as 'more than that of teachers', 'equal to that of teachers', and 'less than that of teachers'. Question number 16 probes whether they have any parent education programmes in their school.

Items 17 to 24 are concerned with the question whether the teachers have given any training to parents to develop basic living skills in their retarded children. All these items were provided with two alternative responses, 'yes' and 'no'.

The last part of this schedule, that is items 25 to 34 deals with the perception of teachers on the parental need for guidance and counselling. These items probe whether parents need guidance and counselling for-increasing their self-confidence, understanding clearly about their child's abilities and inabilities, having a correct perception about their child's education, ensuring proper involvement in the educational process, preventing disruption of social relationships, maintaining healthy family relationships, alleviating difficulties in caring for the retarded children, preventing chances of ignoring other family members, avoiding anxieties about the child's future, making aware of various services that are available in the society. These items also were provided with two alternative responses, 'yes' and 'no'.

This schedule is also prepared only after the thorough review of related literature of discussion with special teachers and experts. It has also been field tested prior to the finalization.

The Sample

Regardless of the technique to be used in selecting a sample, the first step in sampling is definition of the population; which is the group on which the researcher would like to generalise the results. The parents and teachers of mentally retarded children studying in the special schools of Kerala state is the population for the present investigation.

Selection of a sample is a very important step in conducting any research study. The quality of the sample determine the possibility for generalisation of the results. In the words of Gay (1990, p. 101), "sampling is the process of selecting a number of individuals for a study in such a way that the individual represents the larger group from which they were selected".

From the different sampling techniques the investigator selected random sampling procedures for selection of the sample of parents for the present study. Random sampling method ensures every individual the same probability of being selected and selection of one individual in no way affects selection of another individual. Parents of 170 mentally retarded children studying in various special schools of Ernakulam and Kottayam districts of Kerala state and 85 special teachers working in these school constitute the sample of the study. The details of the sample selected for study are given in Table 3.1.

Table 3.1 : *Details Regarding the Sample Selected for the Study*

Sr. No.	*Name of the Special School*	*Sample Obtained*	
		Parents	*Teachers*
1.	Raksha Institute of Special Education, Chullikal, Ernakulam.	36	11
2.	Pratheeksha, Rotary School for the mentally retarded children, N. Parur, Eranakulam.	13	4
3.	Snehasadan, Angamaly, Ernakulam.	11	4
4.	Nirmala Sadan, Muvattupuzha, Ernakulam.	10	20
5.	Sevagram, Vettimukal, Kottayam.	10	6
6.	Vikas Vidyalaya, Kottayam.	35	10
7.	YMCA Bodhinilayam, Kottayam.	10	5
8.	Jeevodaya Centre, Kurumpanadom, Kottayam.	20	5
9.	Ashanilayam, Ponkunnam, Kottayam.	13	11
10.	Shalom DCMR, Puliyannoor, Pala, Kottayam.	8	5
11.	Santhwanam Special School, Kottayam.	4	4
	Total	170	85

The details of the break-up of the sample are given in Table 3.2.

Procedure for Data Collection

The investigator personally contacted the special school authorities. The scope of the study was explained to them and their permission

Table 3.2 : *Break-up of the Sample of Parents and Retarded Children*

Category	*Number*	*Percentage*
Sex of mentally retarded children		
Male	105	61.76
Female	65	38.24
Age of children		
6–10	46	27.06
11–15	59	34.71
16–20	43	25.29
Above 20	22	12.94
Birth order of children		
First born	64	37.65
Middle born	36	21.18
Last born	70	41.17
Degree of mental retardation		
Mild	59	34.71
Moderate	92	54.12
Severe	19	11.17
Religion		
Hindu	53	31.18
Muslim	18	10.59
Christian	99	58.23
Location of residence		
Urban	62	36.47
Rural	108	63.53
Age of Father		
Younger age group (below 35 years)	10	5.88
Middle age group (35–49)	103	60.59
Old age group (50 and above)	41	24.12
Died/Divorced	16	9.41
Age of Mother		
Younger age group (below 35 years)	36	21.18
Middle age group (35–49)	100	58.82
Old age group (50 and above)	34	20.00

(Contd.)

Table 3.2 : *(Contd.)*

Category	*Number*	*Percentage*
Education of Father		
Low education group (0–IX Standard)	62	36.47
Middle education group (SSLC–Degree)	85	50.00
High education group (PG/Professional)	7	4.12
Education of Mother		
Low education group (0–IX Standard)	71	41.76
Middle education group (SSLC–Degree)	92	54.12
High education group (PG/Professional)	7	4.12
Occupation of Father		
Group I (Coolie, etc.)	82	48.24
Group II (Clerk, etc.)	36	21.18
Group III (Gazetted Officers, etc.)	21	12.35
Group IV (Unemployed)	15	8.83
Occupation of Mother		
Group I (Coolie, etc.)	6	3.53
Group II (Clerk, etc.)	14	8.24
Group III (Gazetted Officers, etc.)	7	4.12
Group IV (Unemployed)	143	84.11
Monthly income group (Rs. 0–750)	94	55.29
Middle income group (Rs. 751–3,000)	49	28.82
High income group (Above Rs. 3,000)	27	15.89

was sought for collecting data from the parents through their institutions and from teachers of those institutes directly. Permission of the parents was also sought either through the school authorities or directly from parents.

After getting permission from the parents, the investigator contacted them personally either by visiting their homes or the institutions. After establishing proper rapport the investigator supplied the general data sheet and got it filled. The interview was conducted by using the structured parent involvement interview schedule. The questionnaire was also supplied after the interview and most of the parents returned it duly filled in immediately after the interview, and the others sent it by post.

The interest shown by the school authorities ensured the cent per cent return of the filled questionnaires. In many cases, it was the mothers who responded, in some cases it was the fathers alone and in the rest both the parents together participated in the interview and completed the questionnaire. However, out of the final sample if 170, in the case of 16, it was the mother alone who responded as the fathers were either dead or divorced. It was striking that some of the parents especially mothers were found to be emotional describing their children's problems and on such occasions the interviewer allowed them to take their own time to become normal before proceeding with the interview.

During the visits to the special schools, the investigator conducted interview with the teachers by using the structured interview schedule prepared for the purpose.

Even though all the 200 parents who were interviewed responded to the questionnaires and the general data sheet, only 170 of them were included in the final sample. Thirty of them were deleted owing to incomplete questionnaires.

Scoring and Processing of Data

Each subject of the sample was given an identification number by serially numbering from one to 170. Against the identification number of each subject the data pertaining to that subject were entered in a single line on consolidated data sheet. At first the data collected through the General Data Sheet were entered followed by the data obtained through the Parent Involvement Interview Schedule and that of the Parent Involvement Questionnaire.

All the items of the Parent Involvement Interview Schedule were followed by four alternative responses such as 'high', 'average', 'low', and 'nil'. These scale points were assigned values of three, two, one, and zero respectively. All the items of the interview schedule were scored in a similar way. The total score for each section, except for Section VII, obtained by summing up the scores of the items of that section. The total score for Section VII was obtained by summing up the scores of first nine items of the section and adding the highest score from any one of the remaining 15 items. As the items from 9 to 24 were given as choice, only one of these items were considered for calculating the total score for the section. The total score for each subject was obtained by summing up the scores of all sections except Section VII. Thereby each subject has got its own Parent Involvement Score.

All items of the questionnaire were scored in such a way that the total frequency of different responses to different items were obtained.

Similarly, each of the 85 Interview Schedules for Teachers was given an identification number by serially numbering from one to 85 and the relevant data were entered as explained in the case of questionnaire.

Classification of data: The data were classified according to the different variables studied, viz., age, sex, birth order, and degree of mental retardation of the children; religion, number of siblings, years of schooling, location of residence; age, education, and occupation of fathers and mothers, and monthly income of parents. Instead of considering the socio-economic status as a single variable, the level of education, occupation, and monthly income of parents were taken separately, as it would specify more clearly the relation of the variables with the parental involvement.

The educational level of fathers and mothers was categorised into three groups as follows:

Low education group: Illiterates to IX Standard

Middle education group: SSLC to Bachelor's degree

High education group: Post Graduates and Professional degrees

Similarly, the occupational level of fathers and mothers was categorised into four groups as follows:

Group I: Coolie, driver, petty shop business, mason, painter, carpenter, fisherman, goldsmith, agricultural labourer.

Group II: Businessman with monthly income between Rs. 1,000 and Rs. 3,000, clerk, mechanic, fitter, accountant, retired people, vendor, farmer, with monthly income between Rs. 1,000 and Rs. 3,000, police army, laboratory assistant, junior nurse, lady health inspector.

Group III: Office Superintendent, businessman with monthly income of more than Rs. 3,000, gazetted officer, gulf employee, farmer with monthly income of more than Rs. 3,000, teacher, engineer, doctor, medical representative, senior nurse.

Group IV: Unemployed

Monthly income of parents was categorised into three groups as follows:

Low income group: Monthly income of Rs. 750 or less.

Middle income group: Monthly income between Rs. 751 and Rs. 3,000.

High income group: Monthly income above Rs. 3,000.

Out of the total sample of 170, forty–six were the parents of children who are less than 10 years old. As the children belonging to this age group are usually not considered for the vocational training, their parents' responses were not considered for calculating the parent involvement score in vocational skills. So the sample size for this particular skill is 124. Of this, 124, fathers of 14 children were either dead or divorced. So, while calculating parent involvement score for vocational skills with respect to father-related variables sample size was further reduced to 110.

Similarly, out of the total sample of 170, the fathers of sixteen children were either dead or divorced. So, while calculating parent involvement score with respect to age, education, and occupation of father, these sixteen, subjects were kept out of the total sample and thereby reduced the sample size to 154.

In order to find out the different levels of parental involvement the total sample was divided into three groups as 'high involvement group', 'average involvement group', and 'low involvement group'. This classification was done on the basis of considering a parent involvement score of 70 per cent and above as high involvement, 40 per cent and above but less than 70 per cent as average involvement, and below 40 per cent as low involvement.

Statistical Techniques Used for Analysis

The collected data were analysed with respect to a number of background variables. The following statistical techniques were used for this purpose:

(a) Computation of frequencies and percentages.

(b) Computation of arithmetic mean and standard division.

(c) Computation of 't' value to test the significance of difference between the means of two groups of data.

(d) The method of logarithmic transformation was used to transform the data prior to the application of ANOVA as the data show high variability.

(e) One-way analysis of variance to test the significance of difference between the means of three or more groups of data.

(f) Whenever a statistically significant 'F' value was observed, test of Least Significant Difference was used for post hoc comparisons. Procedure given by Steel and Torie (1980, p. 137) has been used for this purpose.

(g) Karl Pearson's product-moment coefficient of correlation was computed to study the nature and intensity of relationship between parental involvement and certain selected variables.

(h) Chi-square test was used to test the significance of difference between the frequencies of different levels of parental involvement and different types of perceptions on various issues.

(i) In order to compare the proportion of numbers in the existing and expected levels of parental involvement, 'Z' test of double proportion was used. Procedure given by Gupta and Kapoor (1973, pp. 662-66) has been used for this purpose.

4

Analysis and Interpretations

This chapter deals with the analysis and interpretations of the data collected using different tools. The analysis and interpretations of the results have been presented under the following heads:

1. Parental involvement in developing the basic living skills in their mentally retarded children.
2. Parental perceptions with regard to their existing and expected levels of involvement in the educational decision-making.
3. Perceptions of parents and teachers with regard to the efforts taken by the teachers and school authorities for enhancing parental involvement.
4. Parental perceptions with regard to the effect of associated problems in the education of their retarded children and services available for their education.
5. Parental satisfaction in the method of the training provided to the mentally retarded children.
6. Perceptions of the parents and teachers with regard to parental guidance and counselling.

Parental Involvement in Developing the Basic Living Skills in their Mentally Retarded Children

As this section deals with the most important part of this study, the investigator has done an exhaustive analysis of data using different statistical techniques and presented the findings under three heads as shown below.

1. Total and skill-wise analysis of parental involvement in developing basic living skills in mentally retarded children.
2. Parental involvement with respect to certain child-related and parent-related variables.
3. Relationship between parental involvement and certain parent-related variables and age of mentally retarded children.

1. Total and Skill-wise Analysis of Parental Involvement in Developing Basic Living Skills in Mentally Retarded Children

Frequencies, percentages, mean values, and standard deviations have been computed, and bar diagrams and pie diagrams have been provided. The details of these analysis are presented in Table 4.1–4.11 and Figures 4.1–4.10. The percentages of parental involvement are calculated using the obtained mean involvement scores and maximum possible involvement scores.

Table 4.1 : *Mean, Standard Deviation and Percentage of Total Parental Involvement Scores (excluding Vocational Skills) in Developing Basic Living Skills in Mentally Retarded Children*

	Mean	*SD*	*Percentage*
Total parental involvement (excluding vocational skills)	96.68	38.63	50.40

Table 4.1 shows the mean value as 96.98 for the total parental involvement score (excluding vocational skills) with a standard deviation of 38.63. The large value of standard deviation indicates that the parental involvement scores are more spread out. The percentage of parent involvement obtained is 50.40, which shows that the general trend of the involvement of parents in developing basic living skills in their mentally retarded children is neither high nor very low.

Table 4.2 and Fig. 4.1 reveal that among the various skills, the involvement of parents in developing the self-care skills is highest (66.60%), followed by that in social skills (59.90%), health and safety skills (53.90%), and motor skills (52.30%). In all the other skills the parental involvement was found to be less than 50 per cent, and the

Table 4.2 : *Mean, Standard Deviation and Percentage of Parental Involvement in Developing Different Basic Living Skills in Mentally Retarded Children*

Skills	*Number*	*Mean*	*SD*	*Percentage*
Self-care	170	19.97	8.84	66.60
Social	170	16.18	8.08	59.90
Health and Safety	170	11.32	6.03	53.90
Motor	170	9.42	4.65	52.30
Leisure time	170	14.74	7.59	49.10
Vocational	124	14.65	7.78	48.80
Reading and Writing	170	10.95	7.11	45.60
Numerical	170	14.10	14.16	33.60

lowest involvement was found in developing numerical skills (33.60%). However, Table 4.1 and Fig. 4.1 show that the total parental involvement in developing basic living skills (excluding vocational skills) in their mentally retarded children is just above 50 per cent (50.40%).

The vertical bar graph shown in Fig. 4.1 represents the percentage of parental involvement in developing different basic living skills in the mentally retarded children.

As it is evident from Table 4.3 and Fig. 4.2 the majority of the parents belong to the 'average' involvement group (52.90%), followed by 'low' involvement group (30.60%) and only 16.50 per cent of the parents belong to the 'high' involvement group. Further, as the

Table 4.3 : *Frequencies, Percentages, and Chi-square Value with regard to Different Levels of Total Parental Involvement in Developing Basic Living Skills (excluding Vocational Skills)*

Level of Involvement	*Number*	*Percentage*	*Chi-Square*
High (a score of 70% and above, i.e., ≥ 134)	28	16.50	
Average (a score of 40% and about but < 70%, i.e., 77–133)	90	52.90	34.49**
Low (a score below 40%, i.e,. 0–76)	52	30.60	
Total	**170**	**100**	

** Significant at 0.01 level.

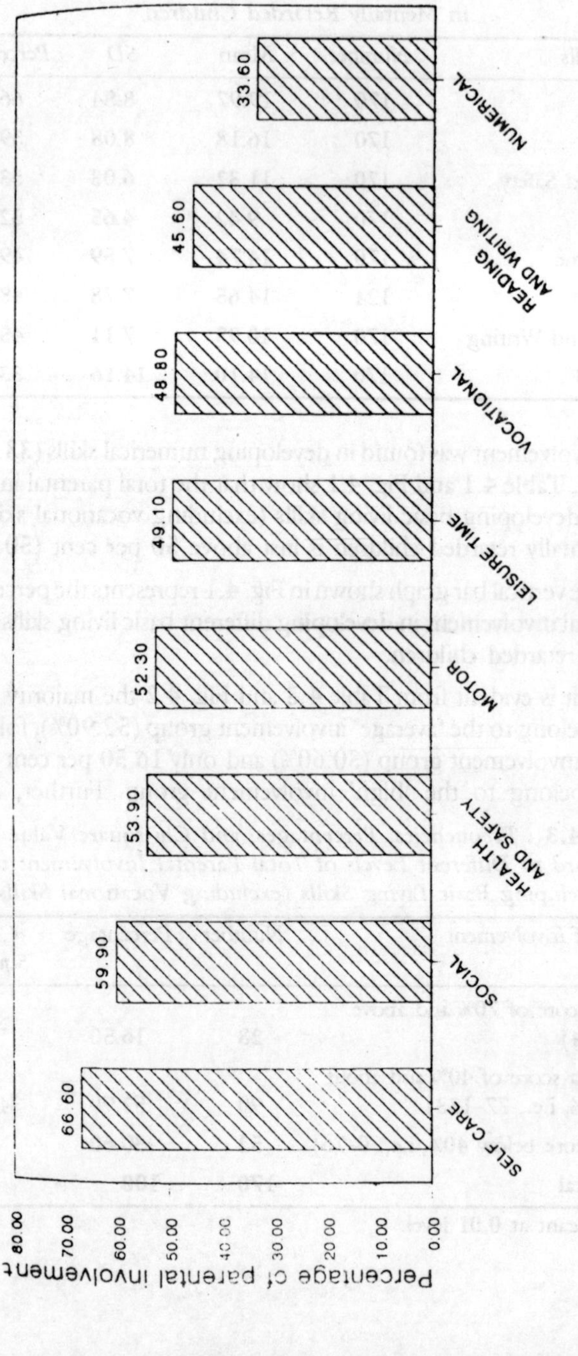

Fig. 1 : Percentages of Parental Involvement in Developing Basic Living Skills

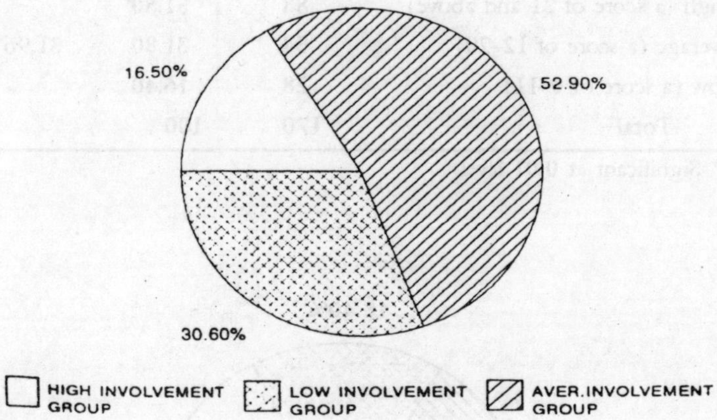

Fig. 4.2 : *Different Levels of Total Parental Involvement in Developing Basic Living Skills (excluding vocational skills)*

chi-square value obtained is found to be significant at 0.01 level, it can be concluded that difference between the observed frequencies of the three groups of parents with respect to the different levels of involvement in developing basic living skills is statistically significant.

Table 4.4 and Fig. 4.3 show that majority of the parents (51.80%) 'highly' involve in developing self-care skills, whereas involvement of 31.80 per cent of the parents is of 'average' level and the remaining 16.40 per cent of the parents have only a 'low' level of involvement.

The result of the chi-square test of significance indicates that there is significantly higher difference ($p < 0.01$) between the frequencies of the three groups of parents with respect to their level of involvement in developing self-care skills in mentally retarded children.

Table 4.4 : *Frequencies, Percentages, and Chi-square Value with Regard to Different Levels of Parental Involvement in Developing Self-care Skills*

Level of Involvement	*Number*	*Percentage*	*Chi-Square*
High (a score of 21 and above)	88	51.80	
Average (a score of 12–20)	54	31.80	31.96**
Low (a score of 0–11)	28	16.40	
Total	170	100	

** Significant at 0.01 level.

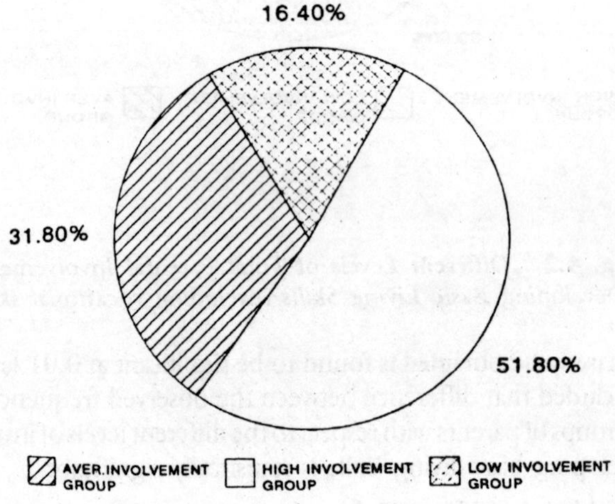

Fig. 4.3 : *Different Levels of Parental Involvement in Developing Self-Care Skills*

Table 4.5 : *Frequencies, Percentages, and Chi-square Value with Regard to Different Levels of Parental Involvement in Developing Motor Skills*

Level of Involvement	*Number*	*Percentage*	*Chi-Square*
High (a score of 13 and above)	39	22.90	
Average (a score of 7–12)	86	50.60	23.08**
Low (a score of 0–6)	45	26.50	
Total	170	100.00	

** Significant at 0.01 level.

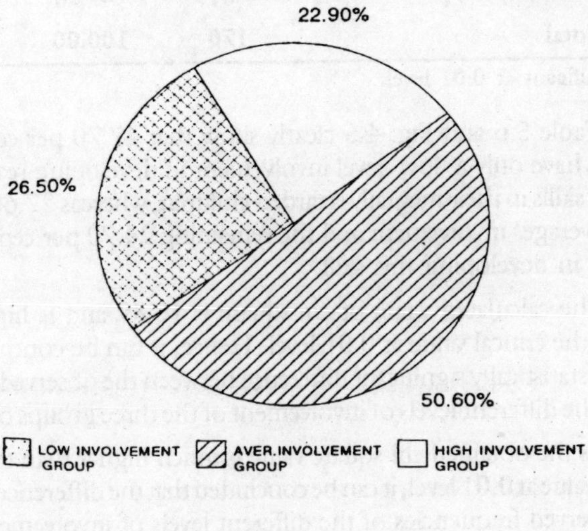

Fig. 4.4 : *Different Levels of Parental Involvement in Developing Motor Skills*

According to Table 4.5 and Fig. 4.4, majority (50.60%) of the parents belong to the 'average' involvement group, and 26.50 per cent belong to the 'low' involvement group; and only 22.90 per cent of the parents have 'high' involvement in developing motor skills in their mentally retarded children. The obtained chi-square value is 23.08 which is much higher than that of the critical value at 0.01 level. Hence, it can be concluded that there is statistically significant difference between the observed frequencies of the three groups of parents with respect to their level of involvement in developing motor skills in mentally retarded children.

Table 4.6 : *Frequencies, Percentages, and Chi-square Value with Regard to Different Levels of Parental Involvement in Developing Reading and Writing Skills*

Level of Involvement	*Number*	*Percentage*	*Chi-Square*
High (a score of 17 and above)	42	24.70	
Average (a score of 10–16)	47	27.60	15.89**
Low (a score of 0–9)	81	47.70	
Total	**170**	**100.00**	

** Significant at 0.01 level.

Table 5.6 and Fig. 4.5 clearly show that 47.70 per cent of the parents have only a 'low' level involvement in developing reading and writing skills in their mentally retarded children, whereas 27.60 per cent have 'average' involvement and the remaining 24.70 per cent 'highly' involve in developing this skill.

The calculated value of chi-square is 15.89 and is higher than that of the critical value at 0.01 level. Hence, it can be concluded that there is statistically significant difference between the observed frequencies of the different levels of involvement of the three groups of parents.

As the obtained chi-square value is much higher than that of the critical value at 0.01 level, it can be concluded that the difference between the observed frequencies of the different levels of involvement of the three groups of parents is statistically significant.

From Table 4.7 and Fig. 4.6, it can be seen that the majority of the parents (67.60%) have only a 'low' level involvement in developing numerical skills in their mentally retarded children, whereas 21.20 per cent have 'high' involvement and 11.20 per cent have 'average' involvement.

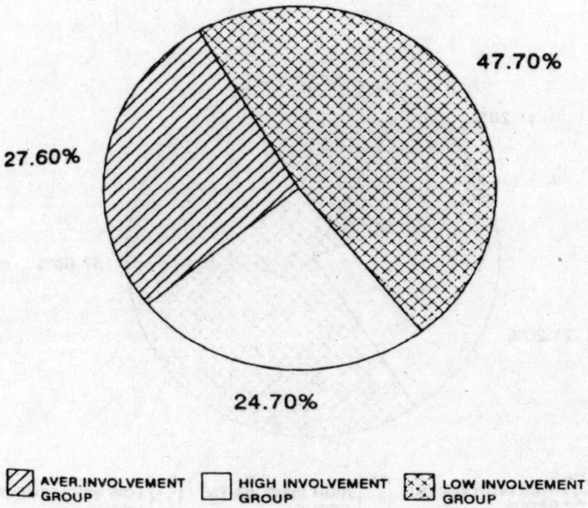

Fig. 4.5 : *Different Levels of Parental Involvement in Developing Reading and Writing Skills*

Table 4.7 : *Frequencies, Percentages, and Chi-square Value with Regard to Different Levels of Parental Involvement in Developing Numerical Skills*

Level of Involvement	*Number*	*Percentage*	*Chi-Square*
High (a score of 29 and above)	36	21.20	
Average (a score of 17–28)	19	11.20	92.61**
Low (a score of 0–16)	115	67.60	
Total	**170**	**100.00**	

** Significant at 0.01 level.

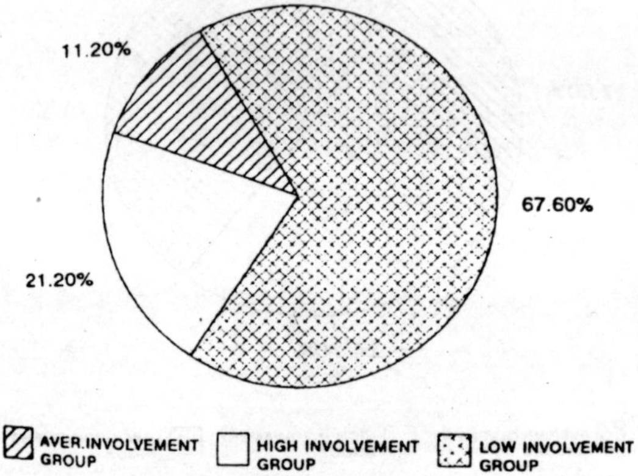

Fig. 4.6 : *Different Levels of Parental Involvement in Developing Numerical Skills*

Table 4.8 : *Frequencies, Percentages, and Chi-square Value with Regard to Different Levels of Parental Involvement in Developing Health and Safety Skills*

Level of Involvement	*Number*	*Percentage*	*Chi-Square*
High (a score of 15 and above)	51	30.00	
Average (a score of 8–14)	74	43.50	8.27*
Low (a score of 0–7)	45	26.50	
Total	**170**	**100.00**	

* Significant at 0.05 level.

Table 4.8 and Fig. 4.7 show that the 43.50 per cent of the parents have an 'average' level involvement in developing health and safety skills

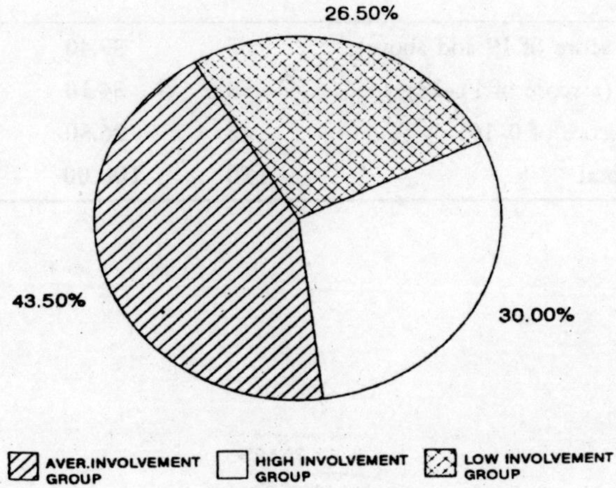

Fig. 4.7 : *Different Levels of Parental Involvement in Developing Health and Safety Skills*

in their retarded children. However, 30.00 per cent of the parents have 'high' level involvement while the remaining 26.50 per cent have only 'low' level involvement.

The result of the chi-square test shows that there exists statistically significant difference ($p < 0.05$) between the observed frequencies of the three groups of parents with respect to the different levels of involvement in developing health and safety skills in their mentally retarded children.

Table 4.9. and Fig. 4.8 show that 39.40 per cent of the parents have 'high' involvement in developing social skills in their mentally retarded children, while 34.10 per cent have 'average' level of involvement and 26.50 per cent have only 'low' level of involvement.

Table 4.9 : *Frequencies, Percentages, and Chi-square Value with Regard to Different Levels of Parental Involvement in Developing Social Skills*

Level of Involvement	*Number*	*Percentage*	*Chi-Square*
High (a score of 19 and above)	67	39.40	
Average (a score of 11–18)	58	34.10	4.32
Low (a score of 0–10)	45	26.50	
Total	170	100.00	

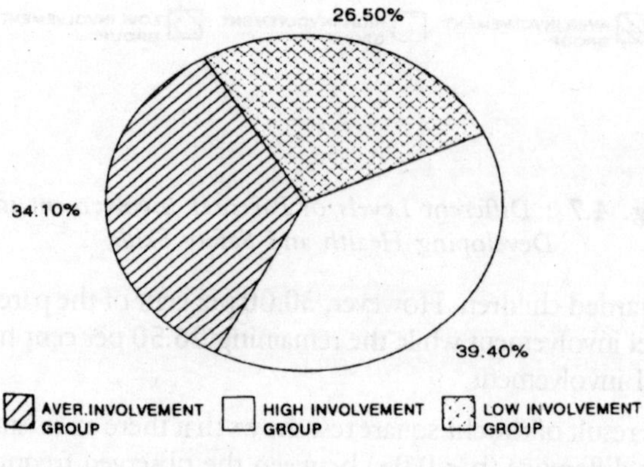

Fig. 4.8 : *Different Levels of Parental Involvement in Developing Social Skills*

As the calculated chi-square value is less than that of the critical value either at 0.01 level or at 0.05 level, it can be concluded that in developing social skills in their mentally retarded children, the observed frequencies of the three levels of parents involvement do not differ significantly.

Table 4.10 and Fig. 4.9 show that only 23.40 per cent of the parents have 'high' involvement in developing vocational skills in their mentally retarded children, whereas 40.30 per cent have 'average' level involvement and 36.30 per cent have only 'low' involvement.

Table 4.10 : *Frequencies, Percentages, and Chi-square Value with Regard to Different Levels of Parental Involvement in Developing Vocational Skills*

Level of Involvement	*Number*	*Percentage*	*Chi-Square*
High (a score of 21 and above)	29	23.40	
Average (a score of 12–20)	50	40.30	5.82
Low (a score of 0–11)	45	36.30	
Total	**124**	**100.00**	

It is evident from Table 4.10 that the calculated value of the chi-square is not significant. This means that the difference between the observed frequencies of the three levels of parental involvement is not statistically significant.

Table 4.11 and Fig. 4.10 clearly show that 49.40 per cent of the parents have 'average' level involvement in developing leisure time skills in their mentally retarded children, while 30.60 per cent of the parents have only 'low' level involvement. Only 20.00 per cent of the parents have 'high' level involvement.

As the obtained chi-square value is significant at 0.01 level, it an be concluded that the difference between the observed frequencies of the different levels of involvement of the three groups of parents is statistically significant.

A close analysis of the above findings throws light into many interesting facts First of all, it can be seen that only in developing self-care skills, more than 50 per cent of the parents (51.80%) have 'high' level involvement. In social skills and health and safety skills it was found to be 39.40 per cent and 30.00 per cent respectively. However, in all the other skills, less than 25 per cent of the parent were found to be

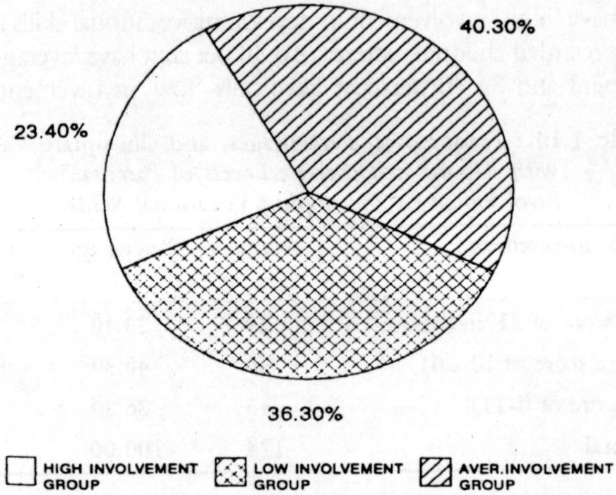

Fig. 4.9 : *Different Levels of Parental Involvement in Developing Vocational Skills*

Table 4.11 : *Frequencies, Percentages, and Chi-square Value with Regard to Different Levels of Parental Involvement in Developing Leisure Time Skills*

Level of Involvement	*Number*	*Percentage*	*Chi-Square*
High (a score of 21 and above)	34	20.00	
Average (a score of 12–20)	84	49.40	22.62**
Low (a score of 0–11)	52	30.60	
Total	**170**	**100.00**	

** Significant at 0.01 level

having 'high' level involvement (reading and writing—24.70%, vocational—23.40%, motor—22.90%, numerical—21.20%, and leisure

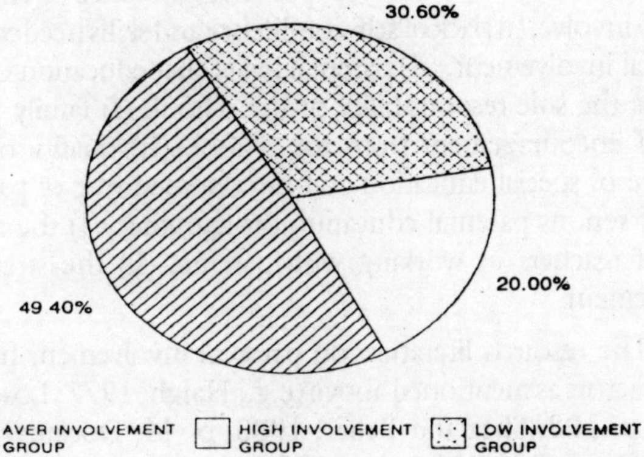

Fig. 4.10 : *Different Levels of Parental Involvement in Developing Leisurem Time Skills*

time—20.00%). When all the skills (excluding vocatio: !) are taken together, only 16.50 per cent of the parents have 'high' level involvement.

Secondly, in developing numerical skills and reading and writing skills it can be seen that the majority of the parents (6˜.6(%. and 47.70%) have only 'low' level involvement.

This mediocre level of parental involvement points out that the prevailing special education system for the mentally retarded children in the state does not lay much emphasis on the development of parents. Moreover, the parents themselves are not so much concerned about their own involvement. They may be interested only in the day caring of their retarded children, in order to be relieved from the burden of care and supervision.

Many factors might have contributed to this lack of active parental involvement. This may include: (a) inadequate knowledge of parents about the methods of special education, (b) parental ignorance about the benefits of involvement, (c) parental ignorance or confusion about how to involve, (d) lack of self-confidence and skills needed for successful parental involvement, (d) parental belief that education of the retarded child is the sole responsibility of the school, (f) family problems, (g) lack of encouragement from the school, (h) quality of the existing practice of special education and the assumed role of parents in it, (i) lack of serious parental education programmes, (j) the ability level or skill of teachers in working with parents, (k) the stress of parental involvement.

The research literature on parental involvement have shown so many factors as mentioned above (e.g., Haigh, 1977; Losen and Losen, 1985, p. 108; Shea and Bauer, 1985, p. 44; Dorgu, 1993; Grizzle, 1993; Quick, 1993; Thorne, 1993; Levenson, 1994; O'Meara, 1994; and Macfarlane, 1996). Further research is needed to elicit the specific factors that contribute to the lack of active parental involvement in developing basic living skills in the mentally retarded children.

2. *Parental Involvement with respect to Certain Child-Related and Parent-Related Variables*

The details of the comparisons of parental involvement made with respect to different child-related and parent-related variables are presented in Tables 4.12–4.54.

Table 4.12 gives the means, standard deviations, and 't' values of total parental involvement scores (excluding vocational skills) and that of different skills with respect to the sex of mentally retarded children. The test of significance for difference between the means shows that only the mean scores of motor skills and leisure time skills differ significantly ($p < 0.05$) with respect to the sex of the children. In both the skills higher mean values are obtained for the male groups, which indicate that parents of the male mentally retarded children are involved significantly higher than that of female counterparts in developing motor skills, and leisure time skills. Even though in all the other skills and in total, mean values are higher for the male groups, the 't' value obtained do now show statistically significant differences between the two groups of parents. However, the higher mean values indicate the trend of parents of male mentally retarded to get more involved than the parents of the female counterparts in developing all the basic living skills.

Table 4.12 : *Means, Standard Deviations, and 't' Values of Parental Involvement Scores with Respect to the Sex of Mentally Retarded Children*

Skill	*Male*			*Female*			't'
	N	*Mean*	*SD*	N	*Mean*	*SD*	value
Self-care	105	20.46	8.96	65	19.14	8.58	0.94
Motor	105	10.02	4.76	65	8.38	4.28	2.24*
Reading and Writing	105	11.33	7.58	65	10.23	6.18	0.98
Numerical	105	14.31	14.75	65	13.80	12.93	0.22
Health and Safety	105	11.52	6.14	65	10.94	5.81	0.62
Social	105	16.68	7.97	65	15.38	8.20	1.01
Vocational	74	15.04	8.05	50	14.06	7.25	0.87
Leisure time	105	15.80	7.34	65	12.88	7.63	2.47*
Total (excluding Vocational)	**105**	**100.12**	**40.29**	**65**	**90.91**	**35.05**	**1.51**

* Significant at 0.05 level.

This observed higher level of involvement of parents of male mentally retarded children is in agreement with the general trend in the field of education. Again, Table 3.1 (p. 62) shows that 61.76 per cent of the sample studied were the parents of male mentally retarded children. These results indicate the parental preference for the education of male mentally retarded children instead of the female ones. It may also be possible that the population of the mentally retarded include more males than females. Research conducted by Sen (1992, p. 157) revealed a higher prevalence rate for males than for females. Directory of Special Schools in Kerala (1995) also indicates higher enrolment of male mentally retarded children than of the female ones. Even then, well-designed research studies are needed in this direction, at least in this part of the country to find out the sex ratio of the mentally retarded and the attitude of parents towards their education.

Table 4.13 shows the arithmetic means, logarithmic means, and standard deviations of the parental involvement scores in developing basic living skills with respect to different age groups of mentally retarded children. Since the data has high variability, the technique of logarithmic transformation was applied to make the data more normal and make

Table 4.13 : *Means, Logarithmic Means, and Standard Deviations, of Parental Involvement Scores with Respect to the Age of the Mentally Retarded Children*

Skill	*6–10 Years (N=46)*		*11–15 Years (N=59)*		*16–20 Years (N=43)*		*Above 20 Years (N=22)*	
	Mean	*SD*	*Mean*	*SD*	*Mean*	*SD*	*Mean*	*SD*
Self-care	20.83 (1.2981)	7.38	19.88 (1.2314)	8.47	19.05 (1.1645)	10.05	20.09 (1.2061)	9.83
Motor	9.35 (0.9457)	4.91	9.95 (0.9757)	4.51	9.00 (0.9253)	4.42	8.77 (0.9171)	4.76
Reading and Writing	10.65 (0.9306)	7.78	10.31 (0.9360)	6.77	11.33 (0.9723)	7.36	12.14 (1.0799)	5.28
Numerical	14.24 (0.8842)	16.06	12.02 (0.8553)	12.54	14.23 (0.9788)	13.45	19.73 (1.1696)	13.82
Health and Safety	11.20 (0.9816)	6.48	10.61 (1.0118)	5.19	11.49 (1.0101)	6.27	13.00 (1.0700)	6.28
Social	16.09 (1.1226)	8.67	16.51 (1.1887)	7.24	15.42 (1.0943)	8.40	17.14 (1.1595)	8.61
Vocational	NA	NA	14.56 (1.1235)	7.76	14.37 (1.1103)	7.90	15.41 (1.1374)	7.38
Leisure time	15.28 (1.0839)	8.66	14.90 (1.1315)	7.08	14.56 (1.1108)	7.21	13.09 (1.0691)	6.97
Total (excluding Vocational)	**97.63 (1.9385)**	**44.75**	**94.12 (1.9466)**	**34.65**	**95.07 (1.9351)**	**39.14**	**104.09 (2.0025)**	**32.44**

Note : Logarithmic means are given in parenthesis.

it appropriate for applying the statistical technique of analysis of variance.

Table 4.14 shows that all the F-ratios obtained are far below the critical value of significance either at 0.01 level or at 0.05 level. Hence, it can be concluded that parental involvement in developing basic living skills in this mentally retarded children does not differ significantly with respect to the age of mentally retarded children. Findings of Pillay (1984) are in agreement with the present results.

Table 4.14 : *Summaries of Analysis of Variance (ANOVA) for the Parental Involvement in Developing Basic Living Skills with Respect to the Age of the Mentally Retarded Children*

Skill	*Source*	*Sum of squares*	*d.f.*	*Mean square*	*F-ratio*
Self-care	Between groups	0.4107	3	0.1369	
	Within groups	23.0690	166	0.1390	<1
	Total	23.4797	169		
Motor	Between groups	0.0886	3	0.0295	
	Within groups	14.3361	166	0.0864	<1
	Total	14.4247	169		
Reading and Writing	Between groups	0.3951	3	0.1317	
	Within groups	22.1601	166	0.1335	<1
	Total	22.5552	169		
Numerical	Between groups	1.7871	3	0.5957	
	Within groups	42.8144	166	0.2579	2.31
	Total	44.6015	169		
Health and Safety	Between groups	0.1165	3	0.0388	
	Within groups	15.8846	166	0.0957	<1
	Total	16.0011	169		
Social	Between groups	0.2500	3	0.0833	
	Within groups	20.8717	166	0.1257	<1
	Total	21.1217	169		
Vocational	Between groups	0.0111	2	0.0056	
	Within groups	10.2055	121	0.0843	<1
	Total	10.2166	123		
Leisure Time	Between groups	0.0914	3	0.0305	
	Within groups	20.2537	166	0.1220	<1
	Total	20.3451	169		
Total (excluding Vocational)	Between groups	0.0768	3	0.0256	
	Within groups	7.0478	166	0.0423	<1
	Total	7.1246	169		

These results indicate that irrespective of the age of retarded children, parental involvement in uniform is developing basic living skills. This may be due to the 'ever dependent' nature of their retarded children whose age, therefore, becomes irrelevant for parental involvement. Unlike in the care of normal children who as they grow older become more and more independent so that parental involvement becomes lower, in mentally retarded children dependence do not decrease considerably as they grow older and this warrants the continuous involvement and supervision of parents.

Table 4.15 provides the arithmetic means, logarithmic means, and standard deviations of the parental involvement scores in developing basic living skills with respect to the birth order of their mentally retarded children.

It may be seen from Table 4.16 that the parental involvement in developing basic living skills do not differ significantly with the birth order of mentally retarded children. All the F-ratios obtained are found to be far below the critical value of significance either at 0.01 level or at 0.05 level. It can, therefore, be concluded that the birth order of mentally retarded children is not a factor in deciding the nature of parental involvement in developing basic living skills. The mean values (Table 4.15) also do not show any specific trend.

These findings indicate that whether the child is first born, middle born, or last born is immaterial for parents to be involved in developing basic living skills. Also, all retarded children need parental involvement and all of them have to develop basic living skills too. So the birth order of the mentally retarded children is not a predictor of the nature of parental involvement.

Table 4.17 provides the arithmetic means, logarithmic means, and standard deviations of the parental involvement scores in developing basic living skills with respect to religion.

Table 4.18 indicates that parental involvement in developing social skills significantly differ ($p < 0.05$) with religion, whereas in all other skills the F-ratios obtained are found to be not significant either at 0.01 level or at 0.05 level. Hence it can be concluded that except in developing social skills, parental involvement in developing basic living skills does not differ with reference to religion.

The result indicates that among the different skills studied, the social skills is more related to religion than the other skills.

Table 4.15 : *Means, Logarithmic Means, and Standard Deviations of Parental Involvement Scores with Respect to the Birth Order of the Mentally Retarded Children*

Skill	First born			Middle born			Last born		
	N	Mean	SD	N	Mean	SD	N	Mean	SD
Self-care	64	21.80 (1.3119)	7.30	36	19.86 (1.2203)	9.11	70	18.33 (1.1586)	9.62
Motor	64	9.53 (0.9801)	4.19	36	9.50 (0.9876)	3.75	70	9.43 (0.9015)	5.75
Reading and Writing	64	11.56 (0.9762)	7.49	36	10.92 (1.0097)	5.59	70	10.31 (0.9261)	7.36
Numerical	64	16.22 (1.0011)	15.36	36	14.14 (0.9600)	12.76	70	12.30 (0.8614)	13.39
Health and Safety	64	11.25 (0.9962)	6.56	36	11.67 (1.0475)	5.20	70	11.16 (1.0051)	5.90
Social	64	15.86 (1.1392)	8.27	36	15.72 (1.1290)	8.04	70	16.51 (1.1494)	7.84
Vocational	38	13.97 (1.0968)	7.91	32	16.06 (1.1876)	6.72	54	14.28 (1.0994)	8.10
Leisure time	64	15.44 (1.1195)	7.66	36	13.17 (1.0736)	6.79	70	14.77 (1.1087)	7.80
Total (excluding Vocational)	**64**	**101.66 (1.9595)**	**42.79**	**36**	**94.94 (1.9567)**	**30.30**	**70**	**92.83 (1.9348)**	**37.93**

Note : Logarithmic means are given in parenthesis.

Table 4.16 : *Summaries of ANOVA for the Parental Involvement in Developing Basic Living Skills with Respect to the Birth Order of the Mentally Retarded Children*

Skill	*Source*	*Sum of squares*	*d.f.*	*Mean square*	*F-ratio*
Self-care	Between groups	0.79	2	0.40	
	Within groups	22.69	167	0.14	2.82
	Total	23.48	169		
Motor	Between groups	0.27	2	0.14	
	Within groups	14.37	167	0.09	1.50
	Total	14.64	169		
Reading and Writing	Between groups	0.18	2	0.09	
	Within groups	22.42	167	0.13	<1
	Total	26.60	169		
Numerical	Between groups	0.68	2	0.34	
	Within groups	43.89	167	0.26	1.31
	Total	44.57	169		
Health and Safety	Between groups	0.06	2	0.03	
	Within groups	15.94	167	0.10	<1
	Total	16.00	169		
Social	Between groups	0.01	2	0.01	
	Within groups	20.98	167	0.13	<1
	Total	20.99	169		
Vocational	Between groups	0.19	2	0.10	
	Within groups	10.03	121	0.08	1.15
	Total	10.22	123		
Leisure Time	Between groups	0.05	2	0.03	
	Within groups	20.30	167	0.12	<1
	Total	20.35	169		
Total (excluding Vocational)	**Between groups**	**0.02**	**2**	**0.01**	
	Within groups	**7.10**	**167**	**0.04**	**<1**
	Total	**7.12**	**169**		

The least significant difference test for paired comparisons yielded a significant difference at 0.05 level between the involvement scores of Hindus and Muslims, with Hindus showing higher involvement than Muslims. Similarly, significant difference was obtained at 0.05 level between the involvement scores of Muslims and Christians, with

Table 4.17 : *Means, Logarithmic Means, and Standard Deviations of Parental Involvement Scores with Respect to Religion*

Skill	*Hindu*			*Muslim*			*Christian*		
	N	*Mean*	*SD*	*N*	*Mean*	*SD*	*N*	*Man*	*SD*
Self-care	53	20.64 (1.2649)	8.31	18	18.67 (1.1875)	9.56	99	19.82 (1.2178)	8.94
Motor	53	9.04 (0.9307)	4.67	18	9.06 (0.9334)	4.31	99	9.65 (0.9586)	4.68
Reading and Writing	53	11.66 (0.9722)	8.13	18	10.78 (0.9350)	7.43	99	14.58 (0.9822)	30.55
Numerical	53	15.81 (0.9482)	16.39	18	13.33 (0.8689)	14.57	99	13.56 (0.9448)	12.60
Health and Safety	53	10.62 (0.9855)	6.06	18	9.39 (0.8993)	6.09	99	12.01 (1.0445)	5.87
Social	53	17.28 (1.1815)	7.41	18	11.83 (0.9684)	8.43	99	16.56 (1.1672)	7.91
Vocational	38	15.74 (1.1326)	9.06	12	11.92 (1.0217)	6.33	74	14.53 (1.1318)	7.09
Leisure time	53	15.57 (1.1281)	8.05	18	12.50 (1.0794)	6.06	99	14.61 (1.0978)	7.50
Total (excluding Vocational)	**53**	**100.72 (1.9635)**	**44.67**	**18**	**84.33 (1.8591)**	**45.66**	**99**	**96.63 (1.9571)**	**32.85**

Note : Logarithmic means are given in parenthesis.

Table 4.18 : *Summaries of ANOVA for the Parental Involvement in Developing Basic Living Skills with Respect to Religion*

Skill	*Source*	*Sum of squares*	*d.f.*	*Mean square*	*F-ratio*
Self-care	Between groups	0.11	2	0.05	
	Within groups	23.37	167	0.14	<1
	Total	23.48	169		
Motor	Between groups	0.03	2	0.02	
	Within groups	14.39	167	0.09	<1
	Total	14.42	169		
Reading and Writing	Between groups	0.03	2	0.02	
	Within groups	26.05	167	0.16	<1
	Total	26.08	169		
Numerical	Between groups	0.10	2	0.05	
	Within groups	44.50	167	0.27	<1
	Total	44.60	169		
Health and Safety	Between groups	0.37	2	0.19	
	Within groups	15.63	167	0.09	2.06
	Total	16.00	169		
Social	Between groups	0.68	2	0.34	
	Within groups	19.08	167	0.11	3.09*
	Total	19.76	169		
Vocational	Between groups	0.13	2	0.07	
	Within groups	10.09	121	0.08	<1
	Total	10.22	123		
Leisure Time	Between groups	0.05	2	0.03	
	Within groups	20.30	167	0.12	<1
	Total	20.35	169		
Total (excluding Vocational)	**Between groups**	**0.16**	**2**	**0.08**	
	Within groups	**6.96**	**167**	**0.04**	**2.00**
	Total	**7.12**	**169**		

* Significant at 0.05 level.

Christians showing higher involvement than Muslims. However, the difference between Hindus and Christians was found to be not statistically significant.

An explanation of these results is rather difficult, but further research could explore the specific reasons for these differences among parents of different religions.

Table 4.19 : *Test of Least Significant Difference for Significance between Pairs of Mean Scores of Parent Involvement in Developing Social Skills with Respect to Religion*

Pairs	Logarithmic Mean	Difference between Pairs	Critical difference
Hindus and Muslims	1.1815 0.9684	0.2131	0.1810*
Hindus and Christians	1.1815 1.1672	0.0143	0.1130
Muslims and Christians	0.9684 1.1672	0.1988	0.1700*

* Significant at 0.01 level

Table 4.20 shows the arithmetic means, logarithmic means, and standard deviations of the parental involvement scores in developing basic living skills with respect to number of siblings of the mentally retarded children.

As it is evident from Table 4.21, parental involvement in developing self-care skills differ significantly ($p < 0.05$) with the difference in the number of siblings. The test of significance for difference between the means of parental involvement score in developing all other basic livings skills studied indicate the nature of involvement do not differ significantly with respect to the number of siblings of the mentally retarded children.

The least significant difference test for paired comparisons shows that a significant difference at 0.05 level exists between the involvement scores of parents of 'no sibling group and three siblings group', with 'no sibling' group showing higher involvement than the other group. Similarly, the test yielded a significant difference between the involvement scores of parents of 'no siblings group and four and more siblings group' ($p<0.05$) with the 'no siblings group' showing higher involvement. Another significant difference was obtained between 'one sibling group and four and more siblings group' ($p < 0.05$) with the former having higher involvement. Again, it was observed that 'two siblings group and three siblings group' differ significantly at 0.05 level with the former showing higher involvement; and lastly, 'two siblings group'

Table 4.20 : *Means, Logarithmic Means, and Standard Deviations, of Parental Involvement Scores with Respect to Number of Siblings of the Mentally Retarded Children*

Skill	No siblings			One sibling			Two siblings			Three siblings			Four and above siblings		
	N	*Mean*	*SD*	*N*	*Mean*	*SD*	*N*	*Mean*	*SD*	*N*	*Mean*	*SD*	*N*	*Mean*	*SD*
Self-care	16	22.31 (1.3129)	7.73	58	19.09 (1.2261)	8.14	62	21.84 (1.2991)	8.01	19	16.74 (1.0412)	10.45	15	17.07 (0.8669)	10.82
Motor	16	9.88 (0.9941)	4.12	58	8.02 (0.8804)	4.40	62	10.27 (0.9859)	4.72	19	10.58 (1.9989)	4.77	15	9.07 (0.7347)	4.33
Reading and Writing	16	10.31 (0.9344)	7.26	58	9.93 (0.8762)	7.77	62	11.06 (1.0010)	6.48	119	11.84 (0.9890)	7.34	15	13.53 (0.8966)	5.23
Numerical	16	14.88 (0.8611)	17.91	58	13.67 (0.8846)	14.85	62	13.60 (0.9472)	12.74	19	16.89 (0.9650)	16.16	15	16.33 (0.9122)	10.48
Health and Safety	16	10.50 (0.9471)	7.01	58	13.76 (0.9708)	28.15	62	11.79 (1.0614)	5.09	19	13.53 (1.0816)	6.31	15	11.80 (0.8057)	5.86
Social	16	14.25 (1.0690)	9.13	58	16.19 (1.1580)	7.80	62	16.24 (1.1576)	7.20	19	18.16 (1.1715)	9.21	15	15.47 (0.8438)	9.24
Vocational	7	13.43 (1.0328)	10.79	37	14.05 (1.0932)	8.44	48	13.19 (1.1024)	6.33	17	18.35 (1.2426)	8.25	15	16.60 (1.0308)	6.60
Leisure time	16	16.31 (1.1442)	8.11	58	13.69 (1.0580)	7.80	62	17.33 (1.1068)	3.38	19	17.26 (1.1960)	8.40	15	14.13 (0.8888)	5.90
Total (excluding Vocational)	**16**	**98.44 (1.9235)**	**48.51**	**58**	**90.90 (1.9184)**	**39.45**	**62**	**99.18 (1.9715)**	**34.00**	**19**	**103.42 (1.9655)**	**45.70**	**15**	**97.40 (1.5613)**	**27.32**

Note : Logarithmic means are given in parenthesis.

Table 4.21 : *Summaries of ANOVA for the Parental Involvement in Developing Basic Living Skills with Respect to Number of Siblings of the Mentally Retarded Children*

Skill	*Source*	*Sum of squares*	*d.f.*	*Mean square*	*F-ratio*
Self-care	Between groups	1.3295	4	0.3324	
	Within groups	22.1502	165	0.1342	2.48*
	Total	23.4797	169		
Motor	Between groups	0.4421	4	0.1105	
	Within groups	13.9826	165	0.0847	1.30
	Total	14.4247	169		
Reading and Writing	Between groups	0.9991	4	0.2498	
	Within groups	21.6013	165	0.1309	1.91
	Total	22.6004	169		
Numerical	Between groups	0.9882	4	0.2471	
	Within groups	44.0676	165	0.2671	<1
	Total	45.0558	169		
Health and Safety	Between groups	0.4032	4	0.1008	
	Within groups	17.3461	165	0.1051	<1
	Total	17.7493	169		
Social	Between groups	0.2118	4	0.0530	
	Within groups	20.8611	165	0.1264	<1
	Total	21.0729	169		
Vocational	Between groups	0.4451	4	0.1113	
	Within groups	10.9472	119	0.0920	1.21
	Total	11.3923	123		
Leisure Time	Between groups	0.3170	4	0.0793	
	Within groups	20.0281	165	0.1214	<1
	Total	20.3451	169		
Total (excluding Vocational)	**Between groups**	**0.1134**	**4**	**0.0284**	
	Within groups	**7.0112**	**165**	**0.0425**	**<1**
	Total	**7.1246**	**169**		

* Significant at 0.05 level.

and 'four and more siblings group' also show a significant difference ($p < 0.05$) between them in the parental involvement in developing self-care skills in the mentally retarded children, with the 'two siblings' group showing higher involvement.

Table 4.22 : *Test of Least Significant Difference for Significance between Pairs of Mean Scores of Parent Involvement in Developing Self-care Skills with Respect to Number of Siblings of the Mentally Retarded Children*

Pairs	*Logarithmic Mean*	*Difference between Pairs*	*Critical difference*
No siblings and one sibling	1.3129 1.2261	0.0868	0.2068
No siblings and two siblings	1.3129 1.2991	0.0138	0.2054
No siblings and three siblings	1.3129 1.0412	0.2717	0.2486*
No siblings and four and more siblings	1.3129 0.8699	0.4430	0.2634*
One siblings and two siblings	1.2261 1.2991	0.0730	0.1336
One siblings and three siblings	1.2261 1.0412	0.1849	0.1936
One siblings and four and more siblings	1.2261 0.8699	0.3562	0.2122*
Two siblings and three siblings	1.2991 1.0412	0.2579	0.1920*
Two siblings and four and more siblings	1.2991 0.8699	0.4292	0.0222*
Three siblings and four and more siblings	1.0412 0.8699	0.1713	0.2530

* Significant at 0.05 level

No statistically significant difference was observed between the other five pairs compared.

The results indicate a trend that as the difference in number of siblings increases between the pairs, there exists a significant difference in the parental involvement. Moreover, the mean value clearly reveal that the parent groups with 'nil or lesser number of siblings' are having higher level of involvement in developing self-care skills when compared to the parent groups with greater number of siblings. This may be because the parents have no other children or lesser number of children to look after which in turn gives them enough time and energy to spend for their retarded child leading to their higher level of involvement. At the same time, involvement in none of the other skills show a similar trend. As no other research findings are available to support or oppose these findings, further research is needed to endorse these results.

Table 4.23 shows the arithmetic means, logarithmic means and standard deviations of the parental involvement scores in developing basic living skills with respect to the number of years of schooling of mentally retarded children.

Table 4.24 clearly reveals that the parental involvement in developing basic living skills does not differ significantly with the number of years of schooling of the mentally retarded children. All the F-ratios obtained are found to be far below the critical value of significance either at 0.01 level or at 0.05 level. Hence, it can be concluded that the number of years of schooling of mentally retarded children is not a factor in deciding the level of parental involvement.

The popular expectation may be that as the child spends more years in the special school, the amount of parental involvement required in his/her education becomes reduced. But the results obtained are not in agreement with such a conclusion. Also, these findings lead to the following assumptions:

(a) The more years a retarded child attends a special school, the greater would be his/her exposure to special training which may make the child independent enough to reduce the level of further parental involvement in developing basic living skills.

(b) As the retarded child and its parents grow in years simultaneously, the level of their involvement tend to go down. However, the grown-up siblings of the retarded child may take over certain roles from the parents and this may be instrumental in reducing the amount of involvement of parents as the child attends more years in the special school.

(c) Decrease in the level of parental involvement and increase in the number of years of schooling of the retarded child may be because parents are mainly concerned with the training in self-care skills

Table 4.23 : *Means, Logarithmic Means, and Standard Deviations, of Parental Involvement Scores with Respect to Number of Years of Schooling*

Skill	*One Year*			*2–3 Years*			*4–5 Years*			*6–8 Years*			*9 and more Years*		
	N	*Mean*	*SD*	*N*	*Mean*	*SD*	*N*	*Mean*	*SD*	*N*	*Mean*	*SD*	*N*	*Mean*	*SD*
Self-care	24	21.75 (1.2930)	7.81	58	19.22 (1.1874)	9.08	40	18.68 (1.2099)	9.03	32	21.91 (1.2805)	8.96	16	19.19 (0.6158)	7.49
Motor	24	9.33 (0.9609)	4.07	58	8.72 (0.8955)	5.10	40	9.47 (0.9420)	4.87	32	13.19 (1.0117)	19.97	16	11.00 (0.5298)	3.59
Reading and Writing	24	19.42 (1.0081)	43.23	58	10.34 (0.9270)	7.17	40	10.32 (0.9191)	7.36	32	11.41 (1.0236)	6.24	16	13.19 (0.5352)	6.59
Numerical	24	11.58 (0.8585)	12.88	58	15.09 (0.9435)	15.20	40	14.30 (0.9209)	14.34	32	12.38 (0.8873)	13.00	16	18.06 (0.5750)	12.52
Health and Safety	24	9.88 (0.9427)	6.02	58	11.74 (1.0336)	5.80	40	10.35 (0.9748)	5.73	32	12.53 (1.0631)	6.24	16	11.75 (0.5074)	6.32
Social	24	14.04 (1.0140)	9.11	58	17.33 (1.2065)	7.25	40	15.78 (1.1213)	8.09	32	17.03 (1.1908)	8.29	16	16.25 (0.5541)	8.55
Vocational	10	16.80 (1.1060)	9.36	35	14.03 (1.1393)	6.21	34	14.32 (1.1004)	7.93	29	13.28 (1.0769)	7.52	16	17.81 (0.6714)	8.55
Leisure time	24	13.92 (1.0797)	7.58	58	14.66 (1.0817)	8.04	40	14.82 (1.1173)	7.59	32	14.72 (1.1084)	7.35	16	15.50 (0.5965)	6.14
Total (excluding Vocational)	**24**	**91.58 (1.9238)**	**39.36**	**58**	**97.10 (1.9483)**	**38.72**	**40**	**93.72 (1.9380)**	**39.26**	**32**	**98.88 (1.9668)**	**35.35**	**16**	**104.94 (0.9892)**	**40.05**

Note : Logarithmic means are given in parenthesis.

Table 4.24 : *Summaries of ANOVA for the Parental Involvement in Developing Basic Living Skills with Respect to the Number of Years of Schooling*

Skill	*Source*	*Sum of squares*	*d.f.*	*Mean square*	*F-ratio*
Self-care	Between groups	0.2982	4	0.0746	
	Within groups	23.1815	165	0.1405	<1
	Total	23.4797	169		
Motor	Between groups	0.4900	4	0.1225	
	Within groups	15.2070	165	0.0922	1.33
	Total	15.6970	169		
Reading and Writing	Between groups	0.4981	4	0.1245	
	Within groups	23.8383	165	0.1445	<1
	Total	24.3364	169		
Numerical	Between groups	0.9654	4	0.2414	
	Within groups	43.6361	165	0.2645	<1
	Total	44.6015	169		
Health and Safety	Between groups	0.2812	4	0.0703	
	Within groups	15.7199	165	0.0953	<1
	Total	16.0011	169		
Social	Between groups	0.7421	4	0.1855	
	Within groups	20.4238	165	0.1238	1.50
	Total	21.1659	169		
Vocational	Between groups	0.2321	4	0.0580	
	Within groups	9.9845	119	0.0839	<1
	Total	10.2166	123		
Leisure Time	Between groups	0.1773	4	0.0443	
	Within groups	20.1678	165	0.1222	<1
	Total	20.3451	169		
Total (excluding Vocational)	**Between groups**	**0.0441**	**4**	**0.0110**	
	Within groups	**7.0805**	**165**	**0.4720**	**<1**
	Total	**7.1246**	**169**		

which in almost all the cases starts and ends within the initial years of schooling. The parents may not have taken all the other aspects of curriculum seriously because of their misconception about the utility of teaching those things to a retarded child. Results shown in Table 4.2 (p. 71) promotes such a thinking as the percentage of parental involvement score in developing self-care skills is the highest (66.57%).

(d) The lack of simultaneous increase in the amount of the parental involvement with the increase in the number of years of schooling may be because of the parental thinking that, irrespective of the age or number of years of schooling, the retarded children need a uniform amount of parental involvement in developing basic living skills.

(e) Contrary to the above assumptions, another line of thought suggests that unlike in the case of normal children, more years of schooling do not ensure self-dependent to the retarded because they need supervision, care and involvement of parent in almost all their daily activities even after they grow older. Also, as they overcome their years of childhood, they need training in pre-vocational and vocational skills. This warrants increased parental involvement with increased years of schooling.

(f) Finally, the more years a retarded child attends a special school, the greater would be the chances for teachers and parents to contact and understand each other and build a healthy partnership; parents have more time to develop a clear awareness about the aims and methods of education suitable for their child and pick up the nature of involvement necessary for their child. This naturally should produce a higher level of parental involvement. But the results obtained reveal a bleak picture. Moreover, a closer analysis of the logarithmic mean values of parental involvement scores (Table 4.23) shows that parents of children with nine and more years of schooling had comparatively lower scores in all the skills. This again confirms that as the children spend more years in the special schools, the parental involvement becomes lower.

Even though, none of the F-values shows a significant difference among different groups of parents, as none of the above assumptions has any empirical evidence to support these assumptions need to be studied scientifically.

The mean values and standard deviations obtained for the involvement scores of urban and rural parents in developing basic living skills in their mentally retarded children are given in Table 4.25. The test of significance for difference between the means of parental involvement scores of different skills studied indicate that parental involvement does not differ significantly with respect to location of residence.

Table 4.25 : *Means, Standard Deviations, and 't' Values of Parental Involvement Scores with Respect to Location of Residence*

Skill	*Urban*			*Rural*			't'
	N	*Mean*	*SD*	*N*	*Mean*	*SD*	*value*
Self-care	62	19.35	9.24	108	20.06	8.73	0.50
Motor	62	9.76	4.63	108	9.19	4.65	0.77
Reading and Writing	62	11.15	6.89	108	10.78	7.21	0.32
Numerical	62	15.81	14.61	108	13.24	13.81	1.14
Health and Safety	62	11.02	6.26	108	11.60	5.94	0.60
Social	62	15.60	8.25	108	16.52	7.96	1.40
Vocational	47	14.11	8.04	77	14.97	7.55	0.36
Leisure time	62	15.39	7.44	108	14.28	7.64	0.92
Total (excluding Vocational)	**62**	**98.06**	**40.72**	**108**	**95.76**	**37.36**	**0.62**

This finding may be explained in terms of the uniqueness of the area studied. In most of the urban and rural areas of Kerala, one cannot notice much difference between the life-style and availability of facilities. An exception to this may be noted in the remote hill areas and coastal areas. This uniform pattern of attitude and life-style may be the reason for the lack of significant difference in the parental involvement or urban and rural samples.

Table 4.26 provides the arithmetic means, logarithmic means, and standard deviations of the parental involvement scores in developing basic living skills with respect to the age of father.

From Table 4.27, it may be seen that statistically significant difference ($p < 0.01$) exists between the different age groups of parents in their involvement in developing reading and writing skills as well as health and safety skills in their mentally retarded children. Hence it can be concluded that the age of the father is a significant factor in the parental involvement in developing reading and writing as well as health and safety skills. Similarly, the three different age groups of parents are found to differ significantly ($p < 0.05$) in their involvement in developing basic living skills when the total score (excluding vocational)

Table 4.26 : *Means, Logarithmic Means, and Standard Deviations of Parental Involvement Scores with Respect to the Age of Father*

Skill	Younger Age Group			Middle Age Group			Old Age Group		
	N	*Mean*	*SD*	*N*	*Mean*	*SD*	*N*	*Mean*	*SD*
Self-care	10	20.00 (1.2382)	9.07	103	21.16 (1.2758)	7.97	41	18.12 (1.1524)	9.91
Motor	10	9.10 (0.9424)	4.83	103	9.61 (0.9589)	4.73	41	9.29 (0.9462)	4.38
Reading and Writing	10	8.00 (0.6861)	8.83	103	10.33 (0.9350)	7.05	41	12.41 (1.0686)	6.39
Numerical	10	8.10 (0.7047)	12.06	103	12.44 (0.8729)	13.32	41	17.15 (1.0485)	14.31
Health and Safety	10	6.60 (0.7056)	6.37	103	11.48 (1.0301)	5.63	41	11.63 (1.0375)	6.20
Social	10	12.60 (0.9695)	9.95	103	16.81 (1.1758)	7.59	41	16.46 (1.1691)	7.74
Vocational	2	10.50 (0.9404)	7.50	67	14.63 (1.1405)	7.16	41	15.61 (1.1599)	7.85
Leisure time	10	12.50 (0.9893)	9.09	103	14.50 (1.0937)	7.56	41	16.27 (1.1699)	8.20
Total (excluding Vocational)	**10**	**76.90 (1.7800)**	**52.03**	**103**	**96.49 (1.9505)**	**37.40**	**41**	**101.22 (1.9827)**	**36.89**

Note : Logarithmic means are given in parenthesis.

Table 4.27 : *Summaries of ANOVA for the Parental Involvement in Developing Basic Living Skills with Respect to the Age of Father*

Skill	*Source*	*Sum of squares*	*d.f.*	*Mean square*	*F-ratio*
Self-care	Between groups	0.4467	2	0.2234	
	Within groups	19.9410	151	0.1321	1.69
	Total	20.3877	153		
Motor	Between groups	0.0063	2	0.0032	
	Within groups	12.2850	151	0.0814	<1
	Total	12.2913	153		
Reading and Writing	Between groups	1.2936	2	0.6468	
	Within groups	19.3080	151	0.1279	5.06**
	Total	20.6016	153		
Numerical	Between groups	1.3493	2	0.6747	
	Within groups	39.2916	151	0.2602	2.59
	Total	40.6409	153		
Health and Safety	Between groups	0.9988	2	0.4994	
	Within groups	12.3298	151	0.0817	6.11**
	Total	13.3286	153		
Social	Between groups	0.3920	2	0.1960	
	Within groups	16.0140	151	0.1061	1.85
	Total	16.4060	153		
Vocational	Between groups	0.0941	2	0.0471	
	Within groups	6.3675	107	0.0595	<1
	Total	6.4616	109		
Leisure Time	Between groups	0.3188	2	0.1594	
	Within groups	18.6083	151	0.1232	1.29
	Total	18.9271	153		
Total (excluding Vocational)	**Between groups**	**0.3322**	**2**	**0.1661**	
	Within groups	**6.1594**	**151**	**0.0408**	**4.07***
	Total	**6.4916**	**153**		

* Significant at 0.05 level. ** Significant at 0.01 level.

was considered. With all the other skills, the F-ratios obtained are found to be below the critical value of significance either at 0.01 level or at 0.05 level. This indicates that the age of the father is not a discriminating factor in the parental involvement in developing these skills.

Table 4.28 : *Test of Least Significant Difference for Significance between Pairs of Mean Scores of Parent Involvement in Developing Reading and Writing Skills with Respect to the Age of Father*

Pairs	*Logarithmic Mean*	*Difference between Pairs*	*Critical difference*
Younger age group and middle age group	0.6861 0.9350	0.2489	0.2370**
Younger age group and old age group	0.6861 1.0686	0.3825	0.2522**
Middle age group and old age group	0.9350 1.0686	0.1336	0.1320**

** Significant at 0.01 level

The least significant difference test for paired comparisons yielded a significant difference at 0.01 level between all the three pairs of different age groups compared. A closer analysis of the mean values (Table 4.26) reveal higher level of involvement by parents of 'old age group', followed by that of 'middle age group' and 'younger age group' respectively. In other words, the results indicate that as the age of father increases, there is a significant tendency to involve more in developing reading and writing skills in their mentally retarded child.

The least significant difference test for paired comparisons shows that a significant difference at 0.01 level exists between the mean involvement scores of 'younger age group and middle age group' with the later showing higher involvement than the former group. Similarly, the test yielded a significant difference between the mean involvement scores of 'younger age group and old age group' ($p < 0.01$) with 'old age group' showing higher involvement in developing health and safety skills in their mentally retarded children. However, no statistically significant difference was observed between the mean involvement scores of 'middle age group and old age group'.

The mean values (Table 4.26) favour the trend that as the age of the father increases, the amount of parental involvement also is found to increase in developing health and safety skills in their mentally retarded children.

Table 4.29 : *Test of Least Significant Difference for Significance between Pairs of Mean Scores of Parental Involvement in Developing Health and Safety Skills with Respect to the Age of Father*

Pairs	*Logarithmic Mean*	*Difference between Pairs*	*Critical difference*
Younger age group and middle age group	0.7056 1.0301	0.3245	0.1894**
Younger age group and old age group	0.7056 1.0375	0.3319	0.2016**
Middle age group and old age group	1.0301 1.0375	0.0074	0.1056

** Significant at 0.01 level

Table 4.30 : *Test of Least Significant Difference for Significance between Pairs of Mean Scores of Total Parental Involvement in Developing Basic Living Skills (excluding vocational) with Respect to the Age of Father*

Pairs	*Logarithmic Mean*	*Difference between Pairs*	*Critical difference*
Younger age group and middle age group	1.7800 1.9505	0.1705	0.1340*
Younger age group and old age group	1.7800 1.9827	0.2027	0.1424*
Middle age group and old age group	1.9505 1.9827	0.0322	0.0746

* Significant at 0.05 level

Post hoc comparisons using the test of least significant difference yielded a significant difference at 0.05 level between the mean of the total parental involvement scores (excluding vocational skills) of 'younger age group of fathers and middle age group of fathers' with the latter showing higher involvement in developing basic living skills in their mentally retarded children. Similarly, significant difference at 0.05 level was also observed between the 'younger age group and old age group' with the 'old age group' showing higher involvement than the 'younger age group'. However, no significant difference was obtained between the involvement scores of 'middle age group and old age group'.

The mean values (Table 4.26) show an increase in the level of parental involvement in developing basic living skills (excluding vocational) with the increase in the age of father.

Findings of the analysis of variance test indicate three significant F-ratios. All the three sets of post hoc comparisons reveal that as the age of the father increases, the level of parental involvement also increases. Again, a close observation of Table 4.26 shows that out of the nine sets of mean values, six sets have higher mean values for the old age groups. All the above observations strongly suggest that the level of parental involvement increase as the age of the father increases. However, the remaining three sets of mean values do not show any specific trend.

While analysing the parental involvement scores with respect to the number of years of schooling (Table 4.23 and 4.24) it was found that, as the number of years of schooling increases, the amount of parental involvement tend to decrease. Contrary to that observation, here somewhat a reverse relation has emerged. This may be because increase in age makes the fathers more and more aware of the aims and methods of education for their child, and also, they may be getting more acquainted with the ways and means of involvement resulting in the increased level of their participation. Hence the assumption number six in the discussion of the results of Table 4.24 get substantiated.

Table 4.31 shows the arithmetic means, logarithmic means, and standard deviations of the parental involvement scores in developing basic living skills with respect to the age of mother.

Table 4.32 shows that the obtained F-ratios for involvement in reading and writing skills, numerical skills, social skills, and for total parental involvement (excluding vocational skills) are significant at 0.05 level. Similarly, F-ratios obtained for involvement in health and safety skills were found to be significant at 0.01 level. However, from Table 4.32 it can be seen that the F-ratios obtained for involvement in self-care skills, motor skills, vocational skills, and leisure time skills are not significant either at 0.01 level or at 0.05 level.

Table 4.31 : *Means, Logarithmic Means, and Standard Deviations of Parental Involvement Scores with Respect to the Age of Mother*

Skill	*Younger Age Group*			*Middle Age Group*			*Old Age Group*		
	N	*Mean*	*SD*	*N*	*Mean*	*SD*	*N*	*Mean*	*SD*
Self-care	36	20.19 (1.2530)	8.51	100	20.91 (1.2657)	8.24	34	16.88 (1.0969)	10.09
Motor	36	8.83 (0.9259)	4.73	100	9.86 (0.9672)	4.63	34	9.03 (0.9458)	4.27
Reading and Writing	36	9.31 (0.8619)	7.02	100	10.69 (0.9498)	7.26	34	13.21 (1.1057)	6.00
Numerical	36	10.78 (0.8243)	12.59	100	13.99 (0.9067)	14.52	34	18.32 (1.1355)	13.59
Health and Safety	36	8.31 (0.8554)	5.79	100	12.21 (1.0603)	5.74	34	12.35 (1.0408)	6.84
Social	36	13.14 (1.0105)	8.60	100	17.19 (1.1920)	7.40	34	15.68 (1.1060)	8.82
Vocational	12	14.17 (1.0836)	8.33	78	14.58 (1.1289)	7.55	34	15.09 (1.0999)	7.79
Leisure time	36	12.33 (0.9919)	7.95	100	15.39 (1.1313)	7.54	34	15.09 (1.1490)	6.80
Total (excluding Vocational)	**36**	**83.61 (1.8692)**	**39.70**	**100**	**100.20 (1.9660)**	**39.07**	**34**	**99.76 (1.9824)**	**32.82**

Note : Logarithmic means are given in parenthesis.

Table 4.32 : *Summaries of ANOVA for the Parental Involvement in Developing Basic Living Skills with Respect to the Age of Mother*

Skill	*Source*	*Sum of squares*	*d.f.*	*Mean square*	*F-ratio*
Self-care	Between groups	0.75	2	0.38	
	Within groups	22.73	167	0.14	2.68
	Total	23.48	169		
Motor	Between groups	0.05	2	0.03	
	Within groups	13.52	167	0.08	<1
	Total	13.57	169		
Reading and Writing	Between groups	1.08	2	0.54	
	Within groups	21.50	167	0.13	4.20*
	Total	22.58	169		
Numerical	Between groups	1.89	2	0.95	
	Within groups	42.71	167	0.26	3.70*
	Total	44.60	169		
Health and Safety	Between groups	1.14	2	0.57	
	Within groups	15.10	167	0.09	6.31**
	Total	16.24	169		
Social	Between groups	0.91	2	0.46	
	Within groups	20.77	167	0.12	3.66*
	Total	21.68	169		
Vocational	Between groups	0.04	2	0.02	
	Within groups	10.33	121	0.09	<1
	Total	10.37	123		
Leisure Time	Between groups	0.59	2	0.02	
	Within groups	19.76	167	0.12	2.49
	Total	20.35	169		
Total (excluding Vocational)	**Between groups**	**0.30**	**2**	**0.15**	
	Within groups	**6.83**	**167**	**0.04**	**3.62***
	Total	**7.13**	**169**		

* Significant at 0.05 level. ** Significant at 0.01 level.

Hence it can be concluded that the age of the mother is a significant factor in determining the nature of parental involvement in developing reading and writing skills, numerical skills, health and safety skills, and social skills in their mentally retarded children. As per the results, it can be stated that age of the mother is a significant factor in developing basic living skills in general, though the age of the mother is not a discriminating factor in deciding the nature of the parental involvement in developing skills such as self-care, motor, vocational, and leisure time.

The least significant difference test for paired comparisons yielded significant difference at 0.05 level between the mean parent involvement scores of mothers of 'younger and old age groups' and 'middle and old age groups'. In both the pairs it is the 'old age group' that shows a higher level of involvement in developing reading and writing skills. Hence it can be concluded that the age of the mother is a significant factor in deciding the level of involvement in developing reading and writing skills in their mentally retarded children.

Table 4.33 : *Test of Least Significant Difference for Significance between Pairs of Mean Scores of Parental Involvement in Developing Reading and Writing Skills with Respect to the Age of Mother*

Pairs	*Logarithmic Mean*	*Difference between Pairs*	*Critical difference*
Younger age group and middle age group	0.8619 0.9498	0.0879	0.1402
Younger age group and old age group	0.8619 1.1057	0.2438	0.1724*
Middle age group and old age group	0.9498 1.1057	0.1559	0.1432*

* Significant at 0.05 level

Paired comparisons with the least significant difference test show that there exists a significant difference at 0.05 level between the mean parental involvement scores of 'younger and old age groups' and 'middle and old age groups'. Further, the mean values (Table 4.32) show that in both the pairs, it is the 'older age groups' that show higher level of involvement in developing numerical skills. This result suggests that the age of the mother is an influential factor in deciding the level of parental involvement in developing numerical skills in their mentally retarded children.

Post hoc comparisons using the least significant difference test reveal that the mean parent involvement scores of 'younger and middle age groups' as well as 'younger and old age groups' differ significantly at 0.01 level. Also, no significant difference is obtained between the

Table 4.34 : *Test of Least Significant Difference for Significance between Pairs of Mean Scores of Parental Involvement in Developing Numerical Skills with Respect to the Age of Mother*

Pairs	*Logarithmic Mean*	*Difference between Pairs*	*Critical difference*
Younger age group and middle age group	0.8243 0.9067	0.0824	0.1982
Younger age group and old age group	0.8243 1.1335	0.3112	0.2440*
Middle age group and old age group	0.9067 1.1355	0.2288	0.2024*

* Significant at 0.05 level

'middle and old age groups'. The mean values (Table 4.31) indicate the parental involvement score of 'middle age groups' as the highest followed by that of the 'old age groups' and the score of the 'younger age groups' as the lowest. Hence, it may be concluded that the age of the mother is an important factor in deciding the level of parental involvement in developing health and safety skills in their mentally retarded children.

Table 4.35 : *Test of Least Significant Difference for Significance between Pairs of Mean Scores of Parental Involvement in Developing Health and Safety Skills with Respect to the Age of Mother*

Pairs	*Logarithmic Mean*	*Difference between Pairs*	*Critical difference*
Younger age group and middle age group	0.8554 1.0603	0.2049	0.1166**
Younger age group and old age group	0.8554 1.0408	0.1854	0.1434**
Middle age group and old age group	1.0603 1.0408	0.0195	0.1190

** Significant at 0.01 level

Table 4.36 : *Test of Least Significant Difference for Significance between Pairs of Mean Scores of Parental Involvement in Developing Social Skills with Respect to the Age of Mother*

Pairs	*Logarithmic Mean*	*Difference between Pairs*	*Critical difference*
Younger age group and middle age group	1.0105 1.1920	0.1815	0.1346*
Younger age group and old age group	1.0105 1.1060	0.0955	0.1656
Middle age group and old age group	1.1920 1.1060	0.0860	0.1376

* Significant at 0.05 level

Results of the least significant difference test for the paired comparisons reveal that the mean parent involvement scores of 'younger age group and middle age group' differ significantly at 0.05 level with the latter showing higher level of involvement. The difference between the other two pairs compared does not show any statistical significance. Hence, it can be concluded that the age of the mother has certain influence in deciding the level of parental involvement in developing social skills in their mentally retarded children.

The least significant difference test for paired comparisons yielded significant difference at 0.05 level between the mean parent involvement scores of 'younger and middle age groups' as well as 'younger and old age groups;' with the 'middle age groups' and 'old age groups' showing higher level of involvement respectively. Hence, it can be concluded that the age of mother is a significant factor in deciding the level of parental involvement in developing basic living skills in general (excluding vocational skills) in their mentally retarded children.

Out of the nine-F-ratios calculated for the parental involvement scores in developing different skills with respect to the age of the mother, five were found to be statistically significant either at 0.05 level or at 0.01 level. An analysis of the mean values (Table 4.31) shows that the involvement score is the lowest for the 'younger age groups' in all these

Table 4.37 : *Test of Least Significant Difference for Significance between Pairs of Mean Scores of Parental Involvement in Developing Basic Living Skills (excluding vocational skills) with Respect to the Age of Mother*

Pairs	*Logarithmic Mean*	*Difference between Pairs*	*Critical difference*
Younger age group and middle age group	1.8692 1.9660	0.0968	0.0786*
Younger age group and old age group	1.8692 1.9824	0.1132	0.0968*
Middle age group and old age group	1.9660 1.9824	0.0164	0.0802

* Significant at 0.05 level

five instances, and is higher for either the 'middle age groups' or for the 'old age groups'. Hence, it may be concluded that the levels of parental involvement in developing the basic living skills are likely to increase with the increase in the 'age of the mother' of the retarded children.

As in the context of relation between the age of the father and parental involvement (Table 4.26–4.30), here also, it may be argued that an increase in the age of the mother provides the chance for increased awareness of the special education methods and the role of the mother. This may enhance their level of involvement in developing basic living skills in retarded children.

Table 4.38 shows the arithmetic means, logarithmic means, and standard deviations of parental involvement scores in developing basic living skills in mentally retarded children with respect to the education of the father.

As seen in Table 4.39, all the F-ratios obtained are far below the critical value of significance either at 0.01 level or at 0.05 level. Hence it can be concluded that parental involvement in developing basic living skills in mentally retarded children does not differ with variation in the educational level of father.

Table 4.38 : *Means, Logarithmic Means, and Standard Deviations of Parental Involvement Scores with Respect to the Education of Father*

Skill	*Low Education Group*			*Middle Education Group*			*High Education Group*		
	N	*Mean*	*SD*	N	*Mean*	*SD*	N	*Mean*	*SD*
Self-care	62	20.74 (1.2566)	8.52	85	19.87 (1.2255)	8.84	7	21.57 (1.2855)	8.28
Motor	62	9.23 (0.9580)	4.29	85	9.65 (0.9473)	4.95	7	10.00 (1.0082)	3.62
Reading and Writing	62	10.06 (0.9313)	6.59	85	11.24 (0.9786)	7.36	7	11.43 (1.0099)	6.18
Numerical	62	12.13 (0.8789)	13.11	85	14.13 (0.9187)	14.23	7	15.43 (1.0491)	10.18
Health and Safety	62	10.77 (0.9772)	6.13	85	11.66 (1.0401)	5.85	7	10.71 (1.0351)	4.56
Social	62	15.61 (1.1074)	8.66	85	17.16 (1.1986)	7.11	7	16.00 (1.1423)	8.54
Vocational	44	14.02 (1.1064)	7.68	60	15.33 (1.1612)	7.44	6	17.33 (1.2498)	4.82
Leisure time	62	14.37 (1.1069)	7.27	85	14.80 (1.0934)	8.08	7	17.14 (1.2482)	3.72
Total (excluding Vocational)	**62**	**92.97 (1.9324)**	**37.43**	**85**	**98.61 (1.9553)**	**40.41**	**7**	**101.57 (1.9971)**	**25.97**

Note : Logarithmic means are given in parenthesis.

Table 4.39 : *Summaries of ANOVA for the Parental Involvement in Developing Basic Living Skills with Respect to Education of Father*

Skill	*Source*	*Sum of squares*	*d.f.*	*Mean square*	*F-ratio*
Self-care	Between groups	0.0493	2	0.0247	
	Within groups	20.3586	151	0.1348	<1
	Total	20.4079	153		
Motor	Between groups	0.0253	2	0.0126	
	Within groups	12.2660	151	0.0812	<1
	Total	12.2913	153		
Reading and Writing	Between groups	0.0979	2	0.0490	
	Within groups	19.4594	151	0.1289	<1
	Total	19.5573	153		
Numerical	Between groups	0.2017	2	0.1009	
	Within groups	40.3833	151	0.2653	<1
	Total	40.5850	153		
Health and Safety	Between groups	0.1447	2	0.0724	
	Within groups	13.0330	151	0.0863	<1
	Total	13.1777	153		
Social	Between groups	0.3003	2	0.1502	
	Within groups	16.9735	151	0.1124	1.34
	Total	17.2738	153		
Vocational	Between groups	0.1472	2	0.0736	
	Within groups	6.3144	107	0.0590	1.25
	Total	6.4616	109		
Leisure Time	Between groups	0.1551	2	0.0776	
	Within groups	18.6043	151	0.1232	<1
	Total	18.7594	153		
Total (excluding Vocational)	**Between groups**	**0.0364**	**2**	**0.0182**	
	Within groups	**6.4552**	**151**	**0.0427**	**<1**
	Total	**6.4916**	**153**		

Even though in most of the skills studied, a higher mean value is found for parent groups with fathers having 'higher education' when compared with the other two groups, the results of the analysis of variance do not show any significantly higher level of involvement of these groups. This in someway may contradict the population expectation that a higher level of parental educational status may lead to higher level of parental involvement in their children's education. Findings of Wells (1994) support this popular belief. However, the results of the study conducted by Grizzle (1993) support the present findings.

The present finding attempts to substantiate the argument that in teaching the mentally retarded children what matters most is a higher level of patience, love, and commitment than an improvement in parental education.

Table 4.40 shows the arithmetic means, logarithmic means, and standard deviations of parental involvement scores in developing basic living skills in mentally retarded children with respect to the education of mother.

Table 4.41 shows that all the F-ratios obtained are not statistically significant as they are found to be far below the critical value of significance either at 0.01 level or at 0.05 level. Hence it can be concluded that parental involvement in developing basic living skills in mentally retarded children does not vary with the educational level of mother.

As in the case of the parental involvement with respect to education of father, here also most of the mean values are higher for high education groups, but none of the F-ratios is found to be statistically significant. As explained earlier, it may assumed that more than the educational status of mothers, it is their ability to show patience, love, and readiness to accept the realities of retardation which becomes more crucial in deciding their level of involvement in developing basic living skills in the retardation children.

It can be seen from Table 4.42 that the 't' value obtained for the two groups is not statistically significant either at 0.01 level or at 0.05 level. Hence it can be concluded that whether or not the father is employed is not a significant factor in deciding the nature of parental involvement in developing basic living skills in their mentally retarded children.

But the mean values suggest a higher involvement level for 'unemployed' group. This is contrary to the earlier findings of Countryman (1994) which indicated parental unemployment as an obstacle for parents to participate in school based parental activities. An explanation for this finding is that the unemployed fathers find more time to spend for their retarded children's development, which result in increased level of involvement.

Table 4.40 : *Means, Logarithmic Means, and Standard Deviations of Parental Involvement Scores with Respect to the Education of Mother*

Skill	*Low Education Group*			*Middle Education Group*			*High Education Group*		
	N	*Mean*	*SD*	*N*	*Mean*	*SD*	*N*	*Mean*	*SD*
Self-care	71	20.49 (1.2529)	8.53	92	19.71 (1.2045)	9.09	7	21.86 (1.3507)	4.61
Motor	71	9.63 (0.9674)	4.61	92	9.09 (0.9238)	4.71	7	10.71 (1.0401)	3.77
Reading and Writing	71	10.58 (0.8860)	6.23	92	12.05 (1.0257)	6.86	7	10.14 (0.9487)	6.64
Numerical	71	12.27 (0.8941)	13.12	92	15.76 (0.9596)	15.09	7	12.71 (1.0273)	7.63
Health and Safety	71	10.86 (0.9950)	5.98	92	11.59 (1.0163)	6.17	7	12.00 (1.0968)	3.82
Social	71	15.30 (1.1024)	8.16	92	16.71 (1.1642)	8.20	7	18.00 (1.2668)	4.47
Vocational	57	13.09 (1.0685)	7.62	63	15.79 (1.1593)	7.70	4	18.25 (1.2649)	5.85
Leisure time	71	13.65 (1.0786)	7.36	92	15.36 (1.1167)	7.88	7	16.29 (1.2271)	3.77
Total (excluding Vocational)	**71**	**91.73 (1.9260)**	**37.38**	**92**	**99.97 (1.9623)**	**40.06**	**7**	**101.71 (2.0008)**	**23.69**

Note : Logarithmic means are given in parenthesis.

Table 4.41 : *Summaries of ANOVA for the Parental Involvement in Developing Basic Living Skills with Respect to Education of Mother*

Skill	*Source*	*Sum of squares*	*d.f.*	*Mean square*	*F-ratio*
Self-care	Between groups	0.20	2	0.10	
	Within groups	23.34	167	0.14	<1
	Total	23.54	169		
Motor	Between groups	0.14	2	0.07	
	Within groups	14.27	167	0.09	<1
	Total	14.41	169		
Reading and Writing	Between groups	0.78	2	0.39	
	Within groups	21.75	167	0.13	3.00
	Total	22.53	169		
Numerical	Between groups	0.23	2	0.12	
	Within groups	44.37	167	0.27	<1
	Total	44.60	169		
Health and Safety	Between groups	0.07	2	0.04	
	Within groups	15.93	167	0.10	<1
	Total	16.00	169		
Social	Between groups	0.27	2	0.14	
	Within groups	20.83	167	0.12	1.13
	Total	21.10	169		
Vocational	Between groups	0.33	2	0.17	
	Within groups	9.88	121	0.08	2.04
	Total	10.21	123		
Leisure Time	Between groups	0.17	2	0.09	
	Within groups	20.18	167	0.12	<1
	Total	20.35	169		
Total (excluding Vocational)	**Between groups**	**0.07**	**2**	**0.04**	
	Within groups	**7.05**	**167**	**0.04**	**1**
	Total	**7.12**	**169**		

Table 44 : *Mean, Standard Deviation and 't' value of Parental Involvement Scores with Respect to the Employment Status of Father*

Employment Status	*N*	*Mean*	*SD*	*'t' value*
Employed	139	95.53	38.52	
Unemployed	15	105.27	40.13	0.96
Total	154			

Table 4.43 provides the arithmetic means, logarithmic means, and standard deviations of parental involvement scores in developing basic living skills in mentally retarded children with respect to the occupation of father.

Table 4.44 shows that all the F-ratios obtained are not significant as they are found to be far below the critical value of significance either at 0.01 level or at 0.05 level. A close analysis of the mean values (Table 4.43) shows a slightly higher involvement scores in most of the skills for the group with unemployed fathers (Group IV). However, the differences between the mean values are not found to be statistically significant. Hence it can be concluded that the nature of occupation of fathers in no way affects the involvement of parents in developing basic living skills in mentally retarded children.

The mean values obtained for parental involvement scores with respect to 'employed' mothers and 'unemployed' mothers are found to be 102.50 and 95.53 with standard deviations 33.23 and 39.43 respectively. The test of significance for difference between the two means indicates that the nature of parental involvement in developing basic living skills in mentally retarded children does not differ significantly with respect to the employment status of mother.

Contrary to the findings of level of parental involvement with respect to the employment status of fathers, here the group with 'employed' mothers has higher mean value. Countryman's (1994) findings is in agreement with this result.

Table 4.46 shows the arithmetic means, logarithmic means, and standard deviations of parental involvement scores in developing basic living skills in mentally retarded children with respect to the nature of occupation of mother.

Table 4.47 shows that the obtained F-ratios for involvement in numerical skills and social skills are significant at 0.05 level. However, the table also shows that the F-ratios obtained for self-care skills, motor skills, reading and writing skills, health and safety skills, vocational skills, leisure time skills, and for the total parent involvement score (excluding vocational) are not significant either at 0.01 level or at 0.05 level.

Hence it can be concluded that the nature of occupation of mother is a significant factor in the involvement of parent in developing numerical and social skills in their mentally retarded children. However, the nature of occupation of mother does not influence the nature of

Table 4.43 : *Means, Logarithmic Means, and Standard Deviations, of Parental Involvement Scores with Respect to the Nature of Occupation of Father*

Skill	*Group I*			*Group II*			*Group III*			*Group IV*		
	N	*Mean*	*SD*	*N*	*Mean*	*SD*	*N*	*Mean*	*SD*	*N*	*Mean*	*SD*
Self-care	82	20.28 (1.2454)	8.35	36	20.56 (1.2077)	9.16	21	21.76 (1.3114)	7.96	15	29.07 (1.3324)	19.43
Motor	82	9.10 (0.9470)	4.52	36	10.19 (0.9671)	4.77	21	9.90 (0.9654)	4.96	15	9.40 (0.9492)	4.32
Reading and Writing	82	10.54 (0.9504)	6.74	36	11.11 (0.9586)	7.74	21	10.71 (0.9650)	6.77	15	11.40 (1.0120)	7.40
Numerical	82	12.40 (0.8899)	12.80	36	13.92 (0.8619)	15.25	21	16.24 (1.0632)	13.24	15	14.40 (0.9165)	15.60
Health and Safety	82	10.70 (0.9914)	5.76	36	11.81 (1.0192)	6.26	21	10.86 91.0234)	5.43	15	13.60 (1.1174)	6.01
Social	82	15.38 (1.1079)	8.45	36	17.72 (1.1979)	7.40	21	16.86 (1.2116)	6.41	15	18.47 (1.2563)	6.79
Vocational	57	14.86 (1.1363)	7.57	27	15.81 (1.1740)	7.47	14	15.79 (1.1870)	6.95	12	12.17 (1.0639)	6.83
Leisure time	82	14.34 (1.1051)	7.23	36	15.28 (1.0774)	8.89	21	14.00 (1.1157)	6.29	15	18.33 (1.2606)	6.72
Total (excluding Vocational)	**82**	**92.73 (1.9290)**	**36.41**	**36**	**99.08 (1.9493)**	**45.44**	**21**	**100.33 (1.9850)**	**32.10**	**15**	**105.27 (1.9966)**	**40.13**

Note : (i) Logarithmic means are given in parenthesis. (ii) Group I denotes Coollies and Labourers, Group II denotes Clerks and Other Office Employees, Group III denotes Gazetted Officers, High Level Professionals, etc. and Group IV denotes Unemployed Fathers.

Table 4.44 : *Summaries of ANOVA for the Parental Involvement in Developing Basic Living Skills with Respect to the Nature of Occupation of Father*

Skill	*Source*	*Sum of squares*	*d.f.*	*Mean square*	*F-ratio*
Self-care	Between groups	0.2446	3	0.0815	
	Within groups	21.1073	150	0.1407	<1
	Total	21.3519	153		
Motor	Between groups	0.0132	3	0.0044	
	Within groups	12.2781	150	0.0819	<1
	Total	12.2913	153		
Reading and Writing	Between groups	0.0487	3	0.0162	
	Within groups	19.6392	150	0.1309	<1
	Total	19.6879	153		
Numerical	Between groups	0.6096	3	0.2032	
	Within groups	40.1929	150	0.2680	<1
	Total	40.8025	153		
Health and Safety	Between groups	0.2050	3	0.0683	
	Within groups	12.9727	150	0.0865	<1
	Total	13.1777	153		
Social	Between groups	0.4680	3	0.1560	
	Within groups	16.8164	150	0.1121	1.39
	Total	17.2844	153		
Vocational	Between groups	0.1307	3	0.0436	
	Within groups	6.3309	106	0.0597	<1
	Total	6.4616	109		
Leisure Time	Between groups	0.3767	3	0.1256	
	Within groups	17.2486	150	0.1150	1.09
	Total	17.6253	153		
Total (excluding Vocational)	**Between groups**	**0.0938**	**3**	**0.0313**	
	Within groups	**6.3978**	**150**	**0.0427**	**<1**
	Total	**6.4916**	**153**		

Table 4.45 : *Means, Standard Deviation and 't' value of Parental Involvement Scores with Respect to the Employment Status of Mother*

Employment Status	*N*	*Mean*	*SD*	*'t' value*
Employed	26	102.50	33.23	0.92
Unemployed	144	95.53	39.43	
Total	170			

Table 4.46 : *Means, Logarithmic Means, and Standard Deviations, of Parental Involvement Scores with respect to the Nature of Occupation of Mother*

Skill	Group I			Group II			Group III			Group IV		
	N	Mean	SD	N	Mean	SD	N	Mean	SD	N	Mean	SD
Self-care	6	19.00 (1.1372)	9.73	13	21.69 (1.2421)	9.66	7	17.14 (1.2015)	7.10	144	19.97 (1.2333)	8.76
Motor	6	8.67 (0.9429)	3.86	13	8.92 (0.9453)	3.93	7	8.71 (0.9325)	4.13	144	9.50 (0.9483)	4.76
Reading and Writing	6	10.00 (0.9144)	5.54	13	11.85 (1.0854)	3.78	7	11.86 (0.9905)	8.08	144	10.82 (0.9523)	7.32
Numerical	6	11.17 (0.7990)	12.23	13	22.46 (1.2758)	12.85	7	19.86 (1.2397)	11.85	144	13.28 (0.8951)	14.13
Health and Safety	6	7.00 (0.7576)	5.10	13	13.69 (1.1223)	6.02	7	13.14 (1.1235)	5.05	144	11.17 (1.0057)	5.98
Social	6	9.50 (0.7851)	7.02	13	18.46 (1.2248)	7.85	7	18.43 (1.2768)	4.44	144	16.15 (1.1442)	8.12
Vocational	6	12.00 (1.0155)	8.19	12	15.00 (1.1259)	6.03	4	19.00 (1.2847)	5.43	102	14.52 (1.1109)	8.01
Leisure time	6	14.33 (1.1453)	6.18	13	15.15 (1.1795)	5.08	7	15.29 (1.1728)	5.55	144	14.60 (1.0930)	7.91
Total (excluding Vocational)	**6**	**79.67 (1.8386)**	**33.60**	**13**	**112.00 (2.0378)**	**29.16**	**7**	**104.43 (2.0048)**	**30.62**	**144**	**95.53 (1.9426)**	**39.43**

Note : (i) Logarithmic means are given in parenthesis. (ii) Group I denotes Coollies and Labourers, Group II denotes Clerks and Other Office Employees, Group III denotes Gazetted Officers, High Level Professionals, etc., and Group IV denotes Unemployed Fathers.

Table 4.47 : *Summaries of ANOVA for the Parental Involvement in Developing Basic Living Skills with Respect to the Nature of Occupation of Mother*

Skill	*Source*	*Sum of squares*	*d.f.*	*Mean square*	*F-ratio*
Self-care	Between groups	0.0608	3	0.0203	
	Within groups	23.4189	166	0.1411	<1
	Total	23.4797	169		
Motor	Between groups	0.0018	3	0.0006	
	Within groups	14.4229	166	0.0869	<1
	Total	14.4247	169		
Reading and Writing	Between groups	0.2308	3	0.0769	
	Within groups	22.3716	166	0.1348	<1
	Total	22.6004	169		
Numerical	Between groups	2.5003	3	0.8334	
	Within groups	42.1012	166	0.2536	3.29*
	Total	44.6015	169		
Health and Safety	Between groups	0.6391	3	0.2130	
	Within groups	15.3620	166	0.0925	2.30
	Total	16.0011	169		
Social	Between groups	0.9808	3	0.3269	
	Within groups	20.0921	166	0.1210	2.70*
	Total	21.0729	169		
Vocational	Between groups	0.1774	3	0.0591	
	Within groups	11.4075	120	0.0951	<1
	Total	11.5849	123		
Leisure Time	Between groups	0.1348	3	0.0449	
	Within groups	20.2059	166	0.1217	<1
	Total	20.3407	169		
Total (excluding Vocational)	**Between groups**	**0.2034**	**3**	**0.0678**	
	Within groups	**6.9212**	**166**	**0.0417**	**1.63**
	Total	**7.1246**	**169**		

* Significant at 0.05 level

parental involvement in developing other basic living skills already mentioned.

Post hoc comparisons using least significant difference test indicate significant difference at 0.05 level between the mean parental involvement scores of 'Group I and Group III' with the latter showing a higher level of involvement. Similarly, the test yielded a significant difference between the 'Group II and Group IV', with the former showing higher level of involvement in developing numerical skills in their mentally retarded children. None of other four pairs compared show the existence of significant difference between their involvement scores.

Hence, it can be concluded that mothers with 'higher level of occupation' (Group III) involve significantly more than the mothers with 'lower level of occupation' (Group I) in developing numerical skills in their mentally retarded children. Similarly, mothers with an 'average occupational' status (Group II) involve significantly more than that of 'unemployed mothers' (Group IV).

A closer analysis of the mean values indicates the lowest parental involvement score for the group with mothers having 'low level of occupation' (Group I).

Table 4.48 : *Test of Least Significant Difference for Significance between Pairs of Mean Scores of Parental Involvement in Developing Numerical Skills with Respect to the Nature of Occupation of Mother*

Pairs	*Logarithmic Mean*	*Difference between Pairs*	*Critical difference*
Group I and Group II	0.7990 1.2758	0.4768	0.4970
Group I and Group III	0.7990 1.2397	0.4407	0.2822*
Group I and Group IV	0.7990 0.8951	0.0961	0.4196
Group II and Group III	1.2758 1.2397	0.0361	0.4722
Group II and Group IV	1.2758 0.8951	0.3807	0.2916*
Group III and Group IV	1.2397 0.8951	0.3446	0.3898

* Significant at 0.05 level

Paired comparisons with the least significant difference test include the existence of statistically significant difference ($p<0.05$) between the parental involvement scores of 'Group I and Group II', with the latter showing higher level of involvement. Also, 'Group I and Group III' was found to differ significantly ($p<0.05$) with the latter showing more involvement. Again, the test yielded a significant difference (($p<0.05$) between 'Group I and Group IV', with the latter group showing higher level of involvement. However, the test does not show statistically significant difference among the other three pairs compared.

Hence it can be concluded that in all the three pairs compared, the three groups, viz., mothers with an 'average level of occupation' (Group II), mothers with 'high level of occupation' (Group III) and the 'unemployed mothers' (Group IV) were found to be having significantly higher level of involvement than the mothers with 'low level of occupation' (Group I) in developing social skills in their mentally retarded children.

Table 4.49 : *Test of Least Significant Difference for Significance between Pairs of Mean Scores of Parental Involvement in Developing Social Skills with Respect to the Nature of Occupation of Mother*

Pairs	*Logarithmic Mean*	*Difference between Pairs*	*Critical difference*
Group I and Group II	0.7851 1.2248	0.4397	0.3434*
Group I and Group III	0.7851 1.2768	0.4917	0.1950*
Group I and Group IV	0.7851 1.1442	0.3591	0.0420*
Group II and Group III	1.2248 1.2768	0.0520	0.3262
Group II and Group IV	1.2248 1.1442	0.0806	0.2014
Group III and Group IV	1.2768 1.1442	0.1326	0.2692

* Significant at 0.05 level

A closer analysis of the mean values indicates the highest parental involvement score for the group with mothers having 'high level occupation', followed by the group with mothers having 'average level occupation', and by the 'unemployed mothers', and as Table 4.46 shows in most of the cases the mean value is found to be the lowest for the group with mothers having 'low level occupation'. This specific trend may be due to the fact that the mothers with 'low level occupation' like coolies or labourer hardly get any time for involving in their retarded children's educational activities. Moreover, usually mothers belonging to the low socio-economic status families go for the level jobs, and this too for meeting their primary requirements of daily life. This may be cited as another reason for the failure of these mothers to involve highly in developing basic living skills in their mentally retarded children.

Table 4.50 provides the arithmetic means, logarithmic means, and standard deviations of parental involvement scores in developing basic living skills in mentally retarded children with respect to the monthly income of parents.

Table 4.51 shows that all the F-ratios obtained are far below the critical value of significance either 0.01 level or at 0.05 level. This indicates that the parental involvement in developing basic living skills in mentally retarded children does not differ with the variation in monthly income of parents.

But a close observation of the mean values indicates a trend towards higher level of involvement for the 'high income group' of parents as most of the mean values are higher for 'high income group'. However, as far as no significant F-ratios are obtained this trend cannot be considered seriously.

When reviewing the results of the analysis of parental involvement with respect to the three key constituent aspects of socio-economic status, viz., education, occupation, and income of parents, it can be seen that only two statistically significant F-ratios were obtained, one involving numerical skills with respect to the nature of occupation of mother and the other involving social skills with respect to the nature of occupation of the mother. The remaining 34 F-ratios and two 't' values calculated were found to be statistically insignificant. Hence, it can be inferred that neither the educational level of father and mother, nor the occupational status of both the parents, nor the monthly income of parents has any significant role to play in deciding the level of parental involvement in developing basic living skills in mentally retarded

Table 4.50 : *Means, Logarithmic Means, and Standard Deviations of Parental Involvement Scores with Respect to the Monthly Income of Parents*

Skill	*Low Education Group*			*Middle Education Group*			*High Education Group*		
	N	*Mean*	*SD*	*N*	*Mean*	*SD*	*N*	*Mean*	*SD*
Self-care	94	19.79 (1.2343)	8.60	49	19.43 (1.1735)	9.82	27	21.48 (1.3128)	7.50
Motor	94	9.24 (0.9499)	4.57	49	9.47 (0.9302)	4.73	27	9.78 (0.9690)	4.75
Reading and Writing	94	10.53 (0.9403)	7.07	49	11.00 (0.9621)	7.49	27	11.56 (1.0091)	6.65
Numerical	94	12.86 (0.8948)	13.50	49	14.76 (0.9152)	15.28	27	17.74 (1.1141)	13.56
Health and Safety	94	10.54 (0.9744)	5.94	49	12.65 (1.0570)	6.40	27	11.59 (1.0554)	5.29
Social	94	15.06 (1.0906)	8.50	49	17.55 (1.1924)	7.98	27	17.59 (1.2364)	5.91
Vocational	67	13.24 (1.0731)	7.53	38	16.71 (1.1853)	8.39	19	15.79 (1.1947)	6.21
Leisure time	94	14.90 (1.1220)	7.26	49	14.59 (1.0611)	8.89	27	14.07 (1.1275)	5.92
Total (excluding Vocational)	**94**	**93.04 (1.9303)**	**36.44**	**49**	**99.45 (1.9552)**	**44.99**	**27**	**103.81 (2.0011)**	**31.45**

Note : Logarithmic means are given in parenthesis.

Table 4.51 : *Summaries of ANOVA for the Parental Involvement in Developing Basic Living Skills with Respect to the Monthly Income of Parents*

Skill	*Source*	*Sum of squares*	*d.f.*	*Mean square*	*F-ratio*
Self-care	Between groups	0.3433	2	0.1717	
	Within groups	23.1364	167	0.1385	1.24
	Total	23.4797	169		
Motor	Between groups	0.0277	2	0.0139	
	Within groups	14.3970	167	0.0862	<1
	Total	14.4247	169		
Reading and Writing	Between groups	0.1006	2	0.0503	
	Within groups	22.7815	167	0.1370	<1
	Total	22.8821	169		
Numerical	Between groups	1.0377	2	0.5189	
	Within groups	43.5327	167	0.2607	1.99
	Total	44.5704	169		
Health and Safety	Between groups	0.2827	2	0.1414	
	Within groups	15.7566	167	0.0944	1.50
	Total	16.0393	169		
Social	Between groups	0.6131	2	0.3066	
	Within groups	20.4598	167	0.1225	2.50
	Total	21.0729	169		
Vocational	Between groups	0.5321	2	0.2661	
	Within groups	10.7222	121	0.0866	3.00
	Total	11.2543	123		
Leisure Time	Between groups	0.1353	2	0.0677	
	Within groups	20.2098	167	0.1210	<1
	Total	20.3451	169		
Total (excluding Vocational)	**Between groups**	**0.1080**	**2**	**0.0540**	
	Within groups	**7.0166**	**167**	**0.0423**	**1.28**
	Total	**7.1246**	**169**		

children. The findings of Pillay (1984), Grizzle (1993), and O'Toole (1990a, 1990b) support this conclusion.

This lack of influence of educational, occupational, and income levels of parents in the nature of their involvement may be attributed to the following fact. Unlike in the general education or education of other disabled children, the curriculum content for mentally retarded children is only a functional one. That is, no formal academic subjects are being taught and the emphasis is on the acquisition of functional or the basic living skills. It they have enough time, patience, understanding, and willingness, parents belonging to all levels of educational, occupational, and income levels can easily follow this curriculum. So more than the educational, occupational, and economic status of parents, it is the availability of time, patience, understanding, and willingness that matters more for the active parental involvement in developing the basic living skills in their mentally retarded children.

Table 4.52 shows the arithmetic means, logarithmic means, and standard deviations of parental involvement scores in developing basic living skills in mentally retarded children with respect to the level of mental retardation.

As is evident from Table 4.53, only the F-ratio for reading and writing skills is found to be significant at 0.05 level. All the other F-ratios are found to be far below the critical value of significance either at 0.01 level or at 0.05 level. The mean values of the involvement scores with respect to the different skills too do not indicate any specific trend. Hence it can be concluded that the level of mental retardation of the children is a significant factor in the parental involvement in developing reading and writing skills but this does not influence the nature of parental involvement in developing all other basic living skills. Findings of O'Toole (1990a, 1990b) support the present results, as he found that the severity of the child's disability does not help to predict the level of parental involvement.

The least significant difference test for paired comparisons yielded statistically significant difference at 0.05 level between the mean involvement scores of parents of children with 'mild and moderate' level of retardation, with the 'mild group' showing higher level of involvement in developing reading and writing skills. However, the test does not indicate any significant difference between the other two pairs compared.

A close observation of the mean values reveal that the higher involvement score is obtained by 'mild group' followed by 'moderate group' and the lowest mean value is obtained by the 'severe group'. When considering the nature of the reading and writing skills, it is natural that parents of mildly retarded children involve more, and the level of involvement is seen to decrease as the severity of retardation becomes more serious. This is because, parents may not have high hope of

Table 4.52 : *Means, Logarithmic Means, and Standard Deviations of Parental Involvement Scores with Respect to the Level of Mental Retardation of the Children*

Skill	*Mild*			*Moderate*			*Severe*		
	N	*Mean*	*SD*	*N*	*Mean*	*SD*	*N*	*Mean*	*SD*
Self-care	59	19.27 (1.2025)	9.23	93	20.47 (1.2458)	8.47	18	19.17 (1.2225)	9.31
Motor	59	9.31 (0.9233)	4.96	93	9.30 (0.9501)	4.52	18	10.50 (0.9956)	4.88
Reading and Writing	59	12.14 (1.0591)	6.07	93	10.05 (0.9138)	7.24	18	11.33 (0.8992)	8.68
Numerical	59	15.36 (1.0071)	13.45	93	13.34 (0.9068)	13.97	18	14.61 (0.8447)	16.82
Health and Safety	59	11.36 (1.0216)	5.62	93	11.06 (0.9920)	6.26	18	12.33 (1.0715)	5.94
Social	59	16.17 (1.1530)	7.87	93	15.77 (1.1224)	8.28	18	18.11 (1.2019)	7.82
Vocational	44	15.39 (1.1574)	7.52	67	14.55 (1.1127)	7.83	13	12.62 (1.0442)	7.72
Leisure time	59	15.47 (1.1585)	6.95	93	13.94 (1.0619)	7.81	18	15.39 (1.1426)	7.77
Total (excluding Vocational)	**59**	**99.24 (1.9714)**	**34.85**	**93**	**93.87 (1.9304)**	**39.59**	**18**	**102.06 (1.9691)**	**43.85**

Note : Logarithmic means are given in parenthesis.

Table 4.53 : *Summaries of ANOVA for the Parental Involvement in Developing Basic Living Skills with Respect to the Level of Mental Retardation of the Children*

Skill	*Source*	*Sum of squares*	*d.f.*	*Mean square*	*F-ratio*
Self-care	Between groups	0.06	2	0.03	
	Within groups	23.41	167	0.14	<1
	Total	23.47	169		
Motor	Between groups	0.08	2	0.04	
	Within groups	15.23	167	0.09	<1
	Total	15.31	169		
Reading and Writing	Between groups	0.84	2	0.42	
	Within groups	21.76	167	0.13	3.23*
	Total	22.60	169		
Numerical	Between groups	0.53	2	0.27	
	Within groups	44.07	167	0.26	1.02
	Total	44.60	169		
Health and Safety	Between groups	0.11	2	0.06	
	Within groups	15.89	167	0.10	<1
	Total	16.00	169		
Social	Between groups	0.11	2	0.06	
	Within groups	21.15	167	0.13	<1
	Total	21.26	169		
Vocational	Between groups	0.14	2	0.07	
	Within groups	10.08	121	0.08	<1
	Total	10.22	123		
Leisure Time	Between groups	0.37	2	0.19	
	Within groups	19.89	167	0.12	1.54
	Total	20.26	169		
Total (excluding Vocational)	**Between groups**	**0.06**	**2**	**0.03**	
	Within groups	**7.06**	**167**	**0.04**	**<1**
	Total	**7.12**	**169**		

* Significant at 0.05 level.

developing reading and writing skills in their 'moderately' and 'severely' retarded children as they may have for their 'mildly' retarded children.

In short, the findings from Tables 4.12–4.54 point towards the fact that most of the variables studied do not have much effect on the

Table 4.54 : *Test of Least Significant Difference for Significance between Pairs of Mean Scores of Parental Involvement in Developing Reading and Writing Skills with Respect to the Level of Mental Retardation of the Children*

Pairs	*Logarithmic Mean*	*Difference between Pairs*	*Critical difference*
Mild and Moderate	1.0591 0.9138	0.1453	0.1200*
Mild and Severe	1.0591 0.8992	0.1599	0.1942
Moderate and Severe	0.9138 0.8992	0.0146	0.1858

* Significant at 0.05 level

nature of parental involvement in developing basic living skills in their mentally retarded children. Especially, the difference in; number of years of schooling, location of residence, age and birth order of mentally retarded children were found to be not at all differentiating the nature of parental involvement. Similarly, a difference in education, occupation, and monthly income of parents were also found to have no significant influence in the nature of parental involvement. At the same time, it was observed that the parental involvement in developing motor skills and leisure time skills were changing with the change in the sex of mentally retarded children. Also, involvement in developing social skills was found to be significantly affected by difference in religion, and that self-care skills were found to significantly differ with the difference in the number of siblings. The involvement in developing reading and writing skills, health and safety skills, and the basic living skills in general (excluding vocational) were also found to differ significantly with the difference in the age of father and mother.

Parental involvement in developing numerical and social skills was found to vary significantly with the difference in the age of mother and also with the occupation of mother. Finally, involvement in developing reading and writing skills was found to vary significantly with the difference in the degree of mental retardation of the children. But, none of the 15 variables studied was found to be having any significant influence in deciding the level of parental involvement in developing vocational skills. These results may be an indication of the absence of the serious vocational training programmes and the lack of scientific attitude on the part of parents towards the vocational training of mentally retarded children.

On looking from a different angle, it can be seen that out of a total of 20 't' values computed only two were found to be statistically significant. Similarly, out of the total 117 F-ratios computed, only 13 were found to be statistically significant. Of these 13 significant F-ratios, seven were associated with mother-related variables, whereas only three were associated with father-related variables. This result suggests the changes in the variables related to the mother's influence in the nature of parental involvement rather than that of the father's in the education of the mentally retardation children. The prevailing popular belief may support these findings. Even then, further studies are needed to confirm the higher level of involvement of mothers than of fathers.

3. *Relationship Between Parental Involvement and Certain Parent-Related Variables and Age of Mentally Retarded Children*

The details of the correlational analysis conducted between parental involvement and variables such as age of mentally retarded children, monthly income of parents and age of father and mother are presented in Table 4.55.

Table 4.55 : *Correlation between Parental Involvement and Age of Mentally Retarded Children, Age of Father and Mother and Monthly Income of Parents*

Variables	*N*	*Coefficient of Correlation (r)*
Age of mentally retarded children	170	0.08
Age of father	154	0.14
Age of mother	170	0.13
Monthly income of parents	170	0.11

Table 4.55 shows the values of coefficient of correlation computed between the scores of parental involvement in developing basic living skills in mentally retarded children and age of the retarded children, age of father and mother, and monthly income of parents. It is evident from the table that all the obtained correlation coefficients are far below

the critical value of significance either at 0.01 level or at 0.05 level. Hence it can be concluded that there is no significant relationship between parental involvement and either the age of mentally retarded children or the age of father and mother, or monthly income of parents.

Parental Perceptions with Regard to Their Existing and Expected Levels of Involvement in the Educational Decision-Making

Frequencies and percentages have been computed as well as chi-square test or 'Z' test of double proportion have been used to analyse the parental perceptions regarding their existing and expected levels of involvement in the educational decision-making for their mentally retarded children. The details of analysis are presented in Tables 4.56–4.91.

As shown in Table 4.56, the majority (62.94%) of the parents express 'high level' of existing involvement in taking decisions on assessing the child's abilities. While 21.18 per cent of the parents 'only give information' to authorities, 9.41 per cent 'only receive information' and 6.47 per cent are of the opinion that, at present they are 'not at all' involving themselves in taking decisions related to assessing the child's abilities. Further, as the chi-square value obtained is found to be higher than that of the critical value at 0.01 level, it can be concluded that the difference between the frequencies of the four types of responses is statistically significant.

Table 4.56 : *Frequencies, Percentages, and Chi-square Value with Regard to the Perception of Parents on Their Existing Level of Involvement in Taking Decisions on Assessing the Child's Abilities*

Nature of Involvement	*Number*	*Percentage*	*Chi-square*
High involvement	107	62.94	
Only gives information to authorities	36	21.18	138.75**
Only receives information from authorities	16	9.41	
No involvement	11	6.47	
Total	170	100.00	

** Significant at 0.01 level.

Table 4.57 shows that the obtained value of chi-square is far higher than that of the critical value at 0.01 level. Hence it can be concluded that the difference between the frequencies of the four types of parental responses is statistically significant, with the majority of the parents (79.41%) expecting a higher level of involvement in taking decisions related to the assessment of their retarded children's abilities. It can also be seen from the table that only 6.47 per cent of the parents wish for 'no involvement'. Hence it can be concluded that most of the parents are eager to involve more in their retarded children's assessment decisions.

Table 4.57 : *Frequencies, Percentages, and Chi-square Value with Regard to the Perception of Parents on Their Expected Level of Involvement in Taking Decisions on Assessing the Child's Abilities*

Nature of Involvement	*Number*	*Percentage*	*Chi-square*
High involvement	135	79.41	
Only gives information to authorities	12	7.06	268.45**
Only receives information from authorities	12	7.06	
No involvement	11	6.47	
Total	**170**	**100.00**	

** Significant at 0.01 level.

It is seen from Table 4.58 that the 'Z' values obtained for the difference between the existing and expected levels of parental involvement are statistically significant at 0.01 level for both the responses, namely, 'high involvement' and 'only gives information'. A close observation of the percentages reveals that significantly higher number of parents desire for higher level of involvement in taking decisions related to the assessment of their children's abilities than merely giving or receiving information. Findings of Tomlinson (1981) and Yamilkoski (1983) support these results. This finding may be an indication of the parental feeling that they have an unparalleled amount of experience with their retarded children which the professionals do not have and they should get enough opportunities for expressing and utilising this experience in the process of assessment.

Table 4.58 : *Comparison of Parental Perceptions Regarding Their Existing and Expected Levels of Involvement in Taking Decisions on Assessing the Child's Abilities*

Nature of Involvement	Existing N	Existing %	Expected N	Expected %	'Z' value
High involvement	107	62.94	135	79.41	–3.35**
Only gives information to authorities	36	21.18	12	7.06	3.74**
Only receives information from authorities	16	9.41	12	7.06	0.29
No Involvement	11	6.47	11	6.47	0.00
Total	170	100.00	170	100.00	

** Significant at 0.01 level.

Table 4.59 shows that the obtained chi-square value is not statistically significant either at 0.05 level or at 0.01 level. Hence it can be concluded that the difference between the frequencies of the four types of parental responses is not statistically significant.

Table 4.59 : *Frequencies, Percentages, and Chi-square Value with Regard to the Perception of Parents on Their Existing Level of Involvement in Taking Decisions Related to the Formulation of Individualised Education Programme (IEP)*

Nature of Involvement	Number	Percentage	Chi-square
High involvement	50	29.41	
Only gives information to authorities	40	23.53	1.81
Only receives information from authorities	39	22.94	
No involvement	41	24.12	
Total	170	100.00	

** Significant at 0.01 level.

As shown in Table 4.60, the majority of the parents (60%) want to involve highly in taking decisions related to the formulation of Individualised Education Programme for their retarded children. Only

15.30 per cent of the parents indicate a 'no involvement' response and almost an identical percentage of parents (11.76 and 12.94 respectively) suggest that they want only the role of giving and receiving information. The highly significant chi-square value obtained ($p < 0.01$) indicate that the difference between the frequencies of the four types of parental responses is statistically significant.

Table 4.60 : *Frequencies, Percentages, and Chi-square Value with Regard to the Perception of Parents on Their Expected Level of Involvement in Taking Decisions Related to the Formulation of (IEP)*

Nature of Involvement	*Number*	*Percentage*	*Chi-square*
High involvement	102	60.00	
Only gives information to authorities	20	11.76	111.51**
Only receives information from authorities	22	12.94	
No involvement	26	15.30	
Total	**170**	**100.00**	

** Significant at 0.01 level.

It can be seen from Table 4.61 that the difference between all the four responses with regard to the existing and expected levels of involvement in taking decisions relating to the formulation of IEP are statistically significant either at 0.05 level or at 0.01 level. A close observation of the percentages reveals that the majority of the parents (60%) expect significantly higher level of involvement in taking these decisions than at the existing level. Consequently, in all the other three expected parental responses, the percentages are significantly reduced and only 15.30 per cent of the parents desire 'no involvement'.

The finding is consistent with the earlier research findings (Goldstein *et al.*, 1980; Gerber *et al.*, 1986; O'Connell, 1992).

The low percentage of high involvement of parents at the existing level indicate that in the prevailing system of special education there is no significant role for parents to play in the formulation of individualised education programme. This may be the result of the possible negative attitude of teachers and school authorities who feel that the formulation of IEP is the sole responsibility of the teachers. The findings of Grainger

Table 4.61 : *Comparison of Parental Perceptions Regarding Their Existing and Expected Levels of Involvement in Taking Decisions Related to the Formulation of IEP*

Nature of Involvement	*Existing*		*Expected*		*'Z' value*
	N	*%*	*N*	*%*	
High involvement	50	29.41	102	60.00	–5.67**
Only gives information to authorities	40	23.53	20	11.76	2.85**
Only receives information from authorities	39	22.94	22	12.94	2.40*
No Involvement	41	24.12	26	15.30	2.05*
Total	**170**	**100.00**	**170**	**100.00**	

* Significant at 0.05 level. ** Significant at 0.01 level.

(1984) support this assumption. Parental ignorance and lack of self-confidence too might have contributed to this result. At the same time, it was found that significantly higher percentage of parents desire high involvement. This points to the fact that if parents are provided with proper training, they will actively involve in the formulation of IEP.

Table 4.62 : *Frequencies, Percentages, and Chi-square Value with Regard to the Perception of Parents on Their Expected Level of Involvement in Taking Decisions on the Implementation of IEP*

Nature of Involvement	*Number*	*Percentage*	*Chi-square*
High involvement	74	43.53	
Only gives information to authorities	26	15.29	35.41**
Only receives information from authorities	27	15.88	
No involvement	43	25.30	
Total	**170**	**100.00**	

** Significant at 0.01 level.

As shown in Table 4.62, the obtained chi-square value is significant at 0.01 level. Hence it can be concluded that the difference between the frequencies of the four types of parental responses is statistically significant, with 43.53 per cent of the parents showing high level of existing involvement in taking decisions related to the implementation of individualised education programmes. While, 25.30 per cent of the parents do not have any involvement in taking decisions related to the implementation of IEP, 15.29 per cent of the parents only given information and 15.88 per cent only receive information from authorities.

Table 4.63 shows that the difference between the frequencies of the four types of parental responses regarding their expected level of involvement in taking decisions related to the implementation of IEP is statistically significant ($p < 0.01$) It can also be seen that 64.12 per cent of the parents wish for a high level involvement than either only giving information (9.41%), or only receiving information (9.41%). Also, 17.06 per cent of the parents do not want any type of involvement in taking decisions on the implementation of IEP.

Table 4.63 : *Frequencies, Percentages, and Chi-square Value with Regard to the Perception of Parents on Their Expected Level of Involvement in Taking Decisions on the Implementation of IEP*

Nature of Involvement	*Number*	*Percentage*	*Chi-square*
High involvement	109	64.12	
Only gives information to authorities	16	9.41	141.39**
Only receives information from authorities	16	9.41	
No involvement	29	17.06	
Total	**170**	**100.00**	

** Significant at 0.01 level.

Table 4.64 clearly reveals that significantly more number of parents wish for 'high involvement' in taking decisions related to the implementation of IEP ($p < 0.01$) rather than only giving or receiving information.

This result again points towards the nature of existing practice in the special schools. Here also, the attitude of professionals become crucial. Sometimes they may consider the parental role in special education as high, but they may not be willing to allow the parents to teach the children. The findings of Yamilkoski (1983) support this view. But the special educationists world over already recognise the role

Table 4.64 : *Comparison of Parental Perceptions Regarding Their Existing and Expected Levels of Involvement in Taking Decisions on the Implementation of IEP*

Nature of Involvement	Existing		Expected		'Z' value
	N	%	N	%	
High involvement	74	43.53	109	64.12	-3.81**
Only gives information to authorities	26	15.29	16	9.41	1.65
Only receives information from authorities	27	15.88	16	9.41	1.79
No Involvement	43	25.30	29	17.06	1.85
Total	**170**	**100.00**	**170**	**100.00**	

** Significant at 0.01 level.

of parents as teachers and therefore advocate the conduct of educational programmes for parents through which parents can become at least the home teachers of their retarded children. Studies of Goodson and Hess (1976), Brassell (1977), Hanson (1977), Ludlow and Allen (1979), and Sanders and Glynn (1981) have consistently proved the efficacy of parents as home teachers.

Also, the present study indicates that more parents wish to provide actively in the implementation process of their children's individualised education programmes. So, it may be concluded that, if proper training is provided, parents will actively participate in their retarded children's educational programmes.

It can be seen from Table 4.65 that the chi-square value obtained for the difference between the frequencies of the four types of parental responses is found to be significant at 0.01 level. Table 4.65 also reveals that majority of the parents (42.35%) have 'high involvement' at the existing level in taking decisions related to the evaluation of IEP. While, 25.29 per cent of the parents do not involve in taking these decisions, 17.65 per cent of the parents 'only give information' to authorities and 14.71 per cent 'only receive information'.

Table 4.66 shows that there exists significant difference at 0.01 level between the frequencies of the four types of parental responses regarding their expected level of involvement in taking decisions related to the evaluation of IEP.

Table 4.65 : *Frequencies, Percentages, and Chi-square Value with Regard to the Perception of Parents on Their Expected Level of Involvement in Taking Decisions Related to the Evaluation of IEP*

Nature of Involvement	*Number*	*Percentage*	*Chi-square*
High involvement	72	42.35	
Only gives information to authorities	30	17.65	31.36**
Only receives information from authorities	25	14.71	
No involvement	43	25.29	
Total	**170**	**100.00**	

** Significant at 0.01 level.

Table 4.66 : *Frequencies, Percentages, and Chi-square Value with Regard to the Perception of Parents on Their Expected Level of Involvement in Taking Decisions Related to the Evaluation of IEP*

Nature of Involvement	*Number*	*Percentage*	*Chi-square*
High involvement	107	62.94	
Only gives information to authorities	18	10.59	132.26**
Only receives information from authorities	17	10.00	
No involvement	28	16.47	
Total	**170**	**100.00**	

** Significant at 0.01 level.

The findings further reveals that 62.94 per cent of the parents wish for 'high involvement' and 16.47 per cent expect only a 'no involvement' role. However, certain parents expect 'only to give information' to authorities (10.59%), whereas, 10 per cent of the parents expect 'only to receive information'.

Table 4.67 shows that significantly higher percentage of parents (62.94%) desire a high level of involvement in taking decisions related to the evaluation of IEP. Also, the table shows significant reduction in the frequencies of 'no involvement' group. Hence it can be concluded

Table 4.67 : *Comparison of Parental Perceptions Regarding Their Existing and Expected Levels of Involvement in Taking Decisions Related to the Evaluation of IEP*

Nature of Involvement	*Existing*		*Expected*		*'Z' value*
	N	*%*	*N*	*%*	
High involvement	72	42.35	107	62.94	–3.80**
Only gives information to authorities	30	17.65	18	10.59	1.87
Only receives information from authorities	25	14.71	17	10.00	1.32
No Involvement	43	25.29	28	16.47	2.00*
Total	**170**	**100.00**	**170**	**100.00**	

** Significant at 0.01 level.

that more parents wish for active involvement in taking the IEP evaluation decisions.

Like the previous results, these findings also indicate the dearth of appropriate-training and opportunities to parents for involving in the IEP evaluation decisions. The explanation given earlier (Table 4.61 and 4.64) may be considered here also.

Table 4.68 shows that the obtained chi-square value is significant at 0.01 level, which indicates that the difference between the frequencies of the four types of parental responses is statistically significant. The table shows that 35.29 per cent of the parents have 'high involvement' at the existing level in taking decisions related to the class placement, whereas 33.54 per cent have 'no involvement' at all. Similarly, 15.88 per cent 'only give information' to authorities and 15.29 per cent 'only receive information' on class placement decisions.

This result that only about one-third of the parents involve highly in taking class placement decisions in the existing system. This means that majority of the parents have no active involvement in taking class placement decisions in the existing system.

Table 4.69 shows that the difference between the four types of parental responses is statistically significant ($p < 0.01$) It is seen that majority of the parents (54.12%) expect a high level of involvement in taking class placement decisions and only 24.71 per cent expect a

Table 4.68 : *Frequencies, Percentages, and Chi-square Value with Regard to the Perception of Parents on Their Existing Level of Involvement in Taking Decisions on Class Placement*

Nature of Involvement	*Number*	*Percentage*	*Chi-square*
High involvement	60	35.29	
Only gives information to authorities	27	15.88	24.21**
Only receives information from authorities	26	15.29	
No involvement	57	33.54	
Total	170	100.00	

** Significant at 0.01 level.

Table 4.69 : *Frequencies, Percentages, and Chi-square Value with regard to the Perception of Parents on their Expected Level of Involvement in Taking Decisions on Class Placement*

Nature of Involvement	*Number*	*Percentage*	*Chi-square*
High involvement	92	54.12	
Only gives information to authorities	15	8.82	86.33**
Only receives information from authorities	21	12.35	
No involvement	42	24.71	
Total	170	100.00	

** Significant at 0.01 level.

'no involvement' role. Also, 8.82 per cent of the parents wish only the role of giving information to authorities and 12.35 per cent desire only the role of receiving information.

Table 4.70 reveals that the 'Z' value obtained for the difference between the frequencies of the response 'high involvement' at the existing and expected levels is significant at 0.01 level and that of the response, 'only gives information' is significant at 0.05 level.

The significantly significant difference between the frequencies of the 'high involvement' response at the two levels indicate that significantly more parents wish for an improvement in their present role

Table 4.70 : *Comparison of Parental Perceptions Regarding Their Existing and Expected Levels of Involvement in Taking Decisions on Class Placement*

Nature of Involvement	*Existing*		*Expected*		*'Z' value*
	N	*%*	*N*	*%*	
High involvement	60	35.29	92	54.12	–3.49**
Only gives information to authorities	27	15.88	15	8.82	1.97*
Only receives information from authorities	26	15.29	21	12.35	0.79
No Involvement	57	33.54	42	24.71	1.79
Total	**170**	**100.00**	**170**	**100.00**	

* Significant at 0.05 level. ** Singnificant at 0.01 level.

as decision-makers regarding class placement of their retarded children. The following two reasons could have caused this phenomenon. Firstly, the parental attitude that the class placement decisions are the entire responsibility of the teachers and their feeling that no separate classes are needed for the education of mentally retarded children. Secondly, the attitude of teachers that parents are not competent enough to take such decisions and it is only the teachers who should take decisions on class placement.

It can be seen from Table 4.71 that the chi-square value obtained is significant at 0.01 level, which means that the difference between the frequencies of the four different parental responses regarding their existing level of involvement in taking decisions on the disciplinary matters is statistically significant.

A close observation of Table 4.71 reveals that 60.59 per cent of the parents have 'high involvement' at the existing level in taking decisions related to disciplinary matters and only 17.64 per cent of the parents express that they do not have any type of involvement in taking such decisions. As in the previous findings almost an identical percentage of the parents (10.59 and 11.18 respectively) limit their involvement to either giving or receiving information.

Table 4.72 shows that the chi-square value obtained for the difference between the frequencies of the four types of parental responses is statistically significant at 0.01 level. A close observation of Table 4.72

Table 4.71 : *Frequencies, Percentages, and Chi-square Value with Regard to the Perception of Parents on Their Existing Level of Involvement in Taking Decisions on Disciplinary Matters*

Nature of Involvement	*Number*	*Percentage*	*Chi-square*
High involvement	103	60.59	
Only gives information to authorities	18	10.59	116.92**
Only receives information from authorities	19	11.18	
No involvement	30	17.64	
Total	170	100.00	

** Significant at 0.01 level.

Table 4.72 : *Frequencies, Percentages, and Chi-square Value with Regard to the Perception of Parents on Their Expected Level of Involvement in Taking Decisions on Disciplinary Matter*

Nature of Involvement	*Number*	*Percentage*	*Chi-square*
High involvement	118	69.41	
Only gives information to authorities	12	7.06	181.53**
Only receives information from authorities	14	8.24	
No involvement	26	15.29	
Total	170	100.00	

** Significant at 0.01 level.

reveals that the majority of the parents (69.41%) wish for 'high involvement' in taking decisions related to disciplinary m atters, whereas only 15.29 per cent expect a 'no involvement' role. As in the previous findings, almost similar (7.06 and 8.24% respectively) percentages of parents desire the role of either 'only giving information' or 'only receiving information' regarding disciplinary matters.

Table 4.73 shows that none of the 'Z' values obtained are significant either at 0.01 level or at 0.05 level. Hence it can be said that the difference between the frequencies of the four types of parental responses with respect to the existing and expected levels of involvement

Table 4.73 : *Comparison of Parental Perceptions Regarding Their Existing and Expected Levels of Involvement in Taking Decisions on Disciplinary Matters*

Nature of Involvement	*Existing*		*Expected*		*'Z' value*
	N	*%*	*N*	*%*	
High involvement	103	60.59	118	69.41	1.71
Only gives information to authorities	18	•10.59	12	7.06	1.15
Only receives information from authorities	19	11.18	14	8.24	0.92
No Involvement	30	17.64	26	15.29	0.58
Total	**170**	**100.00**	**170**	**100.00**	

** Significant at 0.01 level.

in taking decisions related to the disciplinary matters is not statistically significant. However, a close observation of the table reveals an increase in the percentage of the response 'high involvement' and a decrease in the percentages of the other three responses at the expected level. The table also shows that more than 60 per cent of the parents express 'high involvement' both at the existing and expected levels.

This high percentage of 'high involvement' response may be attributed to the parental awareness that many of the retarded children exhibit behavioural problems and this may cause disciplinary problems in the school which make the involvement of parents a necessity.

Table 4.74 shows that the obtained chi-square value is significant at 0.01 level which means that the difference between the frequencies of the four types of parental responses regarding their existing level of involvement in taking decisions on keeping the record about the child is statistically significant. The table also shows that the majority of the parents (60%) have 'high involvement' at the existing level and 22.35 per cent have 'no involvement' at all. 10 per cent of the parents perceive their existing involvement as 'only giving information' to authorities and 7.65 per cent perceive it as 'only receiving information' from authorities.

It can be seen from Table 4.75 that the obtained chi-square value is significant at 0.01 level, which indicates that the difference between the frequencies of different parental responses regarding their expected

Table 4.74 : *Frequencies, Percentages, and Chi-square Value with Regard to the Perception of Parents on Their Existing Level of Involvement in Taking Decisions on Keeping relevant Records about the Retarded Children*

Nature of Involvement	*Number*	*Percentage*	*Chi-square*
High involvement	102	60.00	
Only gives information to authorities	17	10.00	119.56**
Only receives information from authorities	13	7.65	
No involvement	38	22.35	
Total	**170**	**100.00**	

** Significant at 0.01 level.

Table 4.75 : *Frequencies, Percentages, and Chi-square Value with Regard to the Perception of Parents on Their Expected Level of Involvement in Taking Decisions on Keeping relevant Records about the Retarded Children*

Nature of Involvement	*Number*	*Percentage*	*Chi-square*
High involvement	124	72.94	
Only gives information to authorities	10	5.88	214.09**
Only receives information from authorities	8	4.71	
No involvement	28	16.47	
Total	**170**	**100.00**	

** Significant at 0.01 level.

level of involvement in taking decisions related to keeping records about the child is statistically significant. A close observation of the table reveals that the majority of the parents (72.94%) expect 'high involvement' in taking decisions related to keeping records about their retarded children and only 16.47 per cent expect a 'no involvement' role. The percentage of parents who desire the role of 'only giving information' was found to be 5.88 and another 4.71 per cent of the parents wish for 'only receiving information'.

Table 4.76 shows that the 'Z' value obtained for the difference between the frequencies of the parental response, 'high involvement'

Table 4.76 : *Comparison of Parental Perceptions Regarding Their Existing and Expected Levels of Involvement in Taking Decisions Related to Keeping Relevant Records about the Retarded Children*

Nature of Involvement	*Existing* N	*Existing* %	*Expected* N	*Expected* %	*'Z' value*
High involvement	102	60.00	124	72.94	−2.52*
Only gives information to authorities	17	10.00	10	5.88	1.40
Only receives information from authorities	13	7.65	8	4.71	1.13
No Involvement	38	22.35	28	16.47	1.37
Total	**170**	**100.00**	**170**	**100.00**	

** Significant at 0.01 level.

at the existing and expected levels is statistically significant at 0.05 level. No other 'Z' values are found to be statistically significant either at 0.01 level or at 0.05 level. Hence it can be concluded that significantly more parents wish for 'high involvement' at the expected level in taking decisions relating to keeping records about their retarded children.

The results obtained by Lusthaus and Lusthaus (1982) also show a similar trend. This result may be considered as in line with the popular thinking that the relevant important records about the retarded children should be kept by their parents and also they should have an important role in deciding the nature of records to be kept about their mentally retarded children.

Table 4.77 shows that the obtained chi-square value is significant at 0.01 level, which means that the difference between the frequencies of the four types of parental responses regarding their existing level of involvement in taking decisions related to travelling facilities is statistically significant.

Further observation of the table reveals that the majority of the parents (72.94%) have 'high involvement' at the existing level and 14.70 per cent of the parents do not have any type of involvement. While, 7.65 per cent have the role of 'only giving information' 4.71 per cent are 'only receiving information' from authorities.

It can be seen from Table 4.78 that the obtained chi-square value is significant at 0.01 level, which indicates that the difference between

Table 4.77 : *Frequencies, Percentages, and Chi-square Value with Regard to the Perception of Parents on Their Existing Level of Involvement in Taking Decisions Related to Travelling Facilities*

Nature of Involvement	*Number*	*Percentage*	*Chi-square*
High involvement	124	72.94	
Only gives information to authorities	13	7.65	211.98**
Only receives information from authorities	8	4.71	
No involvement	25	14.70	
Total	170	100.00	

** Significant at 0.01 level.

Table 4.78 : *Frequencies, Percentages, and Chi-square Value with Regard to the Perception of Parents on Their Expected Level of Involvement in Taking Decisions Related to Travelling Facilities*

Nature of Involvement	*Number*	*Percentage*	*Chi-square*
High involvement	132	77.65	
Only gives information to authorities	7	4.12	256.68**
Only receives information from authorities	6	3.53	
No involvement	25	14.70	
Total	170	100.00	

** Significant at 0.01 level.

the frequencies of the four types of parental responses regarding their expected level of involvement in taking decisions related to travelling facilities is statistically significant. The percentages given in the table show that majority of the parents (77.65%) expect 'high involvement' and 14.70% per cent of the parents do not have the desire for any type of involvement. Also, only less than five per cent of the parents are having the desire for the role of 'only giving, (4.12%) or 'only receiving' (3.53%) information.

According to Table 4.79, none of the 'Z', values are significant either at 0.01 level or at 0.05 level. Hence it can be concluded that the difference between the frequencies of different parental responses regarding their existing and expected levels of involvement in taking decisions related to travelling facilities are not statistically significant. However, the percentages of the two sets of responses indicate a trend towards the parental desire for 'high involvement' in taking these decisions.

Table 4.79 : *Comparison of Parental Perceptions Regarding Their Existing and Expected Levels of Involvement in Taking Decisions Related to Travelling Facilities*

Nature of Involvement	*Existing*		*Expected*		*'Z' value*
	N	*%*	*N*	*%*	
High involvement	124	72.94	132	77.65	–1.00
Only gives information to authorities	13	7.65	7	4.12	1.38
Only receives information from authorities	8	4.71	6	3.53	0.55
No Involvement	25	14.70	25	14.70	0.00
Total	170	100.00	170	100.00	

** Significant at 0.01 level.

It can be seen from the table that 72.94 per cent of the parents have 'high involvement' in the existing system in taking decisions related to the travelling facilities. Still higher percentage (77.65) of the parents expressed their desire for 'high involvement' at the expected level. Taking decisions regarding the travelling facilities for their children is an area where, traditionally, parents having a higher level of involvement. The present results confirm this trend.

Table 4.80 clearly shows that the obtained chi-square value is significant at 0.01 level. Hence it can be concluded that the difference between the frequencies of different parental responses regarding their existing level of involvement in taking decisions related to medical treatment of their children is statistically significant. A close observation of the table reveals that a huge majority of the parents (82.35%) have 'high involvement' at the existing level and only 8.83 per cent do not have any type of involvement. 5.88 per cent of the parents are found

Table 4.80 : *Frequencies, Percentages, and Chi-square Value with Regard to the Perception of Parents on Their Existing Level of Involvement in Taking Decisions on Medical Treatment of Their Retarded Children*

Nature of Involvement	*Number*	*Percentage*	*Chi-square*
High involvement	140	82.35	
Only gives information to authorities	10	5.88	299.41**
Only receives information from authorities	5	2.94	
No involvement	15	8.83	
Total	**170**	**100.00**	

** Significant at 0.01 level.

to be having a role of 'only giving information' to authorities and a mere 2.94 per cent have the role of 'only receiving information' from authorities.

According to Table 4.81, the obtained chi-square value is significant at 0.01 level. Hence it can be concluded that the difference between the frequencies of different parental responses regarding their expected level of involvement in taking decisions related to medical treatment of their retarded children is statistically significant. The percentages of different parental responses given in the table clearly reveal that more than 85 per cent of the parents desire 'high involvement' and only 8.83 per cent wish for a 'no involvement' role. Only less than five per cent of the parents are found to be expecting the role of 'only giving information' (2.35%) and 'only receiving information' (3.53%).

According to Table 4.82, none of the 'Z' values are significant either at 0.01 level or at 0.05 level. Hence it can be said that the differences between the frequencies of parental responses of existing and expected levels of involvement in taking decisions related to the medical treatment of their mentally retarded children are not statistically significant.

However, the percentages indicate a trend towards the parental desire for an increased level of 'high involvement'. This lack of significant difference between the scores of two levels of involvement is because of the fact that already a very high percentage (82.35) of the parents are involving in these decisions. As mentioned in the case of decisions

Table 4.81 : *Frequencies, Percentages, and Chi-square Value with Regard to the Perception of Parents on Their Expected Level of Involvement in Taking Decisions on Medical Treatment of Their Retarded Children*

Nature of Involvement	*Number*	*Percentage*	*Chi-square*
High involvement	145	85.29	
Only gives information to authorities	4	2.35	331.22**
Only receives information from authorities	6	3.53	
No involvement	15	8.83	
Total	170	100.00	

** Significant at 0.01 level.

Table 4.82 : *Comparison of Parental Perceptions Regarding Their Existing and Expected Levels of Involvement in Taking Decisions Related to Medical Treatment of Their Retarded Children*

Nature of Involvement	*Existing*		*Expected*		*'Z' value*
	N	*%*	*N*	*%*	
High involvement	140	82.35	145	85.29	–0.74
Only gives information to authorities	10	5.88	4	2.35	1.64
Only receives information from authorities	5	2.94	6	3.53	–0.31
No Involvement	15	8.83	15	8.83	0.00
Total	170	100.00	170	100.00	

** Significant at 0.01 level.

on travelling facilities, this is another area where, traditionally, the parents have almost full responsibility in taking decisions and actions. This could be the reason for the observed 'high involvement' at the two levels.

Table 4.83 shows that the obtained chi-square value is significant at 0.01 level, which means that there exists a statistically significant difference between the frequencies of different parental responses regarding their existing level of involvement in taking decisions related to admitting their retarded children in residential schools. A close

Table 4.83 : *Frequencies, Percentages, and Chi-square Value with Regard to the Perception of Parents on Their Existing Level of Involvement in Taking Decisions Related to Admitting Their Retarded Children in the Residential Schools*

Nature of Involvement	*Number*	*Percentage*	*Chi-square*
High involvement	60	35.29	
Only gives information to authorities	12	7.06	95.51**
Only receives information from authorities	12	7.06	
No involvement	86	50.59	
Total	**170**	**100.00**	

** Significant at 0.01 level.

observation of the percentages shows that the majority of the parents (50.59%) do not have any involvement in this regard, whereas, 35.59 per cent have 'high involvement' in these decisions. However, 7.06 per cent of the parents are 'only giving information' and another 7.06 per cent of the parents are having the role of 'only receiving information'.

According to Table 4.84, the obtained chi-square value is significant at 0.01 level. Hence it can be concluded that the difference between the frequencies of different parental responses regarding their expected level of involvement in taking decisions related to admitting their retarded children in residential schools is statistically significant. A close observation of the percentages given in the table shows that 46.47 per cent of the parents expect 'high involvement' and 43.53 per cent of the parents do not wish for any type of involvement. However, 5.88 per cent of the parents desire only 'the information receiving role' and another 4.12 per cent wanted only 'the information giving role'.

Table 4.85 shows that the 'Z' value obtained for the difference between the frequencies of the parental response 'high involvement' at the existing and expected level is significant at 0.05 level. No other 'Z' value is found to be significant either at 0.01 level or at 0.05 level.

A close observation of the percentages given in the table reveals that significant higher percentage of the parents expect 'high involvement' in deciding whether their retarded children should be admitted to a residential school or not. But it can be seen from the table that

Table 4.84 : *Frequencies, Percentages, and Chi-square Value with Regard to the Perception of Parents on Their Expected Level of Involvement in Taking Decisions related to Admitting Their Retarded Children in the Residential Schools*

Nature of Involvement	*Number*	*Percentage*	*Chi-square*
High involvement	79	46.47	
Only gives information to authorities	7	4.12	109.20**
Only receives information from authorities	10	5.88	
No involvement	74	43.53	
Total	**170**	**100.00**	

** Significant at 0.01 level.

Table 4.85 : *Comparison of Parental Perceptions Regarding Their Existing and Expected Levels of Involvement in Taking Decisions Related to Admitting Their retarded Children in Residential Schools*

Nature of Involvement	*Existing*		*Expected*		*'Z' value*
	N	*%*	*N*	*%*	
High involvement	60	35.29	79	46.47	–2.10*
Only gives information to authorities	12	7.06	7	4.12	1.18
Only receives information from authorities	12	7.06	10	5.88	0.44
No Involvement	86	50.59	74	43.53	1.30
Total	**170**	**100.00**	**170**	**100.00**	

** Significant at 0.01 level.

only 46.47 per cent of the parents desire 'high involvement in taking this decision. At the same time 43.53 per cent of the parents do not perceive any type of involvement in this regard.

This result points towards the parental confusion regarding the type of services that are appropriate for their children. Also, the table shows that more than 50 per cent of the parents do not having any involvement at all in taking this decision at the existing level, which indicates that parents are only acting on the advice of other like teachers, doctors, etc. instead of taking their own decision on admitting their retarded children into a residential school. In order to have their own decisions they should have a clear understanding of the nature of the retardation, advantages and disadvantages of day-care special schools and residential special school, etc. This highlights the need for proper guidance and counselling.

Table 4.86, and the vertical bar graph shown in Fig. 4.11 illustrate the comparison of percentages of parents who expressed 'high involvement' at the existing and expected levels in the different areas of educational decision-making. The graph very clearly reveals that in all the ten areas studied, the percentage of parents at the expected level of involvement is higher than that at the existing level. This indicates that parents wish to involve more than their present level in various educational decisions related to their retarded children. This result is in agreement with the earlier findings of Shellady (1994), Darga (1993), Minikutty (1993), Lusthaus and Lusthaus (1982), and Hardy (1979).

Table 4.86 : Percentages of Existing and Expected Levels of 'High Involvement' Response Expressed by Parents in Different Areas of Educational Decision-making

Areas of Decision-making	*Existing (%)*	*Expected (%)*
Assessing child's abilities	62.94	79.41
IEP Formulation	29.41	60.00
IEP Implementation	43.53	64.12
IEP Evaluation	42.35	62.94
Class Placement	35.29	54.12
Disciplinary Matters	60.59	69.41
Keeping Relevant Records	60.00	72.94
Travelling Facilities	72.94	77.65
Medical Treatment	82.35	85.29
Admission in Residental Schools	35.29	46.47

Even though parents have a minimum level of involvement in most of the areas, their desire for increased level of involvement indicates that they are not satisfied with the existing level. This may be attributed

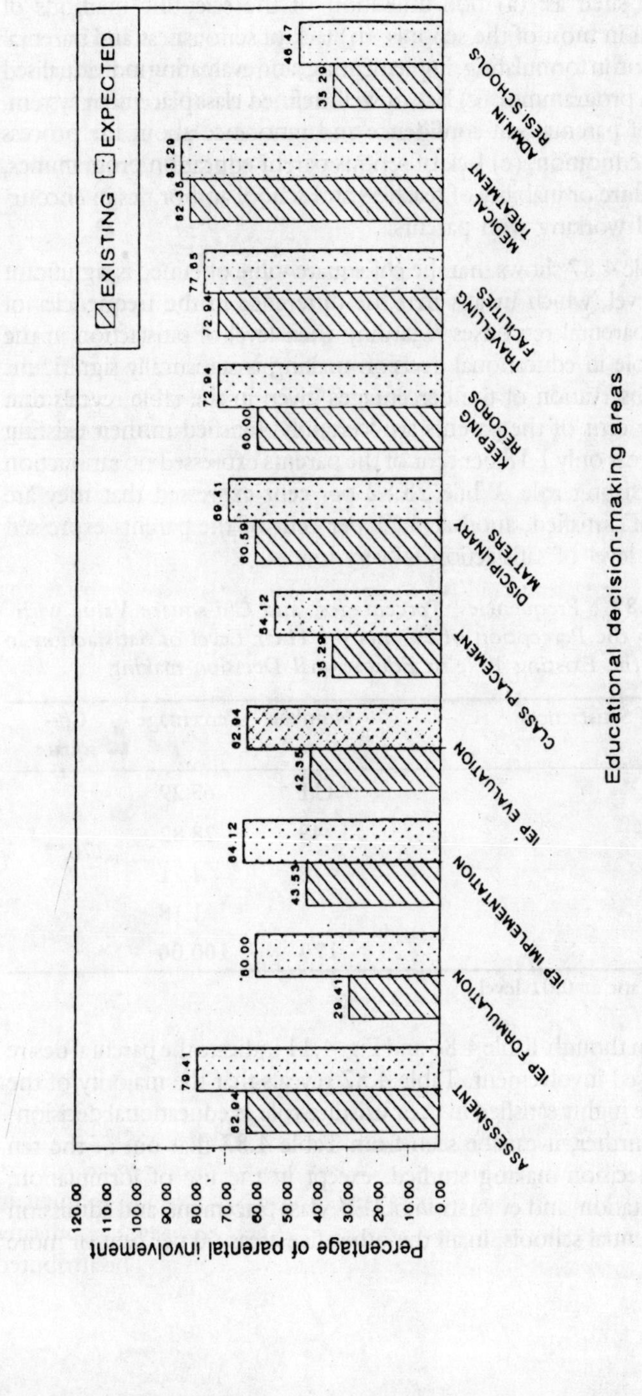

Fig. 4.11 : *Comparison of Existing and Expected Levels of Parental Involvement in Educational Decision-making with Regard to Different Areas*

to factors such as: (a) non-utilisation of the scientific methods of assessment in most of the schools, (b) lack of seriousness and parental participation in formulating, implementing, and evaluating individualised education programmes, (c) lack of well-defined class placement system, (d) lack of parental self-confidence and ignorance about the process of special education, (e) lack of serious parent education programmes, and (f) failure or inability of teachers and school authorities in encouraging and working with parents.

Table 4.87 shows that the chi-square value obtained is significant at 0.01 level, which means that the difference in the frequencies of different parental responses regarding their level of satisfaction in the existing role in educational decision-making is statistically significant. A close observation of the percentages given in the table reveals that 65.29 per cent of the parents are 'certainly' satisfied in their existing role, whereas only 1.18 per cent of the parents expressed no satisfaction in their existing role. While 28.82 per cent expressed that they are 'somewhat' satisfied, another 4.71 per cent of the parents expressed that their level of satisfaction is 'very low'.

Table 4.87 : *Frequencies, Percentages, and Chi-square Value with Regard to the Perception of Parents on Their Level of Satisfaction in the Existing Role in Educational Decision-making*

Level of Satisfaction	*Number*	*Percentage*	*Chi-square*
Certainly	111	65.29	
Somewhat	49	28.82	178**
Very low	8	4.71	
Not at all	2	1.18	
Total	**170**	**100.00**	

** Significant at 0.01 level.

Even though Table 4.86 and Fig. 4.11 indicate the parental desire for increased involvement, Table 4.87 reveals that the majority of the parents are highly satisfied in their existing role as educational decision-makers. Further, it can be seen from Table 4.87 that out of the ten areas of decision-making studied, except in the use of formulation, implementation, and evaluation of IEP, class placement, and admission into residential schools, in all the other five areas 60 per cent or more parents have high level of existing involvement. This may be the reason for the satisfaction of a majority of the parents in the existing role as decision-makers.

It can also be said that parents may express satisfaction if their existing role is very limited. Moreover, it cannot be said that in the existing system, parents have a significant role to play. So this lack of a significant role may be the reason for the higher percentage of parental satisfaction.

As shown in Table 4.88, the chi-square value obtained is significant at 0.01 level. Hence it can be concluded that the difference between the frequencies of different parental responses with regard to their level of satisfaction in the existing rights to participate in the educational decision-making meetings is statistically significant. Percentage-wise analysis reveals that the majority of the parents (77.06%) are 'certainly' satisfied with their existing rights, whereas only 1.17 per cent are 'not at all' satisfied with it. 17.65 per cent are 'somewhat' satisfied and the level of satisfaction of 4.12 per cent of the parents is 'very low'.

Table 4.88 : *Frequencies, Percentages, and Chi-square Value with Regard to the Perception of Parents on Their Level of Satisfaction in the Existing Rights to Participate in the Educational Decision-making Meetings*

Level of Satisfaction	*Number*	*Percentage*	*Chi-square*
Certainly	131	77.06	
Somewhat	30	17.65	256.21**
Very low	7	4.12	
Not at all	2	1.17	
Total	**170**	**100.00**	

** Significant at 0.01 level.

In the normal conditions higher level of satisfaction means the parental views are getting due consideration and they are contributing much in the decision-making process. But in the existing system, one cannot arrive at such as a conclusion. The observed high level of satisfaction of parents in their existing rights may be because of their feelings that making decisions on formulation, implementation and evaluation of IEP and class placement is the sole responsibility of teachers and only a higher level of participation in the other areas of decision-making is expected from them. So, even if their nature of participation in the decision-making meetings are not so contributory, they may feel that their rights are being protected.

Table 4.89 clearly reveals that the obtained chi-square value is significant at 0.01 level, which means that the difference between the four types of parental responses with regard to their own need for more information and training for being able to take educational decisions is statistically significant.

Table 4.89 : *Frequencies, Percentages, and Chi-square Value with Regard to the Perception of Parents on Their Own Need for More Information and Training for Being Able to Take Educational Decisions*

Extend of Need	*Number*	*Percentage*	*Chi-square*
Certainly	146	85.88	
Somewhat	16	9.42	338.52**
Very low	2	1.17	
Not at all	6	3.53	
Total	**170**	**100.00**	

** Significant at 0.01 level.

Percentage-wise analysis shows that the majority of the parents (85.88%) 'certainly' perceive the need for more information and training and 9.42 per cent 'somewhat' perceive this need. While 3.53 per cent do 'not at all' perceive such a need, 1.17 per cent perceive it as a 'very low' need.

This result in some way contradicts the previous one. But the parental need for more training and information may be justified as their existing level of involvement in the decision-making areas of formulation, implementation, and evaluation of individualised educational programmes, class placement, and admission into residential schools is 'very low' (Table 4.86). From Table 4.86, it can also be seen that parents desire more involvement in all the ten decision-making areas. Parents might think that proper training will enable them to have maximum involvement.

According to Table 4.90, the chi-square value obtained is significant at 0.01 level, which means that the difference between the frequencies of different parental perceptions with regard to their role in the selection of teachers is statistically significant.

Table 4.90 : *Frequencies, Percentages, and Chi-square Value with Regard to the Perception of Parents on Their Existing Role in Selection of Teachers*

Extend of Role	*Number*	*Percentage*	*Chi-square*
Certainly	19	11.18	
Somewhat	13	7.65	179.51**
Very low	20	11.76	
Not at all	118	69.41	
Total	**170**	**100.00**	

** Significant at 0.01 level.

Analysis of the percentages obtained reveals that the majority of the parents (69.41%) do not perceive the existence of such a role and only 11.18 per cent of the parents perceive that they have such a role in the existing system. Whereas 7.65 per cent express that they have 'somewhat' such a role to perform in the prevailing system, 11.76 per cent perceive the role as 'very low'. This result is in perfect agreement with the popular expectation and existing practice in the special education as well as general education system.

It can be seen from Table 4.91 that all the obtained chi-square values are significant at 0.01 level, which means that the difference between the frequencies of the different levels of hindrances perceived by the parents with regard to the factors that may cause their non-attendance in the educational decision-making meetings is statistically significant.

Analysis of the percentages obtained reveals that regarding all the ten factors studied, the majority of the parents do 'not at all' perceive them as a hindrance for attending educational decision-making meetings. However, in the case of occupation, 21.18 per cent of the parents perceive it as a definite hindrance, and 20 per cent perceive it as 'somewhat' a hindrance, but another 14.71 per cent perceive it only as 'very low'. In the case of family burden, 15.88 per cent of the parents

Table 4.91 : *Frequencies, Percentages, and Chi-square Values with Regard to Perception of Parents on the Factors that may Prevent Them from Participating in the Educational Decision-making Meetings*

Factors	*Level of Hindrance*								*Chi-square*
	Certainly		*Somewhat*		*Very low*		*Not at all*		
	N	*%*	*N*	*%*	*N*	*%*	*N*	*%*	
Occupation	36	21.18	34	20.00	25	14.71	75	44.11	34.75**
Communication skills	14	8.24	29	17.06	14	8.24	113	66.46	159.00**
Timing of the meeting	21	12.35	27	15.88	25	14.71	97	57.06	93.62**
Language	10	5.88	25	14.71	14	8.24	121	71.17	196.16**
Finance	23	13.53	30	17.65	22	12.94	95	55.88	87.36**
Educational Standard	13	7.65	28	16.47	25	14.71	104	61.17	121.62**
Confusion on how to participate	16	9.41	24	14.12	19	11.18	111	65.29	147.98**
Family burden	27	15.88	30	17.65	29	17.06	84	49.41	54.14**
Other Children's Education	23	13.53	21	12.35	22	12.94	104	61.18	118.71**
Lack of Encouragement from school authorities	13	7.65	7	4.12	17	10.00	133	78.23	258.14**

** Significant at 0.01 level.

perceive it as a definite hindrance, and 17.65 per cent perceive it as 'somewhat' a hindrance, but another 17.06 per cent perceive it only as a 'very low' hindrance. In all the other factors, only less than 14 per cent (5.88-13.53%) of the parents perceive them as a definite hindrance to attending the educational decision-making meetings.

These results contradict the earlier research findings of Lee (1980), and Leyser and Cole (1984), as they found some of these factors as reasons for the lack of more active involvement in educational decision-making meetings. These differences in results may be attributed to the difference in the system of special education, frequency of educational decision-making meetings, and legal provisions of the two places of study.

Perceptions of Parents and Teachers with Regard to the Efforts taken by the Teachers and School Authorities for Enhancing Parental Involvement

The details of the analysis done for studying the perceptions of parents and teachers with regard to the efforts taken by the teachers and school authorities for enhancing parental involvement are included in this section. Table 4.92–4.95 present the frequencies, percentages, chi-square values or 'Z' values.

Table 4.92 clearly shows that excluding the item number two, all the other 'Z' values obtained are significant at 0.01 level. This indicates that in all the items except the second item, the difference between the frequencies of parental perceptions regarding the efforts taken by the teachers and school authorities for enhancing the involvement of parents is statistically significant.

According to Table 4.92, the majority of the parents are of the opinion that: teachers encourage them to participate in the educational decision-making meetings (90.59%), teachers give special training to parents for home-based training (63.53%), teachers and school authorities contact parents to discuss their children (89.41%), teachers encourages parents to keep continuous contact with school (94.71%), and school authorities provide various help for the child in a satisfactory manner (89.41%). So far as a slight majority of the parents (53.53%) are concerned, the teachers disallow them to participate in the IEP formulation. Similarly, a huge majority of the parents (80.00%) complain that their representatives are not included in the committee that select teachers.

Table 4.92 : *Frequencies, Percentages, and 'Z' Values with Regard to Perception of Parents on the Efforts Taken by the Teachers and School Authorities for Enhancing Involvement*

Efforts taken by the teachers and school	Response of Parents				*'Z' Value*
	Yes		*No*		
	N	*%*	*N*	*%*	
Encourage parents for participating in the educational decision-making meetings	154	90.59	16	9.41	10.58**
Allow parents to participate in the IEP formulation	79	46.47	91	53.53	–0.92
Give special training to parents for home based training	108	63.53	62	36.47	3.53**
Contact parents for discussing about their children	152	89.41	18	10.59	10.28**
Encourage parents for keeping continuous contact with school	161	94.71	9	5.29	11.66**
Provide assistance for the child in a satisfactory level	152	89.41	18	10.59	10.28**
Include representatives of parents in the committee that select teachers	34	20.00	136	80.00	–7.82**

** Significant at 0.01 level.

Even as the efforts taken by the teachers and the school authorities are acknowledged, these results highlight the need for a change in the attitude of teachers regarding the role of parents in the IEP formulation and parental participation in the teachers' selection.

It can be seen from Table 4.93 that most of the 'Z' values are significant at 0.01 level, which indicates that differences in the frequencies of teachers' responses regarding the efforts taken by them for enhancing parental involvement are statistically significant.

Percentage-wise analysis reveals that the majority of the teachers include parents in the policy decision-taking councils (69.41%), consider parental views while formulating IEPs (70.59%), include parents in the assessment process (87.06%), include parents in the disciplinary decision councils (57.65%), recognise the importance of parents as home-

Table 4.93 : *Frequencies, Percentages, and 'Z' Values with Regard to Perception of Teachers on the Efforts Taken by Them for Enhancing Involvement*

Efforts taken by teachers	Response of Parents				'Z'
	Yes		*No*		
	N	*%*	*N*	*%*	*Value*
Include parents in the policy decision-taking councils	59	69.41	26	30.59	3.58**
While formulating IEPs consider views of parents	60	70.59	25	29.41	3.80**
Include parents in the assessment process	74	87.06	11	12.94	6.83**
Include parents for deciding the class placements	20	23.53	65	76.47	–4.89**
Include parents in the disciplinary decision councils	49	57.65	36	42.35	1.41
Include parents in the financial committees	39	45.88	46	54.12	–0.76
Include parents in the other administrative matters of the school	27	31.76	58	68.24	–3.36**
Recognises the importance of parents as home-teachers	82	96.47	3	3.53	8.54**
Help the parents to train their children at home	82	96.47	3	3.53	8.54**
Arranges parent education programmes	71	83.53	14	16.47	6.18**

** Significant at 0.01 level.

teachers (96.47%), help the parents to train their children at home (96.47%). Further, according to 83.53 per cent of the teachers, the school arranges parent-education programmes. Whereas 76.47 per cent of the teachers confirm that they do not include the parents while deciding the class placements, 54.12 per cent of the teachers admit that they do not include parents in the financial committees, and 68.24 per cent of the teachers admit they do not include parents in the other administrative matters of the school.

Contrary to the perception of parents (Table 4.91), 70.59 per cent of the teachers perceive that they consider views while formulating IEPs. Only further studies can explain this difference. Another major finding is that the majority of the teachers do not include parents either in the financial decisions or in the class placement decisions, or in the other administrative matters of the school. In all the other areas, the majority of the teachers perceive the efforts taken by them for enhancing parental involvement. These results are in perfect agreement with the general practice.

Table 4.94 : *Frequencies, Percentages, and Chi-square Value with Regard to the Perception of Teachers on the Role of Parents in the Education of Their Mentally Retarded Children*

Role of Parents	*Number*	*Percentage*	*Chi-square*
More than that of teachers	45	52.94	
Equal to teachers	39	45.88	40.19**
Lower than that of teachers	1	1.18	
Total	**85**	**100.00**	

** Significant at 0.01 level.

As the obtained chi-square value is significant at 0.01 level, it can be concluded that the difference between the frequencies of different perceptions of teachers on the role of parents in the education of mentally retarded children is statistically significant. Analysis of the percentages shows that 52.94 per cent of the teachers consider the role of parents in the education of their mentally retarded children as 'more than that of teachers' and 45.88 per cent perceive an 'equal' role for parents and teachers. Only one teacher perceived the role of parents as 'lower than that of teachers'.

This is a healthy sign that almost all the teachers either consider the role of parents as higher than that of teachers or equal to them. This will definitely help in enhancing the parental involvement and thereby benefiting the retarded children.

According to Table 4.95, most of the teachers provide training to parents in different skills, so that the parents can develop the skills in their retarded children. It can be seen from the table that the percentage of teachers who provide training to parents range from 84.17

Table 4.95 : *Frequencies and Percentages of Teachers who Provided Training to Parents for Developing Certain Skills in the Retarded Children*

Skills	Response of Teachers			
	Yes		*No*	
	N	*%*	*N*	*%*
Self-care	83	97.65	2	2.35
Language	77	90.59	8	9.41
Numerical	74	87.06	11	12.94
Health and Safety	83	97.65	2	2.35
Social	80	94.12	5	5.88
Vocational	72	84.71	13	15.29
Self-expressive	77	90.59	8	9.41
Disciplinary	80	94.12	5	5.88

** Significant at 0.01 level.

in vocational skills to 97.65 in self-care and health and safety skills. These results also indicate the positive attitude of teachers which will definitely enhance parental involvement. Results of the Table 4.92–4.95 clearly reveal the perception of parents and teachers regarding the efforts taken by the teachers and school authorities for enhancing parental involvement. Both the parents and teachers have identified the efforts taken by the teachers and schools. The one area that deserves special mention is the comparatively lower level of parental participation in the administrative matters of the school. Both the teachers and the parents have identically responded in this regard.

Parental Perceptions with Regard to the Effect of Associated Problems in the Education of Their Retarded Children and Services Available for Their Education

Frequencies, percentages, and chi-square values have been computed to analyse the parental perceptions regarding the effect of associated problems in the education of their retarded children and services available for their education. The details of analysis are presented in Tables 4.96–4.98.

Table 4.96 shows that all the obtained chi-square values, except in the case of language disabilities are significant either at 0.01 level or at 0.05 level. This indicates that the differences between the

Table 4.96 : *Frequencies, Percentages, and Chi-square Values with Regard to Perception of Parents on the Effect of Associated Problems in the Education of Their Retarded Children*

Problems	Extent of Effect in the Education								Chi-square
	High		Somewhat		Low		Not at all		
	N	%	N	%	N	%	N	%	
Poor ability to learn	61	35.88	54	31.76	40	23.53	15	8.83	17.11**
Poor ability in basic living skills	53	31.18	64	37.65	33	19.41	20	11.76	16.19**
Health Problems	23	13.53	65	38.24	39	22.94	43	25.29	12.45**
Lack of Discipline	21	12.35	58	34.12	39	22.94	52	30.59	11.15*
Behavioural Problems	17	10.00	58	34.12	33	19.41	62	36.47	18.84**
Language Disabilities	44	25.88	54	31.76	34	20.00	38	22.36	3.14

* Significant at 0.05 level. ** Significant at 0.01 level.

frequencies of different parental responses regarding the effect of associated problems in the education of their retarded children are significant at 0.01 level in the case of 'poor ability to learn', 'poor ability in basic living skills', 'health problems', and also 'behavioural problems'. In the case of 'lack of discipline', the difference is found to be significant at 0.05 level.

But the percentage-wise analysis does not show any specific trend. It can be seen from Table 4.96 that 35.88 per cent of the parents perceive that poor ability of the retarded children to learn, 'highly' effects their educational performance, and 31.76 per cent perceive that this problem 'somewhat' affects their education. While 23.53 per cent perceive the effect as 'low', 8.83 per cent of the parents do 'not at all' perceive any effect of this associated problem on the education of their retarded children.

37.65 per cent of the parents perceive that poor ability of the retarded children in basic living skills 'somewhat' affects their educational performance. But 31.18 per cent of the parents feel that this problem 'highly' affects their education. However, 19.41 per cent perceive the effect as 'low' and 11.76 per cent of the parents do 'not at all' perceive any effect of this problem on their education.

38.24 per cent of the parents perceive that the retarded children's health problems 'somewhat' affect their educational performance. While 25.29 per cent of the parents do 'not at all' perceive any such effect, 22.94 per cent perceive the effect as 'low' and only 13.53 per cent of the parents perceive this effect as 'high'.

34.12 per cent of the parents perceive the effect of retarded children's lack of discipline in their educational performance as 'somewhat', whereas 30.59 per cent do 'not at all' perceive any such effect. 22.94 per cent of the parents perceive the effect as 'low', whereas 12.35 per cent of the parents perceive the 'high' effect of lack of discipline in their education.

36.47 per cent of the parents do 'not at all' perceive any effect of behavioural problems in the educational performance of their retarded children. While 34.12 per cent perceive the effect as 'somewhat', and 19.41 per cent perceive the effect as 'low', 10.00 per cent of the parents perceive the effect as 'high'.

31.76 per cent of the parents perceive that the language disabilities 'somewhat' affect the education of their retarded children and 25.88

per cent consider the effect as 'high'. 22.36 per cent do not perceive any effect and for 20.00 per cent of the parents the effect is 'low'.

A close observation of Table 4.96 reveals that the percentages of all the responses are below 40 and it ranges from 8.83 to 38.24. This may be an indication of the parental confusion regarding the effect of retarded children's associated problems in their education.

As it is evident from Table 4.97, all the obtained chi-square values are significant at 0.01 level, which indicates that the differences between the frequencies of different parental responses with regard to the extent of availability of various facilities in the school are statistically significant.

Percentage-wise analysis shows that the majority of the parents (46.48-87.65%) are 'certainly' satisfied with the availability of facilities in all the areas studied. The experience of the investigator suggests that this high level of parental satisfaction need not be because of the adequacy of all the facilities, but rather may be due to their low expectation regarding the requirements.

From Table 4.98, it is seen that all the obtained chi-square values are significant at 0.01 level. Hence it can be concluded that the differences between the frequencies of different parental responses with regard to their perceptions on the necessity of all the six support services studied are statistically significant. Percentage-wise analysis reveals that according to a significant majority of the parents (69.41-88.82%), all the six support services studied are 'certainly' needed for the progress of their retarded children. Only a very small percentage of the parents (0.59-10.00) perceive the need for these services as 'very little' or 'not at all'. These results are in perfect agreement with the professional thinking that all the above mentioned support services have their own role to play in the rehabilitation of the mentally retarded.

Extent of Parental Satisfaction in the Method of Training Provided to the Mentally Retarded Children

This section deals with the analysis of extent of parental satisfaction in the method of training provided to the mentally retarded children. Frequencies, percentage, and chi-square values have been computed. The details are presented in Table 4.99.

As it is evident from Table 4.99, all the obtained chi-square values are significant at 0.01 level, which means that the difference between the frequencies of different responses of parents regarding their extent of satisfaction in the method of training provided to the mentally retarded children are statistically significant.

Table 4.97 : *Frequencies, Percentages, and Chi-square Values with Regard to Parental Satisfaction with the Extent of Availability of Various Facilities in the School*

Facilities	Extent of Availability								Chi-square
	Certainly		Somewhat		Very Little		Not at all		
	N	%	N	%	N	%	N	%	
Competent teachers	149	87.65	19	11.18	2	1.17	0	0.00	212.36**
Appropriate curriculum	127	74.71	36	21.18	5	2.94	2	1.17	141.61**
Individual attention from teachers	149	87.65	17	10.00	2	1.17	2	1.17	211.45**
Scientific Methods of Assessment	92	54.12	55	32.35	18	10.59	5	2.94	63.85**
Medical Care	105	61.76	38	22.35	12	7.06	15	8.83	77.67**
Travelling facilities	102	60.00	31	18.24	13	7.65	24	14.11	67.61**
Guidance and counselling programmes	117	68.82	38	22.36	9	5.29	6	3.53	137.63**
Day care facilities	149	87.65	19	11.18	2	1.17	0	0.00	212.36**
Parent Education Programmes	79	46.48	32	18.82	27	15.88	32	18.82	24.84**

** Significant at 0.01 level.

Table 4.98 : *Frequencies, Percentages, and Chi-square Values with Regard to Perception of Parents on the Necessity of Certain Support Services for the Progress of Their Children*

Support Services	*Extent of Necessity*								*Chi-square*
	Certainly		*Somewhat*		*Very Little*		*Not at all*		
	N	*%*	*N*	*%*	*N*	*%*	*N*	*%*	
Parent education Programmes	145	85.29	13	7.65	1	0.59	11	6.47	195.00**
Formation of Parent Groups	118	69.41	36	21.18	4	2.35	12	7.06	112.87**
Guidance and counselling programmes for siblings	121	71.18	27	15.88	5	2.94	17	10.00	117.10**
Services of Medical Doctors	151	88.82	9	5.29	6	3.54	4	2.35	217.40**
Services of Psychologists	138	81.18	16	9.41	5	2.94	11	6.47	169.17**
Services of voluntary organisations	144	84.71	15	8.82	4	2.35	7	4.12	191.04**

** Significant at 0.01 level.

Table 4.99 : *Frequencies, Percentages, and Chi-square Values with Regard to the Extent of Parental Satisfaction in the Method of Training Provided to the Mentally Retarded Children*

Areas of Training	*Extent of Satisfaction*								*Chi-square*
	Certainly		*Somewhat*		*Very Little*		*Not at all*		
	N	*%*	*N*	*%*	*N*	*%*	*N*	*%*	
Self-care skills	138	81.18	26	15.29	5	2.94	1	0.59	173.32**
Language skills	113	66.47	36	21.18	15	8.82	6	3.53	98.28**
Numerical abilities	106	62.35	34	20.00	18	10.59	12	7.06	77.98**
Health and Safety skills	119	70.00	33	19.41	13	7.65	5	2.94	113.76**
Social skills	120	70.59	27	15.88	11	6.47	12	7.06	113.76**
Vocational skills	100	58.82	37	21.77	15	8.82	18	10.59	64.95**
Skills of Self-expression	120	70.59	31	18.24	11	6.47	8	4.70	115.18**
Disciplinary skills	127	74.71	32	18.82	6	3.53	5	2.94	138.28**

** Significant at 0.01 level.

Percentage-wise analysis reveals that the majority of the parents (58.82-81.18%) are 'certainly' satisfied with the method of training provided to the retarded children for developing different skills. Also, a sizable percentage (15.29-21.77) of parents are 'somewhat' satisfied with the method of training. However, only a very small percentage of the parents (0.59-10.59) perceive as 'not at all' satisfied.

This high satisfaction of parents may be the result of : (a) the scientific nature of the methods, followed, (b) dedication of teachers in following appropriate programmes, (c) improvement noticed in the child, (d) lack of parental knowledge regarding the scientific methods of training, and (e) low level of parental expectation about the training methods. To specify the reasons further research is needed.

Perception of Parents and Teachers with Regard to Parental Guidance and Counselling

This final section of the investigation presents the details of analysis of perception of parents and teachers with regard to the need for parental guidance and counselling. Table 4.100 and 4.101 give the frequencies of percentages of specific items on perceptions of parents and teachers in this area.

Table 4.100 : *Frequencies and Percentages with Regard to Perception of Parents Regarding Their Need for Guidance and Counselling*

Need for Guidance and Counselling	Response of Parents			
	Yes		*No*	
	N	%	N	%
For proper maintenance and progress of the family	137	80.59	33	19.41
For leading a normal social life	133	78.24	37	21.76
For preventing possible emotional problems in the family	129	75.88	41	24.12
For proper development of siblings	113	66.47	57	33.53
For alleviating anxieties about the future of the child	151	88.82	19	11.18

It can be seen from Table 4.100 that the majority of the parents perceive the need for guidance and counselling. Item-wise analysis shows that the percentages range from 66.47 for proper development of siblings to 88.82 for alleviating anxieties about the future of the child. This highlights the need for organising guidance and counselling programmes for parents.

It is evident from Table 4.101 that almost all the teachers perceive the need for parental guidance and counselling: to increase the parental self-confidence, to develop correct understanding about the abilities and disabilities of their children, to develop proper perception about the education of the retarded, to ensure proper parental involvement, to prevent the likelihood of disruptions in the social relations, to keep

Table 4.101 : *Frequencies and Percentages with Regard to Perception of Teachers Regarding the Need for Parental Guidance and Counselling*

Need for Guidance and Counselling	Response of Teachers			
	Yes		*No*	
	N	%	*N*	%
To increase self-confidence	84	98.82	1	1.18
To have a correct understanding about the abilities and disabilities of their children	84	98.82	1	1.18
To develop a proper perception about the education of their children	84	98.82	1	1.18
To ensure proper involvement in the education of their children	84	98.82	1	1.18
To prevent possible disruptions in the social relations of the families due to the retardation of their children	82	96.47	3	3.53
To keep a healthy family atmosphere	82	96.47	3	3.53
To alleviate difficulties in rearing their retarded children	83	97.65	2	2.35
To prevent the chances of ignoring other family members, as the parents have to spend more time for their retarded children	84	98.82	1	1.18
To alleviate anxieties about the future of the retarded children	84	98.82	1	1.18
To make them aware of various services available in the society	84	98.82	1	1.18

a healthy family atmosphere, to alleviate the difficulties in rearing their retarded children, to prevent the chances of ignoring other family members, to alleviate anxieties about the future of the retarded children, and to develop an awareness about the various services available in the society.

These results also indicate the parental need for guidance and counseling to make their day to day life more comfortable, which will indirectly enhance their level of involvement in the education of their mentally retarded children.

5

Summary, Conclusions and Suggestions

The Study in Retrospect

The present study has been designed to investigate the different aspects of involvement of parents in developing basic living skills in their mentally retarded children. This study was also expected to explore the perception of parents and teachers in relation to some of the issues in the education of retarded children. The details of the objectives and methodology followed are given below.

1. Objectives of the Study

The major objectives of the study were:

1. To study the involvement of parents in developing the basic living skills (self-care, motor, language, numerical, health and safety, social, vocational, and leisure) in mentally retarded children.
2. To investigate the existing and expected levels of parental involvement in the educational decision-making.
3. To examine the efforts taken by the teachers and school authorities for enhancing parental involvement.
4. To study the parental perceptions with regard to the effect of associated problems in the education of retarded children and the services available for their education.

5. To study the extent of parental satisfaction in the method of training provided to the mentally retarded children.
6. To study the perceptions of the parents and teachers with regard to parental guidance and counselling.

2. Methodology of Brief

The descriptive survey method was adopted as the method of research. The sample for the present study consists of parents of 170 mentally retarded children studying in various special schools in Ernakulam and Kottayam districts of Kerala state and 85 special teachers working in these schools. Altogether four different tools were used for the collection of data. They are: (1) General Data Sheet, (2) Parent Involvement Interview Schedule, (3) Parent Involvement Questionnaire, and (4) Interview Schedule for Teachers.

The data collected using these tools were analysed using the following statistical techniques:

(a) Computation of frequencies, percentages, arithmetic mean, and standard deviation.
(b) The 't' test of significance.
(c) Logarithmic transformation.
(d) One-way analysis of a variance.
(e) The test of least significant difference for post hoc comparisons.
(f) Karl Pearson's product-moment coefficient of correlation.
(g) The chi-square test.
(h) The 'Z' test of double proportion.

Major Findings

The major findings that have emerged from the study are given below under separate heads.

1. Percentage-wise and Level-wise Analysis of Parental Involvement in Developing the Basic Living Skills

i. Percentage-wise analysis

The parental involvement in general was found to be neither high nor very low (50.40%). The highest percentage of involvement was found to be in developing self-care skills (66.60%), followed by social skills (59.90%), health and safety skills (53.90%), and motor skills (52.30%). In all the other skills, it was found to be less than 50 per cent. In developing leisure time skills parental involvement was 49.10 per cent followed by vocational skills (49\8.80%), reading and writing skills (45.60%), and the lowest percentage of parental involvement was found to be in developing numerical skills (33.60%).

ii. Level-wise Analysis

In general, majority of the parents (52.90%) were found to be in the 'average involvement' group. 30.60 per cent belong to the 'low involvement' group, and 16.50 per cent of the parents belong to the 'high involvement' group.

In developing self-care skills, it was found that 51.80 per cent, 31.80 per cent and 16.40 per cent of the parents belong to the 'high', 'average', and 'low' involvement groups respectively.

In developing motor skills, it was found that 22.90 per cent, 50.60 per cent, and 26.50 per cent of the parents belong to the 'high', 'average', and 'low' involvement groups respectively.

In developing reading and writing skills, it was found that 24.70 per cent of the parents belong to the 'high involvement' group, 27.60 per cent to the 'average involvement' group, and 47.70 per cent to the 'low involvement' group.

In the case of numerical skills, it was found that 21.20 per cent, 11.20 per cent, and 67.60 per cent of the parents belong to the 'high', 'average', and 'low' involvement groups respectively.

In developing health and safety skills, 30.00 per cent of the parents were found to belong to the 'high involvement' group, 43.50 per cent in the 'average involvement' group, and 26.50 per cent in the 'low involvement' group. In the case of social skills, it was 39.40 per cent, 34.10 per cent, and 26.50 per cent respectively.

In developing vocational skills, 23.40 per cent of the parents were found to belong to the 'high involvement' group, 40.30 per cent in the 'average involvement' group and 36.30 per cent in the 'low involvement' group.

In the case of leisure time skills, it was 20.00 per cent, 49.40 per cent, and 30.60 per cent respectively.

2. *Parental Involvement with respect to Certain Child-Related and Parent-Related Variables*

Sex of the mentally retarded children was found to be a significant factor in deciding the nature of parental involvement in developing motor skills (t=2.24, p<0.05) and in developing leisure time skills (t=2.47, p < 0.05). In both the skills parents of male children were found to be involved highly. However, in developing all the other skills studied, sex of the children was found to be an insignificant factor.

Religion was found to be a significant predictor of parental involvement in developing social skills (F=3.09, d.f. = 2;167, p<0.05) with Hindus having highest score, followed by Christians and Muslims. Difference between Hindus and Muslims as well as Muslims and Christians are found to be significant at 0.05 level. In developing all the other skills, religions was found to be an insignificant factor.

Number of siblings of mentally retarded children emerged as a significant factor in the parental involvement in developing self-care skills (F = 2.48, d.f. = 4;165, p<0.05). Difference between parents of 'no sibling group and three siblings group', 'no sibling group and four and more siblings group', 'one sibling group and four and more sibling group', 'two siblings group and three siblings group', as well as, 'two siblings group and four and more siblings group' were found to be significant at 0.05 level, in all these groups the former one having the higher level of involvement. In no other skills, number of siblings had any significant effect.

Age of the father was found to have significant influence in deciding the nature of parental involvement in developing reading and writing skills (F=5.06, d.f. = 2; 151, p<0.01) with the 'old age group' having the highest involvement score, followed by the 'middle age group' and then by the 'younger age group'. Difference between all the three pairs were found to be significant. In developing health and safety skills also, the age of the father was found to have significant effect (F = 6.11, d.f. = 2; 151, p<0.01) with the 'old age group' having the highest involvement score, followed by the 'middle age group' and then by the 'younger age group'. Difference between 'younger age group and middle age group', as well as 'younger age group and old age group' were found to be significant. When the total involvement score (excluding vocational) was considered, then too, the age of the father was found to be a significant factor (F = 4.07, d.f. = 2; 151,

$p < 0.05$) with the 'old age group' having the highest score, followed by the 'middle age group' and the 'younger age group'. Difference between 'younger age group and middle age group' as well as 'younger and old age groups' were found to be significant.

Age of the mother has emerged as the most influencing predictor of parental involvement. This was found in developing reading and writing skills ($F = 4.20$, d.f. = 2; 167, $p < 0.05$), numerical skills ($F = 3.70$, d.f. = 2;167, $p < 0.05$), health and safety skills ($F = 6.31$, d.f. = 2; 167; $p < 0.01$), social skills ($F = 3.66$, d.f. = 2; 167, $p < 0.05$) and basic living skills in general (excluding vocational) ($F = 3.62$, d.f. = 2; 167, $p < 0.05$). Difference between 'younger and old age groups', as well as 'middle and old age groups' were found to be significant in reading and writing skills and numerical skills with the 'old age group' having the highest score in both the cases, followed by the 'middle age group' and then by the 'younger age group'. In the case of the health and safety skills the difference between 'younger and middle', as well as 'younger and old' age groups were found to be significant, with the 'middle age group' showing highest score, followed by the 'old age group' and then by the 'younger age group'. In the case of social skills, the difference between 'younger and middle age groups' was found to be significant, with 'middle age group' showing higher level of involvement, followed by the 'old age group' and then by the 'younger age group'. In the case of basic living skills in general (excluding vocational), the difference between 'younger and middle age groups', as well as 'younger and old age groups' were found to be significant, with the 'old age group' showing the higher level of involvement, followed by the 'middle age group' and then by the 'younger age group' of parents.

Occupation of the mother was found to be a significant predictor of parental involvement in developing numerical skills ($F = 3.29$, d.f. = 3;166, $p < 0.05$). The difference between the scores of 'Group I (coolie, etc.) and Group III (gazetted officers, etc.)' was found to be significant with the later group having higher level of involvement. The difference between 'Group II (clerical and other office employees) and Group IV (unemployed' was also found to be statistically significant with the former group having higher level of involvement.

In developing social skills, occupation of the mother emerged as a significant factor ($F = 2.70$, d.f. = 3; 166, $p < 0.05$). The difference between 'Group I and Group II', 'Group I and Group III' and 'Group

I and Group IV' was found to be significant. In all these pairs, 'Group I' shows the lowest parental involvement score.

Level of mental retardation has emerged as a significant factor in developing reading and writing skills ($F=3.23$, d.f. = 2; 167, $p<0.05$). The difference between the parents of 'mildly and moderately retarded' children was found to be significant with 'mild group' having higher level of involvement.

Variables such as age, birth order, and number of years of schooling of mentally retarded children, location of residence, educational status of father and mother, nature of occupation of father, and monthly income of parents are found to play no significant role in deciding the parental involvement in developing basic living skills.

No significant correlation was found between parental involvement in developing basic living skills and variables such as age of retarded children, age of the father, age of the mother, and monthly income of parents.

3. Parental Perceptions with Regard to Their Existing and Expected Levels of Involvement in the Educational Decision-Making

Parental involvement in the existing and expected levels were studied in relation to ten areas of educational decision-making. Major findings are given below.

(a) Majority of the parents (62.94%) feel that in the existing level, they are 'highly' involved in taking decisions related to assessing the child's abilities. At the same time, significantly higher percentage of parents (79.41%, $Z = -3.35$, $p<0.01$) were found to be longing for 'high' level of involvement.

(b) In the existing system, only 29.41 per cent of the parents perceive that their level of involvement in taking decisions related to the formulation of Individualised Education Programme (IEP) as 'high'. Whereas, 24.12 per cent report that they do not have any type of involvement. However, few parents feel that they are 'only giving' (23.53%) and 'receiving information' (22.94%).

But in the expected level, significantly higher percentage of the parents (60%, $Z= -5.67$, $p<0.01$) wish for 'high' involvement and only 15.30 per cent of the parents expect 'no involvement' ($Z= 2.05$, $p<0.05$). Similarly, the percentage of parents who wish 'only to give or receive information' were also found to be significantly lower than that at the existing level.

(c) In the existing system 43.53 per cent of the parents reported to have 'high' involvement in taking decisions related to the implementation of IEP and 25.30 per cent opined that they do not have any type of involvement in taking these decisions. But, it was found that significantly higher percentage of the parents (64.12%, $Z = -3.81, p < 0.01$) expect 'high' involvement in taking such decisions.

(d) In taking decisions regarding evaluation of the IEP, 42.35 per cent of the parents are found to have 'high' level of involvement in the existing system. Whereas, 25.29 per cent of the parents reported 'no involvement' in the existing system. But a significantly higher percentage of the parents (62.94%, $Z = -3.80$, $p < 0.01$) expressed their desire for 'high' involvement in taking decisions related to evaluation of IEP. Also, the percentage of 'no involvement' group was significantly lower in the expected level than the existing level (16.47%, $Z = 2.00$, $p < 0.05$).

(e) In the existing system, 35.29 per cent of the parents have reported a 'high' level involvement in taking decisions related to class placement, whereas 33.54 per cent reported that they do not have any involvement in taking such decisions. But a significantly higher percentage of the parents (54.12%, $Z = -3.49, p < 0.01$) expressed their desire for a 'higher' level of the involvement.

(f) Comparatively higher percentage of the parents reported to have 'high' level of involvement in taking decisions related to disciplinary matters (60.59%). Even then, higher percentage of parents (69.14%) wish for high level of involvement. But this difference was found to be statistically insignificant.

(g) In the existing system, 60 per cent of the parents are found to have 'high' level of involvement in taking decisions related to keeping records about the child and a significantly higher percentage of the parents (72.94%, $Z = -2.52, p < 0.05$) expressed their desire for 'high' level of involvement.

(h) Comparatively higher percentage of the parents (72.94%) are found to have 'high' level of involvement in taking decisions related to the travelling facilities. At the expected level more parents (77.65%) expressed their desire for 'high' level involvement; but the difference between existing and expected level was found to be statistically insignificant.

(i) High majority of the parents (82.35%) are found to have 'high' level involvement in the existing system in taking decisions related to medical treatments for their children. In the expected level also, most of the parents (85.29%) expressed their desire for a 'high' involvement. But no significant difference was noticed between the existing and expected levels of involvement.

(j) A slight majority of the parents (50.59%) are found to have 'no involvement' at all in taking decisions related to admitting their retarded children in the residential schools and only 35.29 per cent of the parents have 'high' involvement in taking these decisions. But in the expected level, significantly higher percentage of the parents (46.47%, $Z=-2.10$, $p<0.05$) are found to have expressed their desire for 'high' level involvement and the percentage of parents who expressed their desire for 'no involvement' was found to be lower (43.53%) at the expected level; even though this difference was found to be statistically insignificant.

Moreover, majority of the parents (65.29%) are found to be 'certainly' satisfied with their existing role in educational decision-making. At the same time, 85.88 per cent of the parents perceive that they need more information and training in order to become competent educational decision-makers.

Majority of the parents (69.41%) reported that in the existing system, they do no have any role in the selection of teachers.

Significantly higher percentage of the parents (44.11 to 78.23) perceive no hindrances in attending the educational decision-making meetings in the special schools. But a few parents have perceived the following factors as reasons for their non-attending in the decision-making meetings: occupation (21.18%), lack of adequate communication skills (8.24%), time of the meeting (12.35%), language problems (5.88%), financial problems (13.53%), educational standard (7.65%), confusion on how to participate (9.41%), family burden (15.88%), other children's education (13.53%), and lack of encouragement from school authorities (7.65%).

4. *Perception of the Parents and Teaches with Regard to the Efforts Taken by the Teachers and School Authorities for Enhancing Parental Involvement*

Most of the parents perceive that teachers and school authorities are taking a lot of effort for: encouraging parents to participate in the educational decision-making meetings (90.59%), giving special training to parents for home based training (63.53%), contacting parents for discussions regarding their children (89.41%), encouraging parents for keeping continuous contact with the school (94.71%), and providing assistance for the child in a satisfactory level (89.41%). Whereas 53.53 per cent of the parents perceived that teachers and school authorities need not allow parents to participate in the formulation of individualised education programme. But the remaining 46.47 per cent perceive it as the role of teachers. Similarly, 80.00 per cent of the parents perceived that teachers and school authorities need not include representatives of parents in the committee that select teachers.

Most of the teachers positively perceived the need for: including parents in the policy decision-taking councils (69.41%), considering parental views during the formulation of IEP (70.59%), including parents in the assessment process (87.06%), including parents in the disciplinary decision councils (57.65), recognising the importance of the parents as home teachers (96.47%), helping the parents to train their children at home (96.47%) and arranging parent education programmes (83.53%).

Whereas, majority of the teachers reported that they are not including parents: in the class placement decisions (76.47%), in the financial committees (54.12%), and in the other administrative matters of the school (68.24%).

It was found that 52.94 per cent of the teachers perceive the role of parents in the education of their retarded children as 'more than that of teachers', whereas, 45.88 per cent perceive it as 'equal to that of teachers', and only one teacher (1.18%) perceived it as 'less than that of teachers'.

Most of the teachers expressed that they are imparting training to parents for developing the following skills in their mentally retarded children: self-care (97.65), language (90.59%), numerical (87.06%), health and safety (97.65), social (94.12%), vocational (84.71%), self-expression (90.59%), and disciplinary skills (94.12%).

5. *Parental Perceptions with Regard to the Effect of Associated Problems in the Education of Their Retarded Children and Services Available for Their Education*

Majority of the parents do not perceive the effect of associated problems in the education of their retarded children as 'high'. Specific results obtained are given below.

35.88 per cent of the parents feel that their retarded children's poor ability to learn 'highly' affect their education, whereas, only 8.83 per cent reported that this does not have any effect.

31.18 per cent perceived that their retarded children's poor ability in basic living skills has 'high' effect in the education. Whereas, only 11.76 per cent of the parents reported that this does 'not at all' affect the education.

25.29 per cent of the parents do feel that the health problems of their retarded children 'not at all' affect their education. Only 13.53 per cent feel that the education of their mentally retarded children is affected by the children's health problems.

For 30.59 per cent of the parents, lack of discipline does not have any effect in the education of the retarded children. Whereas, for 12.35 per cent it has 'high' effect in the education.

36.47 per cent of the parents feel that the presence of the behavioural problems in mentally retarded children do not affect the education and only 10.00 per cent of the parents reported that it has a 'high' effect in the education of their mentally retarded children.

Only 25.88 per cent of the parents have expressed a 'high' effect of language disabilities in the education of mentally retarded children, whereas, for 22.36 per cent of the parents this has 'no' effect.

Majority of the parents are found to be satisfied with the availability of all the following facilities in the school: competent teachers (87.65%), appropriate curriculum (74.71%), individual attention from teachers (87.65%), scientific methods of assessment (54.12%), medical care (61.76%), travelling arrangements (60.60%), guidance and counselling programmes (68.82%), day care system (87.65%), and parents education programmes (46.48%).

Most of the parents perceive the following support services as 'certainly' needed for the progress of their retarded children: parent education programmes (85.29%), formation of parent groups (69.41%), guidance and counselling programmes for siblings (71.18%), services of medical doctors (88.82%), services of psychologists (81.18%), and services of voluntary organisations (84.71%).

6. *Parental Satisfaction in the Method of Training Provided to the Mentally Retarded Children*

Majority of the parents are found to be satisfied with the method of training provided to the retarded children for developing the following skills: self-care (81.18%), language (66.47%), numerical (62.35%), health and safety (70.00%), social (70.59%), vocational (58.82%), self-expression (70.59%), and discipline (74.71%).

7. Perception of Parents and Teachers with Regard to Parental Guidance and Counselling

Most of the parents positively perceived the need for guidance and counselling. According to majority of the parents guidance and counselling is needed for: proper maintenance and progress of the family (80.59%), leading a normal social life (78.24%), preventing possible emotional problems in the family (75.88%), proper development of siblings (66.47%), and alleviating anxieties about the future of the child (88.82%).

More than 96 per cent of the teachers positively perceived the following needs of parental guidance and counselling: to increase self-confidence, to have a correct understanding about the abilities and disabilities of their children, to develop a proper perception about the education of their children, to ensure proper involvement of parents in the education, to prevent possible disruptions in the social relations of the families, to keep a healthy family atmosphere, to alleviate difficulties in rearing their retarded children, to prevent the chances of ignoring other family members, to alleviate anxieties about the future of the child, and to make the parents aware of the various services available in the society.

The major findings given above illustrate the realisation of all the objectives of the study.

Conclusions and Suggestions

The major conclusions that are arrived at from the present investigation and the suggestions made on the basis of the above conclusions are given below.

The present study revealed that the extent of parental involvement in developing basic living skills in the mentally retarded children is only of an average level. The highest level of involvement was found to be in developing self-care skills followed by social skills, and health and safety skills. The lowest level of involvement was found to be for developing numerical skills. The study elicited the following significant findings.

Parents of male mentally retarded children were found to have higher level of involvement in developing motor and leisure time skills than the involvement of parents who have female retarded children. Parents of retarded children belonging to Hindu religion was found to have a higher level of involvement in developing social skills than parents of Christian and Muslim religions. Parents of mentally retarded children with no siblings were found to be highly involving in developing self-care skills when compared with the parents of retarded children with one or more siblings.

The age of the father was found to be a significant factor in the parental involvement in developing reading and writing skills, health and safety skills, and basic living skills in general (excluding vocational skills), with the old age groups showing higher level of involvement than the middle and younger age groups. Age of the mother was also found to be a significant predictor of parental involvement in developing reading and writing skills, numerical skills, and basic living skills in general (excluding vocational skills) with the old age groups having higher level of involvement than the other two groups. In developing health and safety skills as well as social skills, age of the mother was found to be significantly influential in the parental involvement, with the middle age groups having a higher level of involvement than the other two groups.

Nature of occupation of the mother was found to be a significant predictor of parental involvement in developing numerical and social skills. In the case of numerical skills, mothers having clerical or other types of office work were found to be increasingly involved than other categories of mothers. In developing social skills, mothers who were gazetted officers or other high status professionals were found to have a higher level of involvement than the other types.

Degree of mental retardation was also found to have significant influence in the parental involvement in the developing reading and writing skills with the parents of mildly retarded children involved highly than the parents of moderately or severely retarded children.

However, factors such as age, birth order, and number of years of schooling of mentally retarded children, locality of residence, educational status of father and mother, nature of occupation of father, and monthly income of parents were found to have no significant influence in the parental involvement in developing basic living skills. Similarly, variables such as age of the retarded children, age of the father, age of the mother, and monthly income of parents were not significantly correlated with parental involvement.

A major and interesting observation is that in all the ten areas of educational decision-making studied, parents expressed their desire for more involvement than that of the existing level. Also, majority of the parents perceived that they need more training and information in order to become competent educational decision-makers.

Majority of the parents do not perceive the effect of associated problems in the education as high. Most of the parents were found to be satisfied with the availability of different services in the school and also they perceived the necessity of the support services such as parent education programme, formation of parent groups, guidance and counselling programmes for siblings, services of medical doctors, services of psychologists, and services of voluntary organisations.

Majority of the parents were highly satisfied with the method of training followed in the school. Similarly, majority of both parents and teachers perceived the significant role of teachers and school authorities in enhancing parental involvement, as well as the parental need for guidance and counselling.

In short, the present study gives a cross-sectional picture of the parental involvement in the education of mentally retarded children. On the basis of the above conclusions, the following suggestions are given.

(a) A concentrated effort is needed to prepare and train parents for increasing their level of involvement in the education of their retarded children. This should start from the very beginning of the process of education of their children. Training programme should include the following area as: concept of mental retardation, causes and characteristics, methods of assessment, aims and methods of education, curriculum and techniques of teaching, management of problem behaviour, planning and evaluation, vocational training and placement, role of different disciplines and support services in the successful rehabilitation of the retarded, role of parents such as educational decision-makers; advocates; supporters, resources; teachers; and counsellors, parents' rights and rights of the mentally retarded. Such a training programme will definitely help the parents to develop a scientific attitude. Parental knowledge will increase their self-confidence and level of involvement.

(b) Formulation of small parent groups in all the special schools will provide the parents the well needed stage for expressing their difficulties, sharing their experiences, solving their problems and moreover to develop a mutual help system.

(c) Parent Teacher Association (PTA) should be strengthened, and should function as a link between the special school and the community. PTAs should stand for making the community aware of various aspects of mental retardation and it should take necessary steps for proper vocational training and placement.

(d) Organisations of parents should be formed to fight for the rights of the retarded and their families, and to persuade the government to take action for the implementation of various rehabilitative measures.

(e) Special teachers and school authorities should recognise the important role of parents in the whole process of special education and should keep on motivating the parents for their active participation.

(f) Necessary steps should be taken to ensure the enrolment of all the female retarded children in the special schools and to encourage parents to actively participate in the education of their female mentally retarded children.

(g) There should be provision for the visit of the itinerant teachers to the homes of the mentally retarded children and thereby helping parents in the home based teaching. So that parents with more number of children can become more involved in the education of their retarded children.

(h) The services of professionally qualified counsellors should be available in the special schools so that involvement of younger parents of retarded children could be enhanced.

(i) Adequate support should be provided to the low socio-economic status parents to properly educate their retarded children and increase their involvement in the education.

(j) Steps should be taken to increase the level of involvement of fathers, so that the mothers can relax little more and the responsibility of looking after the mentally retarded child will become a collective one, which will increase the total parental involvement.

(k) All the special schools should strictly follow the principles of need based education and individualised educational programme. This will make the process of special education more scientific and productive. This will attract parents, irrespective of the degree of retardation of their child, and the parents will show more interest in the education.

(j) Just like the individualised education programme there should be individualised family programmes for the families of all the mentally retarded children. Schools should develop these programmes with the fuli participation of parents. This will help in meeting the different needs of different families, which will positively affect the welfare of the retarded children and their family members.

(m) Siblings and other family members should be encouraged and equipped to participate in the educational process of the retarded children. This will help parents to relax and to reduce their anxieties about the future of the children. Also, this will keep the family relationships intact.

(n) Measures should be taken to create a positive attitude among the community members towards the mentally retarded population and the need for their education. This will help to shed their inhibitions and fear of social stigma associated with mental retardation.

(o) Steps should be taken to produce books and other reading materials on education of the mentally retarded in the Malayalam language, and make them available to all the parents which will be of utmost utility to them.

(p) Special teachers training programmes should be given due importance to develop skills in the special teachers trainees for effectively working with parents. This will help the teachers to keep a healthy relationship with parents.

(q) Representatives of the parents should be included in all the administrative as well as academic committees of the school. This is very important for increasing parent participation and satisfaction.

(r) Make special education system scientific and well defined throughout all the special schools and an effective system should be developed to monitor the functioning of all these schools.

(s) All the special schools should be developed as resource centres with the availability of the following facilities: early identification and intervention, scientific tools for assessment, special educators, clinical psychologists, social workers, paediatricians, speech therapists, occupational therapists, physiotherapists, yoga specialists, specially trained teachers in music; arts; physical education; and vocational education, researchers, well equipped library and laboratory.

(t) The special schools should also conduct periodic orientation programmes for parents and community, seminars, and workshops on major issues in the field.

(u) Research studies are to be conducted in different areas in the education of mentally retarded children.

Suggestions for Further Research

In the light of the finding that have emerged from the present study and the valuable experience gained by conducting this investigation, the following topics are suggested for further research.

(a) The present study was conducted on a sample of parents of 170 mentally retarded children selected from two districts of Kerala. The same study may be conducted with a larger sample drawn from all districts of the state, so that more generalisable findings could be obtained.

(b) A similar study with different methods of data collection such as participant observation and unstructured interview will be worth doing.

(c) Further studies may be conducted to find out the factors that influence parental involvement.

(d) An attempt may be made to study the nature of involvement of fathers and mothers in the education of retarded children.

(e) Relationship between parent involvement and variables such as degree of retardation, socio-economic status of parents and age of parents may be examined.

(f) An investigation may be conducted to compare the levels of parental involvement in the education of their normal and retarded children.

(g) Follow-up studies may be conducted to find out the effect of parent education programmes on the involvement in the education of their retarded children.

(h) Effect of parental involvement in the educational decision-making may be investigated.

(i) Role of parents in the different aspects of vocational training and placement of retarded children may be studied.

(k) Role of siblings and grandparents in the education of retarded children may be studied.

(l) An attempt may be made to identify the needs and problems of the mothers of mentally retarded children.

(m) An attempt may be made to identify the attitude of normal children towards involvement in the education of their retarded siblings.

(n) Effectiveness of the functioning of Parent Teacher Associations and different parent groups in the education and rehabilitation of the retarded children may be examined.

(o) The nature of the parent-teacher partnership in the existing special education system may be investigated.

Bibliography

Adams, F. (Ed.) (1986), "Special education". In D. Baker and K. Bovair (Eds.) (1989). *Making the Special Schools Ordinary?* Vol. 1. London: The Falmer Press.

Allen, D.A. and Hudd, S.S. (1987). "Are we professionalising parents? Weighing the benefits and pitfalls," In B.B.Strickland and A.P. Turnbull (1990). *Developing and Implementing Individualised Education Programmes* (3rd edn.). London: Merrill Publishing, Co., p.26.

American Association on Mental Retardation (1992). *Mental Retardation—Definition, Classification, and Systems of Supports* (9th edn.). Washington, DC: AAMR.

Anderson, E. L. (1994). "The effect of parental invovlement on academic achievement." *Dissertation Abstracts International* 55: 4, 251-A.

Anderson, G.R. and Anderson, S.K. (1983). "The exceptional native American." In M.C. Wang, M.C. Reynolds, and H.J. Walberg (Eds.) (1987). *Handbook of Special Education: Research and Practice* Vol. 1. Oxford: Pergamon Press.

Andersson, E. (1993). "Depression and anxiety in families with a mentally handicapped child." *International Journal of Rehabilitation Research* 16:2, 165-169.

Argulewicz, E.N. (1983). "Effects of ethnic membership, socio-economic status, and home language on LD, EMER, and EH placements." *Learning Disabilities Quarterly* 6, 195-200.

Arnold S., Sturgis, E., and Forehand, R. (1977). "Training a parent to teach communication skills." *Behaviour Modification* 1, 259–276.

Auletta, R. and DeRosa, A.P. (1991). "Self-concepts of adolescent siblings of children with mental retardation." *Percept-Mot-Skills* 73: 1, 211-214.

Austin, P.C. (1984). "Parents' attitudes toward mainstreaming their handicapped children in pre-school programmes." *Dissertation Abstracts International* 45:10, 3110-A.

Azad, F.F. (1986). "Effectiveness of Portage home-based training programme on cognitive development of pre-school mentally retarded children." In M.B. Buch (Ed.) (1991). *IV Survey of Research in Eudcation* Vol. 2. New Delhi: NCERT, p. 1323.

Baine, D. (1986). "Early education curriculum design for handicapped children in developing countries." In J. Narayan (1994). "New trends in curriculum and instruction." *Update in Mental Retardation*. Secunderabad: National Institute for the Mentally Handicapped, p.3.

Baker B.L., Heifetz, L.J., and Murphy, D.M. (1980). "Behavioural training for parents of mentaly retarded children: one year follow-up." *American Journal of Mental Deficiency* 85: 1, 31-38.

Baker, D. and Bovair, K. (Eds.) (1989). *Making the Special Schools Ordinary ?* Vol. 1. London: The Falmer Press, p. 90.

Balasundaram, P. (1989). "Experience of developing services for pre-school mentally handicapped children in New Delhi." *Proceedings of the Second National Annual Seminar on Mental Retardation*. Secunderabad: NIMH.

Ballmer, O. (1978). "A comparison of types of parent involvement in selected pre-school special education programmes in the United States." *Dissertation Abstracts International* 39: 10, 6025-A.

Berlett, K. and Smith, P. (1978). "Family counselling for the handicapped child." In: H.W. Sawyer and S.H. Sawyer. "A teacher-parent communication training approach." *Exceptional Children* 47: 4, 305-306.

Bauch, J.P., Vietze, R.M., and Morris, V.D. (1973). "What makes the difference in parental participation ?" *Childhood Education* 49: 47-51.

Beattie, N. (1985). *Professional Parents.* Lewes: Falmer Press.

Begun, A.L. (1989). "Sibling relationships, involving developmentally disabled people." *American Journal of Mental Retardation* 93, 566-574.

Berdine, W.H. and Meyer, S.A. (1987). *Assessment in Special Education.* Boston: Little, Brown and Company.

Berry, P., Gunn, P., Andrews, R., and Price, C. (1981). "Characteristics of Down syndrome infants and their families." *Australian Paediatric Journal* 17, 40-43.

Best, J. W. and Kahn. J.V. (1992). *Research in Education* (6th edn.). New Delhi: Prentice-Hall of India Pvt. Ltd.

Beveridge, M. and Jerrams, A. (1981). "Parental involvement in language development: an evaluation of a school-based parental assistance plan." *The British Journal of Educational Psychology* 51:3,259-260.

Blacher, J. (1984). "Sequential stages of parental adjustment to the birth of a child with handicaps: fact or artifact?" *Mental Retardation* 22, 55-68.

Blacher, J. (Ed.) (1984b). *Severely Handicapped Children and their Families: Research in Review.* New York: Academic Press.

Blacher, J. and Baker, B.L. (1994). "Out-of-home placement for children with retardation: family decision-making and satisfaction." *Family Relations* 43: 1, 10-15.

Blacher, J., Nihira, K., and Meyers, C.E. (1987). "Characteristics of home environment of families with mentally retarded children: comparison across levels of retardation." *American Journal of Mental Deficiency* 91:4, 313-320.

Blacher, J. and Turnbull, A.P. (1982). "Teacher and parent perspectives on selected social aspects of pre-school mainstreaming." *The Exceptional Child* 29:3, 191-199.

Black, D. (1982) "Handicap and family therapy," In A. Bentovim, G. Gorell Barnes, and A. Cooklin (Eds.) *Family Therapy: Complementary Framework of Theory and Practice.* London: Academic Press.

Black, J.M.M. (1978). "Families with handicapped children-who helps whom and how ?" *Child : Care, Health, and Development* 4, 239-245.

Blackstone, T. (1979). "Parental involvement in education." *Education Policy Bulletin* 7:1, 81-98.

Borthwick-Duffy, S., Eyman, R.K., and White, J.F. (1987). "Client characteristics and residential placement patterns." *American Journal of Mental Deficiency* 92: 24-30.

Boyd, R.D. (1980). "Systematic parent training through a home-based model." *Exceptional Children* 45: 8, 647-650.

Brantlinger, E.A. and Guskin, S.L. (1987). "Ethnocultural and socio-psychological effects on learning characteristics of handicapped children." In M.C. Wang, M.C. Reynolds, and H.J. Walberg (Eds.) (1987). *Handbook of Special Education: Research and Practice* Vol. 1. Oxford: Pergamon Press, p.7.

Brassell, W.R. (1977). "Intervention with handicapped infants: correlates of progress." *Mental Retardation* 15, 18-22.

Breslau, N. and Davis, G.C. (1986). "Chronic stress and major depression." *Archives of General Psychiatry* 43, 309-314.

Breslau, N., Weitzman, M., and Messinger, K. (1981). "Psychological functioning of siblings of disabled children." *Pediatrics* 67, 344-353.

Brickey, M., Browning, L., and Campbell, K. (1982). "vocational histories of sheltered workshop employees placed in projects with industry and competitive jobs." *Mental Retardation* 20:2,52-57.

Brickey, M. and Campbell, K. (1981). "Fast food employment for moderately and mildly mentally retarded adults: The McDonald's project." *Mental Retardation* 19:3, 113-116.

Bristol, M.M. and Gallagher, J.J. (1982). "A family focus in intervention." In C. T. Ramey and P.L. Trohanis (Eds.) (1982). *Finding and Educating High Risk and Handicapped Infants.* Baltimore: University Park Press, P. 146.

Bristol, M.M. and Schopler, E. (1984). "A developmental perspective on stress and coping in families of autistic children." In M.C. Wang, M.C. Reynolds, and H.J. Walberg, (Eds.). (1989). *Handbook of Special Education-Research and Practice* Vol.3. Oxford: Pergamon Press, p. 302.

Brolin, D.E. (1983). "Career education: where do wo go from here ?" *Career Development for Exceptional Individuals* 6, 3-15.

Bromley, B.E. and Blacher, J. (1991). "Parental reasons for out-of-home placement of children with severe handicaps." *Mental Retardation* 29: 5, 275-280.

Brooks, M.A. (1984). "Parents as participants in the individual education planning process." *Dissertaion Abstracts International* 45: 6, 1715-A.

Brotherson, M.J. (1985). "Planning for adult futures: parents' self-report of future planning and its relationships to family functioning and stress with sons and daughters who are disabled." *Dissertation Abstracts International* 46: 10, 2992-2993-A.

Brown, S. and Moersch, M. (1982). *Parents on the Team.* Ann Arbor: University of Michigan Press.

Buckley, S. (1985). "Teaching parents to teach reading to teach language: a project with Down's syndrome children and their parents." In D. Baker and K. Bovair (Eds.) (1989). *Making the Special Schools Ordinary* ? Vol. 1. London: The Falmer Press, p. 145.

Buckley, S., Emslie, M., Haslegrave, G., and Le Prevost, P. (1986). "The development of language and reading skills in children with Down's syndrome." In D. Baker and K. Bovair (Es.(1989). *Making the Special Schools Ordinary* ? Vol. 1. London: The Falmer Press, p.145.

Burden, R.L. (1978). "An approach to the evaluation of early intervention projects with mothers of severely handicapped children; the attitude dimension." *Child : Care, Health and Development*, 4, 171-181.

Burton,T.A. and Hirshoren, A. (1979). "Some further thougths and clarifications on the education of severely and profoundly retarded children." *Exceptional Children* 45, 618-625.

Callias, M. and Carr, J. (1975). "Behaviour modification programmes in a community setting." In C.C. Kiernan and F.P. Woodford (Eds.). *Behaviour Modification with the Severely Retarded.* Amsterdam: Associated Scientific Publishers, pp. 147-171.

Cameron, R.J. (1979). "A lot can happen at home too." In J. Dobbing, A.D.B. Clarke, J.A. Corbett, J. Hogg, and R.O. Robinson (Eds.) (1985). *Scientific Studies in Mental Retardation.* London: The Royal Society of Medicine and the Macmillan Press Ltd., p. 449.

Carr, J. (1980). "Helping your handicapped child." In D. Baker and K. Bovair (Eds.) (1989). *Making the Special Schools Ordinary?* Vol.1. London: The Falmer Press, p. 145.

Carr, J. (1985). "Family processes and parent involvement." In J. Dobbing, A. D. B. Clarke, J.A. Corbett, J. Hogg, and R.O. Robinson (Eds.) *Scientific Studies in Mental Retardation.* London: The Royal Society of Medicine and The Macmillan Press Ltd., p. 450.

Carver, J.N. and Carver, N.E. (1972). *The Family of the Retarded Child.* Syracuse, NY: Syracuse University Press, p. 205.

Centre for Educational Research and Innovation (1983). *The Education of the Handicapped Adolescent—The Transition from School to Working Life.* Paris: CERI, Organisation for Economic Cooperation and Development.

Chess, S., Fernandez, P., and Korn, S. (1980). "The handicapped child and his family: consonance and dissonance." *Journal of American Academy of Child Psychiatry* 19, 56-57.

Chetwynd, S. (1985). "Some costs of caring at home for an intellectually handicapped child." *Australia and New Zealand Journal of Developmental Disabilities* 11, 35-40.

Chinitz, S.P. (1981). "A sibling group for brothers and sisters of handicapped children." In M.C. Wang, M.C. Reynolds, and H.J. Walberg (Eds.) (1989). *Handbook of Special Education—Research and Practice* Vol. 3. Oxford: Pergamon Press, p. 299.

Clark, J.R. (1994). "Parent perceptions of actual and ideal levels of involvement in decision-making in Tennessee elementary schools." *Dissertation Abstracts International* 55: 4, 810-A.

Clear, M.E. and Mank, D.M. (1990). "Supported and competitive employment outcomes and sources of support for individuals with disabilities in integrated jobs in New South Wales." *Australia and New Zealand Journal of Developmental Disabilities* 16:3, 245-257.

Cleveland, D.W. and Miller, N. (1977). "Attitudes and life commitments of older sibs of mentally retarded adults: an exploratory study." *Mental Retardation* 15:3, 38-41.

Cleveland, M.P. (1984). "School participation by parents of handicapped and non-handicapped children." *Dissertation Abstracts International* 45: 4, 996-A.

Cone, J.D. Delawyer, D.D., and Wolfe, V.V. (1985). "Assessing parent participation: the parent/family involvement index." *Exceptional Chidren* 51, 417-424.

Connolly, B., Morgan, S., Russell, F.F., and Richardson. B. (1980). "Early intervention with Down's syndrome children. Follow-up report." *Physical Therapy* 60, 1405-1408.

Countryman, G.J. (1994). "A qualitative study of parent involvement in an at-risk pre-school programme." *Dissertation Abstracts International* 55: 8, 2271-A.

Crnic, K.A., Friedrich, W.N., and Greenberg, M.T. (1983). "Adaptation of families with mentally retarded children: a model of stress, coping, and family ecology." *American Journal of Mental Deficiency* 88, 125-138.

Cunningham, C.C., Aumonier, M.E., and Sloper, P. (1982). "Health visitor support for families with Down's syndrome infants." *Child: Care, Health and Development* 8, 1-9.

Cunningham, C.C. and Davis. H. (1985). *Working with Parents: Framework for Collaboration.* Milton Keynes and Philadelphia: Open University Press.

Cuvo A. and Davis. P. (1983). "Behavioural therapy and community living skills." In M. Hersen, R. Eisler, and P. Miller (Eds.) *Progress in Behaviour Modification* Vol. 14. New York: Academic Press, pp. 125-171.

D'Alonzo, B.J. (1982). "Parent involvement in special education." *Journal for Special Educators* 18: 2, 5-13.

Darga, J.R. (1993). "Parent involvement in the decision-making process on issues related to school-based management." *Dissertation Abstracts International* 53:3, 748-A.

Dattilo, J. (1991a). "Recreation and leisure: a review of the literature and recommendations for future directions." In L.M. Meyer, C.A. Peck, and L. Brown (Eds.) *Critical Issues in the Lives of People with Severe Disabilities.* Baltimore: Brookes, pp. 126-37.

Dattilo, J. and Murphy, W.D. (1991). *Leisure Education Programme Planning: A Systematic Approach.* In J. Dattilo and S.J.Schleien (1994). "Understanding leisure services for individuals with mental retardation." *Mental Retardation* 32: 1, 53-59.

Dattilo J. and St. Peter, S. (1991). "A model for including leisure education in transition services for young adults with mental retardation." *Education and Training in Mental Retardation* 26: 4, 420-32.

DES (Department of Education and Science) (1978). *Special Educational Needs.* In T. Booth, P. Potts and W. Swann (1985). *Research and Progress in Special Education* (2nd edn.) Watton Hall: The Open University Press, p.19.

Directory of Special Schools in Kerala (1995). Ernakulam: State Committee of Special Olympics, Kerala.

Doernberg, N.L. (1978). "Some negative effects on family integration of health and education services." *Rehabilitation Literature* 39, 107-110.

Doleys, D.M., Doster, J., and Cartelli, L.M. (1976). "Parent training techniques: effects of lecture role playing followed by feedback and self-recording." *Behaviour Therapy and Experimental Psychiatry* 7, 359-362.

Donnellan, A. M. and Mirenda, P.M. (1984). "Issues related to professional involvement with families of individuals with autism and other severe handicaps." *The Association for Severely Handicapped Journal* 9:2, 16-22.

Donovan, A.M. (1988). "Family stress and ways of coping with adolescents who have handicaps: maternal perceptions." *American Journal on Mental Retardation* 92: 502-509.

Dorgu, S. O. (1993). "Determinants of parental involvement in supported program: a study of communiction behaviour and information sources." *Dissertation Abstracts International* 54: 8, 2796-A.

Downs, C., Taylor and London, E.M. (1981). *Collaboration in Special Education.* Belmont: Pitman Learning Inc.

Dupond, A. (1980) "A study concerning the time-related and other burdens when severely handicapped children are reared at home." In J. Dobbing, A.D.B. Clarke, J.A. Corbett, J. Hogg, and R.O. Robinson (Eds.) (1985). *Scientific Studies in Mental Retardation.* London: The Royal Society of Medicine and The Macmillan Press Ltd., p. 444.

Dutta, R. (1986). "Effect of different Portage training intervention models on motor development of pre-school mentally retarded children." In M.B. Buch (Ed.) (1991). *IV Survey of Research in Education* Vol. 2. p. 1323.

Educational Testing Service (1980). "New Vistas in special education." *Focus* 8: 2, 1-20.

Ellis, N.R., Bostick, G.E., Moore, S.A., and Taylor, J.J. (1981). "A follow-up of severely and profoundly mentally retarded children after short-term institutionalisation." *Mental Retardation* 19, 31-35.

Epstein, J. L. (1983). "Longitudinal effects of family-school-person interactions on student outcomes." In W.S. Grolnick and M.L. Slowiaczek (1991). "Parents' involvement in children's schooling: a multidimensional conceptualisation and motivational model." *Child Development* 65, 237-252.

Epstein, J. L. (1987). "Parent involvement: what research says to administrators." *Education and Urban Society*, 19, 119-136.

Epstein, J.L. (1990). "School and family connections: theory, research, and implications for integrating sociologies of education and family." *Marriage and Family Review* 15, 99-126.

Farber, B. (1975). "Family adaptation to severely mentally retarded children." In M. Begab and S. Richardson (Eds.). *The Mentally Retarded and Society: A Social Science Perspective.* Baltimore; University Park Press.

Farber, B. (1976). "Family process." In N.R. Ellis and N.W. Bray (Eds.) (1986). *International Review of Research in Mental Retardation* 14, 218.

Farber, B. (1986). "Historical contexts of research on families with mentally retarded members." In L. Rowitz (Ed.) (1992). *Mental Retardation in the Year 2000.* New York: Springer-Verlag, p.69.

Farzanch, K.H. (1985). "Impact of retarded children on families in a non-western society." *Dissertation Abstracts International* (1986), 46: 10, 3166-A.

Fehrmann, P.G., Keith, T.Z., and Reimers, T.M. (1987). "Home influence on school learning: direct and indirect effects of parent involvement on high school grades." *Journal of Educational Research* 80, 330-337.

Floyd, F.J. and Zmich, D.E. (1991). "Marriage and the parenting partnership: perceptions and interactions of parents with mentally retarded and typically developing children." *Child Development* 62: 6, 1434-1448.

Ford, J., Mongon, D., and Whelan, M. (1982). "Special education and social control: invisible disaster." In M.C. Wang, M.C. Reynolds, and H.J. Walberg, (Eds.) (1987). *Handbook of Special Education—Research and Practice* Vol. I. Oxford. Pergamon Press, p.8.

Ford, L., Dineen, J., and Hall, J. (1984). "Is there life after placement?" *Education and Training of the Mentally Retarded* 19, 291-296.

Fortier L.M. and Wanlass, R.L. (1984). "Family crisis following the diagnosis of handicapped child." *Family Relations* 33, 13-24.

Friedrich, W.N. and Friedrich, W.L. (1981). "Psychological assets of parents of handicapped and non-handicapped children." *American Journal of Mental Deficiency* 85: 5, 551-553.

Friedrich, W.N., Greenberg, M.T., and Crnick, K. (1983). "A short form of the questionnaire on resources and stress." *American Journal of Mental Deficiency* 88,41-48.

Fulwood, D. (1981). "Mum or Supermum ?" In J. Dobbing, A.D.B. Clarke, J.A. Corbett, J. Hogg, and R.O. Robinson (Eds.) (1985). *Scientific Studies in Mental Retardation.* London: The Royal Society of Medicine and The Macmillan Press Ltd., p. 450.

Fuqua, R.W., Hegland, S.M., and Karas, S.C.(1985). "Processes influencing linkages between pre-school handicap classrooms and home." *Exceptional Children* 51, 307-314.

Gallagher, D., Rappaport, M., Benedict, A.,Lovett, S., Silven, D., and Kramer, H. (1985). *Reliability of Selected Interview and Self-Report Measures with Family Caregivers.* Paper presented at the 38th Annual meeting of the Gerontological Society of America, New Orleans.LA.

Gallagher, J., Beckman,P., and Cross, A. (1983). "Families of handicapped children: sources of stress and its amelioation." *Exceptional Children* 10, 10-19.

Gallagher, J.J. and Bristol, M. (1989). "Families of young handicapped children." In M.C. Wang. M.C. Reynolds, and H.J. Walberg

(Eds.) (1989). *Handbook of Special Education—Research and Practice* Vol. 3. Oxford: Pergamon Press, p. 307.

Gallagher, J.J. (1983). "The Carolina Institute for Research: early educaiton for the handicapped." *Journal of the Division for Early Childhood* 7, 18-24.

Gay L.R.(1990). *Educational Research: Competencies for Analysis and Application* (3rd edn.). New York: Merrill Publishing Co.

Gerber, P.J., Banbury, M.M., Miller, J.H., and Griffin, H.D. (1986). "Special educator's perceptions of parental participation in the individual education plan process." *Psychology in the Schools* 23, 158-163.

German, M.L. and Maisto, A.A.(1982). "The relationship of perceived family support system to the institutional placement of children with mental retardation." *Education and Training of the Mentally Retarded* 17, 17-23.

Glidden, L.M., Valliere, V.N., and Herbert, S.L. (1988). "Adopted children with mental retardation: positive family impact." *Mental Retardation* 25: 3, 122.

Goldstein, S., Strickland, B., Turnbull, A.P., and Curry, L. (1980). "An observational analysis of the IEP conference." *Exceptional Children* 46: 4, 278-286.

Goldstein, S. and Turnbull, A.P. (1982). "The use of two strategies to increase parent participation in the IEP conference." *Exceptional Children* 48: 4, 360-361.

Gomersall, J.D. (1981). "Family psychotherapy and mental handicap." In J. Dobbing, A.D.B. Clarke, J.A. Corbett, J. Hogg, and R.O. Robinson (Eds.) (1985). *Scientific Studies in Mental Retardation*. London: The Royal Society of Medicine and The Macmillan Press Ltd., p. 446.

Goodson, B.D. and Hess, R.D. (1976). "The effects of parent training programmes on child performance and parent behaviour." In J.M. Love and A.V. Biervliet (1984). "Training parents to be home reading tutors: generalisation of children's reading skills from home to school." *The Exceptional Child* 31: 2, 114-127.

Grainger, R.A. (1984). "The participation of parents in local school decision-making." In S. Penney and L. Wilgosh (1995). "Parenting a child with special abilities: a qualitative study of parent-teacher relationships." *International Journal of Special Education* 10: 2,2.

Greenspan, S. and Shoultz, B. (1981). "Why mentally retarded adults lose their jobs: social competence as a factor in work adjustment." *Applied Research in Mental Retardation* 2, 23-38.

Grizzle, K.L. (1993). "Factors influencing school-home communication and parent involvement for children receiving special education services." *Dissertation Abstracts International* (1994), 54: 9, 3328-A.

Gunn, P. and Berry, P. (1990). "Financial costs for home-reared children with Down syndrome: an Australian perspective." In W.I. Fraser (Ed.) (1990). *Key Issues in Mental Retardation Research.* London: Routledge, p. 187.

Gupta, S.C. and Kapoor, V.K. (1973). *Fundamentals of Mathematical Statistics.* New Delhi: Sultan Chand and Co.

Haigh, G. (1977). "Report on the pre-school 'scope' project." In M. Beveridge and A. Jerrams (1981). Parental involvement in language development: an evaluation of a school-based parental assistance plan." *The British Journal of Educational Psychology* 51:3, 259-260.

Hall, C.W. and Richmond, B.O. (1984). "Consultation with parents of handicapped children." *The Exceptional Child* 31:3, 185-191.

Hammer E. (1972). "Families of deaf-blind children: case studies of stress." In T.M. Shea and A.M. Bauer (1985). *Parents and Teachers of Exceptional Students—A Handbook for Involvement.* Boston: Allyn and Bacon, Inc., pp. 41-42.

Hanson, M. (1977). "Teaching your Down's Syndrome infant: a guide for parents." In S.M. Laten (1981). Mothers of Young Handicapped *Children: Their Emotional Responses and Their Perceptions of Needs and Resources.* Microfilm copy of doctoral dissertation. Ann Arbor, Michigan: University Microfilms International.

Hardy, P.G. (1979). "Educational decision-making in special education: parent involvement." *Dissertation Abstracts International* 40: 4, 2000-A.

Hattersley, J., Hosking G.P., Morrow, D., and Myers, M. (1987). *People with Mental Handicap—Perspectives on Intellectual Disability.* London: Faber and Faber Ltd.

Herbert, M. (1985). "Caring for your children: a practical guide." In D. Baker and K. Bavoir (Eds.) (1989). *Making the Special Schools Ordinary ?* Vol.I. London: The Falmer Press, p. 145.

Herstek, F. J. (1985). "A study of three special education Parent Teacher Associations: organisations in transition." *Dissertation Abstracts International* (1986), 46: 9, 2660-2661.

Heyward, W. and Orlansky, M.(1984). "Exceptional children: an introductory survey of special education." In C.R. Reynolds and L. Mann (1987). *Encyclopaedia of Special Education* Vol.2. New York: John Wiley and Sons, p. 1153.

Holland, J. (1981). "The Lancaster Portage Project." *Health Visitor* 54, 486-488.

Hutchison, P. and Lord, J. (1979). "Recreation integration: issues and alternatives in lesiure services and community involvement." In J. Dattilo and S.J. Schleien (1994). "Understanding leisure service for individuals with mental retardation." *Mental Retardation* 32:1, 53-59.

Janis, L.I. (1982). "Decision-making under stress." In G.H.S. Singer, L.K. Irvin and N. Hawkins (1988). "Stress management training for parents of children with severe handicaps." *Mental Retardation* 26:5, 269-277.

Jennings, J. (1987). "Elderly parents as caregivers for adult dependent children." *Social Work* 32, 430-433.

Johnson, M.M. (1982). "Rural families of children receiving special education services—a study of parent knowledge, involvement, and satisfaction." *Disertation Abstracts International* (1983), 43: 9, 2960-A.

Kaczmarek, L. (1985). "Integrating language/communication objectives into the total pre-school curriculum." *Teaching Exceptional Children* 17, 183-189.

Karnes, M.B. and Teska, J.A. (1980). "Toward successful parent involvement in programs for handicapped children." In A.P. Turnbull and H.R. Turbull, III (1982). "Parent involvement in the education of handicapped children: a critique." *Mental Retardation*, 20: 3, 119.

Karnes, M.B., Zehrbach, R.R., and Teska, J.A. (1977). "Involving families of handicapped children." In C.J. Drew, M.L. Hardman,

H.P. Bluhm, and B, Blatt (Eds.) (1977). *Mental Retardation—Social and Educational Perspectives.* Saint Louis: The C.V. Mosby Company, p. 38.

Kazak, A. and Marvin, R. (1984). "Differences, difficulties, and adaptation: stress and social networks in families with a handicapped child." In M.C. Wang, M.C. Reynolds, and H.J. Walberg (Eds.) (1989). *Handbook of Special Education—Research and Practice* Vol.3. Oxford: Pergamon Press, p. 304.

Kibria, G. (1994). "Early intervention of at-risk and developmentally delayed children in the developing countries: myth or reality ?" *International Journal of Special Education* 9:2, 162-169.

Kirk, S., Gallagher, J., and Anastesiew, N. (1993). "Educating exceptional children." In G. Kibria (1994). "Early intervention of at-risk and developmentally delayed children in the developing countries: myth or reality ?" *International Journal of Special Education* 9:2, 167.

Kisanji, J.N. (1993). "Special education in Africa." In M.K. Possi (1994). "Special education in Tanzania: a critical analysis of special education services." *International Journal of Special Education* 9: 1, 46.

Knoblock, P. (1983). "Teaching emotionally disturbed children." In C.R. Reynolds and L. Mann (1987). *Encylopaedia of Special Education* Vol. 2. New York: John Wiley and Sons, p. 153.

Korn, S. and Chess, S., and Fernandez, P. (1978). "The impact of children's physical handicaps on marital quality and family interaction." In R. Lerner and G. Spanier (Eds.) *Child Inferences on Marital and Family Intreraction: A Life-Span Perspective.* New York: Academic Press.

Krauss, M.W. and Mac Eachron, A.E. (1982). "Competitive employment training for mentally retarded adults: the supported work model." *American Journal of Mental Deficiency* 86, 650-653.

Kropf, N.P. (1990). "Stress and social support of parents with an adult mentally retarded child." *Social Work Research and Abstracts,* 26: 4, 83.

Kurtz, P.D. (1983). "Working with the family." In R.M. Smith, J.T. Neisworth, and F.M. Hunt (Eds.) *The Exceptional Child, A. Functional Approach* (2nd edn.). New York: McGraw-Hill, Inc.

Kushlick, A. and Blunder, R. (1974). "The epidemiology of mental subnormality." In A.M. Clarke and A.D.B. Clarke (Eds.). *Mental Deficiency: The Changing Outlook* (3rd edn.). New York: Free Press, pp. 47-65.

Lacoste, R.J. (1978). "Early intervention: can it hurt ?" *Mental Retardation* 16, 266-268.

Lagerkvist, B. (1992). "Community-based rehabilitation for the disabled in the Philippines and Zimbabwe." *Disability and Rehabilitation* 14: 1, 44-50.

Lancioni,G. (1982). "Employment of normal third and fourth grades for training retarded children to solve problems dealing with quantity." *Education and Training of the Mentally Retarded* 17, 93-102.

Langone, J. (1986). *Teaching Retarded Learners.* Boston: Allyn and Bacon, Inc.

Leary, P.M. and Verth, F. (1995). "The effect of mentally retarded child on family functioning in a Third World community." *Early Child Development and Care* 109, 83-88.

Lee, B. (1980). "Materials developed for parent involvement." In T.M. Shea and A.M. Bauer (1985). *Parents and Teachers of Exceptional Students—A Handbook for Involvement.* Boston: Allyn and Bacon, Inc., p. 45.

Lefley, H.P. (1987). "Aging parents as caregivers of mentally ill adult children: an emerging social problem." *Hospital and Community Psychiatry* 38, 1063-1070.

Levenson, C.A. (1994). "Developing parent education course for parents of children with disabilities and/or chronic illness." *Dissertation Abstracts International* (1995), 56: 1, 95-96-A.

Levy-Shiff, R. (1986). "Mother-father-child interactions in families with a mentally retarded young child." *American Journal of Mental Deficiency* 91: 2, 141-149.

Leyser, Y. and Cole, K.B. (1984). "Perceptions of parents of handicaped children about school and parent teacher partnership." *The Exceptional Child* 31: 3, 193-201.

Losen, S.M. and Losen. J.G. (1985). *The Special Education Team.* Boston: Allyn and Bacon, Inc. pp. 58–108.

Love, J.M. and Biervliet, A.V. (1984). "Training parents to be home reading tutors: generalisation of children's reading skills from home to school." *The Exceptional Child* 31: 2, 114-127.

Ludlow, J.R. and Allen, L.M. (1979). "The effect of early intervention and pre-school stimulus on the development of the Down's Syndrome child." *Journal of Mental Deficiency Research* 23, 29-43.

Lusthaus, C. and Lusthaus, E. (1982). "Parents and their involvement in the educational process." *Mental Retardation* 32: 3, 18.

Lusthaus, C.S., Lusthaus, E.W., and Gibbs, H. (1981). "Parent's role in decision process." *Exceptional Children* 48: 3, 256-257.

Lynch, E.W. and Stein, R. (1982). "Perspectives on parent participation in special edcuation." *Exceptional Education Quarterly* 3:2, 56-63.

Maccoby, E.E. and Martin,. J.A. (1983). "Socialisation in the context of the family: parent-child interaction." In W.S. Grolnick and M.L. Slowiaczek (1994). "Parents' involvement in children's schooling: a multidimensional conceptualisation and motivational model." *Child Development* 65, 237-252.

Macfarlane, E.E. (1996). "Reaching reluctant parents." *The Education Digest*, March, 1996, p. 9.

Mare, R. D. (1981). "Change and stability in educational stratification." *American Sociological Review* 46, 72-87.

Margalit, M. and Raviv, A. (1983). "Mothers' perceptions of family climate in families with a retarded child." *The Exceptional Child* 30: 2, 163-169.

Mattson, B. (1977). "Involving parents in special education: did you really reach them ?" *Education and Training of the Mentally Retarded* 12: 4, 358-360.

Mc Dermott, S.W. and Altekruse, J.M. (1994). "Dynamic model for preventing mental retardation in the population: the importance of poverty and deprivation." *Research in Developmental Disabilities* 15: 1, 61.

Mc Kinney, J.D. and Hocutt, A.M. (1982). "Public school involvement of parents of learning disabled children and average achievers." *Exceptional Education Quarterly* 3:2 64-73.

Melton, J.M. (1985). "A qualitative analysis of the effects of the parent-teacher realtionship on parent education behaviour." *Dissertation Abstracts International* (1986), 46: 9, 2643-A.

Meyer, R.J. (1980). "Attitudes of parents of institutionalised mentally retarded individuals toward deinstitutionalisation." *American Journal of Mental Deficiency* 85: 2, 184-187.

Millard, D. (1984). "Daily living with a handicapped child." In D.Baker and K. Bovair (Eds.) (1989). *Making the Special Schools Ordinary ?* Vol.1 London: The Falmer Press, p. 149.

Minikutty, A. (1993). *Involvement of Parents in the Education and Training of Mentally Retarded Children—Perception of Teachers.* Unpublished M. Phil. thesis. School of Behavioural Sciences, Mahatma Gandhi University, Kottayam.

Ministry of Education (1986). "National policy on education." In J. Narayan (1994). "Special education in India." *Action Aid Disability News* 5: 1, 65.

Mithaug, D.E., Horiuchi, C.N., and Fanning, P.N. (1985). "A report on the Colorado statewide follow-up survey of special education students." *Exceptional Children*, 51, 397-404.

Mittler, P. (1979b). "Parents as partners in the education of their handicaped child." In CERI (1983). *The Education of the Handicapped Adolescent—The Transition from School to Working Life.* Paris: Centre for Educational Research and Innovation, pp. 143-144.

Mittler, P., Cheseldine, S., and Mc. Conachie, H. (1983). "The roles and needs of parents of handicapped adolescents." *The Education of the Handicapped Adolescent—The Transition from School to Working Life.* Paris; Centre for Educational Research and Innovation.

Mittler, P., Mittler, H., and Mc Conachie, H. (1986). *Working Together,—Guides for Special Education* No. 2. Paris: UNESCO, pp, 6-12.

Mittler P. and Serpell, R. (1985). "Services for people with intellectual disabilities: an international perspective." In A. Clarke, A.D.B. Clarke, and J. Berg (Eds.). *Mental Deficiency: The Changing Outlook* (4th end.). London: Methuen.

Morgan, D.P. (1982). "Parental participation in the IEP process: does it enhance appropriate education ?" *Exceptional Education Quarterly* 3: 2, 33-40.

Moroney, R.M. (1981). "Public social policy: impact on families with handicapped children." In A.P. Turnbull and H.R. Turnbull (1982). "Parent involvement in the education of handicapped children: a critique." *Mental Retardation* 20:3, 115-122.

Moroney, R.M. (1986). "Family care: toward a responsive society." In J.B. Blacher, R.A. Hanneman, and A.M.B. Rousey (1992). "Out-of-home placement of children with severe handicaps: a comparison of approaches." *American Journal on Mental Retardation* 96: 6, 607.

Morrison, G.S. (1978). "Parent involvement in the home, school, and community." In T.M. Shea and A.M. Bauer (1985). *Parents and Teachers of Exceptional Students—A Handbook for Involvement.* Boston: Allyn and Bacon, Inc., pp. 3-43.

Moulin, L.J. (1984). "Parent participation in IEP development and achievement of educationally handicapped students." *Dissertation Abstracts International* (1985), 46: 4, 949-A.

Myreddi, V. (1992). "Present trends in Mental Handicap in India." *Disabilities and Impairments* 4(2), 5(1&2), 5-14.

Narayan, J. (1994). "Special education in India." *Action Aid Disability News* 5: 1, 65.

Narayan, J. (1994). "New trends in curriculum and instruction." *Update in Mental Retardation.* Secunderabad : NIMH.

National Committee for Citizens in Education (1979). "Unpublished manuscript serving as basis for congressional testimony." In A.P. Turnbull and H.R. Turnbull, III (1982). "Parent involvement in the education of handicapped children : a critique." *Mental Retardation* 20 : 3, 116.

NCERT (1987). *Project Integrated Education for the Disabled—A Document.* New Delhi : NCERT.

Newson, E. and Hipgrave, T. (1982). "Getting through to your handicapped child." In D. Baker and K. Bovair (Eds.) (1989). *Making The Special Schools Ordinary* ? Vol. I. London : The Falmer Press, p. 145.

NIMH (1994). *Mental Retardation in India : Contemporary Scene.* Secunderabad : National Institute for the Mentally Handicapped.

NIMH (1995). "The Persons with Disabilities (Equal Opportunities, Protection of Rights and Full Participation) Act, 1995." *Karavalamban* 8, 1–26.

O'Connell, D.A.G. (1992). "Training parents in the evaluation of the individualised education plan process." *Dissertation Abstracts International* 53: 2, 464-465-A.

O'Meara, T.A. (1994). "Elementary school principles; a rationale for understanding, utilising, and nurturing family and community resources to develop parent involvement programs." *Dissertation Abstracts International* 55: 4, 823-A.

Ora, J. (1973). "Involvement and training of parents and citizen workers in early education for the handicapped." In C.T. Ramey and P.L. Trohanis (Eds.) (1982). *Finding and Educating High-Risk and Handicapped Infants.* Baltimore; University Park Press, p. 153.

O'Reilly, C.A. III and Weitz, B.A. (1980). "Managing Marginal employees: the use of warnings and dismissals." *Administrative Science Quarterly* 25, 467-484.

O'Toole, B. (1990a). "Community-based rehabilitation: the Guyana evaluation project." In D. Buchner (1994). "Community based rehabilitation: issues and considerations for providing rehabilitation services in developing countries." *International Journal of Special Education* 9:2, 113.

O'Toole, B. (1990b). "Step by step—a community based rehabilitation project with disabled children in Guyana." In D. Buchner (1994). "Community based rehabilitation: issues and considerations for providing rehabilitation services in developing countries." *International Journal of Special Education* 9: 2, 113.

Pandit, A.S. (1987). "Assessing the relevance and effect of training rural-based parents from Wai Taluka to manage and educate their mentally retarded children." In M.B. Buch (Ed.) (1991). *IV Survey of Research in Education* Vol. II, p. 1323.

Paul, J.L. and Warnock, N.J. (1980). "Special education: a changing field." *The Exceptional Child* 27: 1, 3-28.

Peshwaria, R. and Venkatesan, S. (1992). *Behavioural Approach in Teaching Mentally Retarded Children—A Manual for Teachers.* Secunderabad: NIMH.

Peshwaria, R. (1994). "Meeting counselling needs of parents having children with disabilities." *Update in Mental Retardation.* Secunderabad: NIMH.

Pillay, A.N. (1984). "A comparison of the perception of inservice needs of teachers of mentally retarded children as perceived by their parents and teachers." *Dissertation Abstracts International* (1985), 46:4, 950-A.

Pink, W.T.(1982). "School effects, academic performance, and school crime." In M.C. Wang, M.C. Reynolds, and H.J. Walberg, (Eds.) (1987). *Handbook of Special Education: Research and Practice* Vol. I. Oxford: Pergamon Press, p.8.

Piper, M.C. and Pless, I.B. (1980). "Early intervention for infants with Down syndrome: a controlled trial." *Pediatrics* 65, 463-468.

Polifka, J.C. (1981). "Compliance with Public Law 94-142 and consumer satisfaction." *Exceptional Children* 48: 3, 250-253.

Polloway, E.A. and Smith. J.D. (1983). "Changes in mild mental retardation: population, programs, and perspectives." *Exceptional Children* 50, 149-159.

Powell, T.H. and Ogle, P.A. (1985). "Brothers and sisters: a special part of exceptional families." In C.R. Reynolds and L. Mann (Eds.) (1987). *Encyclopaedia of Special Education* Vol. 2. New York: John Wiley and Sons, pp. 1151-1152.

Prabhu, G.G. (1977). *Research in the Field of Mental Retardation.* Proceedings of the Third Asian Conference on Mental Retardation. New Delhi: Federation for the Welfare of the Mentally Retarded, p.43.

Preetha Rajam, R. V. (1987). *A Study of the Problems of the Parents of the Mentally Retarded Children in the Institutions in Kerala.* Unpublished M. Ed. thesis, University of Kerala, Trivandrum.

Pulkkinen, L. (1982). "Self-control and continuity from childhood to adolescence." In P.B. Baltes and O.G. Brim (Eds.). *Life Span Development and Behaviour* Vol.4. New York; Academic Press, pp. 63-105.

Quick, J.B. (1993). "A conceptual model to assist elementary principals enhance parental involvement." *Dissertation Abstracts International* (1995), 55: 10, 3057-A.

RCI (1996). *Report on Manpower Development*. New Delhi; Ministry of Welfare.

Reddi, V.S., (1994). "Family's involvement in special education programmes." *Update in Mental Retardation. Secunderabad*: NIMH, p. 20.

Rees, S. and Emerson, A. (1983). "The costs of caring for disabled children at home." *Australian Rehabilitation Review* 7, 26-31.

Reisinger. J.J., Ora, J.P., and Frangia, G.W. (1970). "Parents as change agents for their children: a review." *Journal of Community Psychology* 4, 108-123.

Reynolds, A.J. (1989). "A structural model of first grade outcomes for an urban, low socio-economic status, minority population." *Journal of Educational Psychology* 81, 594-603.

Robert, A. (1994). "The relationship between family-centred school practices and parental involvement in early childhood programmes for children with and without disbailities." *Dissertation Abstracts International* 54: 10, 3670-A.

Robinson, H.B. and Robinson, N.M. (1965). *The Mentally Retarded Child—A Psychological Approach*. New York: McGraw-Hill Book Co., pp. 61-62.

Robinson, J.M. (1994). "Special education teachers' perceptions of parent participation at the IEP conference within inclusive education,." *Dissertation Abstracts International* 55:8, 2240-A.

Roos, P.R. (1983). "Advocate groups." In C.R. Reynolds and L. Mann (Eds.) (1987). *Encylopedia of Special Education* Vol. I. New York: John Wiley and Sons, p. 50.

Rosenberg, S. (1977). *Family and Parent Variables Affected Outcomes of a Parent-Mediated Intervention*. Unpublished doctoral dissertation. Nashville, Tenn.: George Peabody College, p. 154.

Rusch, F.R. and Mithaug, D.E. (1980). "Vocational training for mentally retarded adults; a behavioural analytic approach." In N.R. Ellis and N.W. Bray (Eds.) (1986). *International Review of Research in Mental Retardataion* Vol. 14. New York: Academic Press. p. 226.

Russell, P. (1986). "Parents as partners: the changing scene." In D. Baker and K. Bovair (Eds.) (1989). *Making the Special Schools Ordinary?* Vol.I. London: The Falmer Press, p. 149.

Rynders, J. and Schleien, S. (1988). "Recreation: a promising vehicle for promoting the community integration of young adults with Down's syndorme." In J. Dattilo and S.J. Schleien (1994). "Understanding leisure services for indiviudals with mental retardation." *Mental Retardation* 32: 1, 53-59.

Rynders, J. and Schleien, S. (1991). "Together successfully creating recreational and educational programmes that integrate people with and without disabilities." In J. Dattilo and S.J. Schleien (1994). "Understanding leisure services for individuals with mental retardation." *Mental Retardation* 32: 1, 53-59.

Sanders, M.R. and Glynn, T. (1981). "Training parents in behavioural self-management: an analysis of generalisation and maintenance." *Journal of Applied Behaviour Analysis* 14, 223-237.

Sandow, S.A. and Clarke, A.D.B., Cox, M.V., and Stewart, F.L. (1981). "Home intervention with parents of severely subnormal pre-school children: a final report." *Child: Care, Health, and Development* 7, 135-144.

Scanlon, C.A., Arick, J., and Phelps, N. (1981). "Participation in the development of the IEP: parents' perspective." *Exceptional Children* 47: 5, 373-374.

Schaefer, E.S. (1976). "Parent-professional-child interactions and involvement." In C.T. Ramey and P.L. Trohanis (Eds.) (1982). *Finding and Educating High-Risk and Handicapped Infants.* Baltimore: University Park Press, p. 153.

Schafler, M. (1980). "Individualised educational programmes in a school for the handicapped." *Social Work in Education* 3: 1, 32-43.

Schilling, R.F., Gilchrist, L.D., and Schinke, S.P. (1984). "Coping and social support in families of developmentally disabled children." *Family Relations* 33, 47-54.

Schleien, S., Olson, K., Rogers, N., and McLafferty, M. (1985). "Integrating children with severe handicaps into recreation and physical education programmes." In J. Dattilo and S.J. Schleien (1994). "Understanding leisure services for individuals with mental retardation." *Mental Retardation* 32: 1, 53-59.

Schneider, J. (1983). "The nature of loss, the nature of grief. A comprehensive model for facilitation and understanding." In

E.C. Lynch and N.H. Staloch (1988). "Parental perceptions of physicians' communication in the informing process." *Mental Retardation* 26: 2, 77-81.

Schreibman, L., O'Neill, R.E., and Koegel, R.L. (1983). "Behavioural training for siblings of autistic children." *Journal of Applied Behaviour Analysis* 16, 129-138.

Schutz,. R.P. and Rusch, F.R. (1982). "Competitive employment: toward employment integration for mentally retarded person." In N.R. Ellis and N.W. Bray (Eds.) (1986). *International Review of Research in Mental Retardation* Vol. 14. New York: Academic Press, p. 226.

Scott, K.G. and Carran, D.T. (1989). "Identification and referral of handicapped infants." In M.C. Wang, M.C. Reynolds, and H.J.Walberg (Eds.). *Handbook of Special Education—Research and Practice* Vol. 3. Oxford: Pergamon Press, p. 238.

Seltzer, G.B., Begun, A.L., Seltzer, M.M., and Krauss, M.W. (1991). "Adults with mental retardation and their aging mothers: impact of siblings." *Family Relations* 40, 310-317.

Seltzer, M.M. (1985). "Informal supports for aging mentally retarded persons." *American Journal of Mental Deficiency* 90, 259-265.

Seltzer, M.M. and Krauss, M.W. (1989a). "Aging parents with mentally retarded children: family risk factors and sources of support." *American Journal on Mental Retardation* 94, 303-312.

Sen, A. (1992). *Mental Handicap Among Rural Indian Children*. New Delhi: Sage Publications.

Shea, T.M. and Bauer, A.M. (1985). *Parents and Teachers of Exceptional Students-A Handbook for Involvement*. Boston: Allyn and Bacon, Inc., pp. 44-175.

Shellady,S.M. (1994). "School administrator, special education teacher, general education teacher, support staff, parent, and student perceptions of the IEP process." *Dissertation Abstracts International* 56: 4, 1316-A.

Simeonsson, R.J. and Bailey, D.B. (1986). "Siblings of handicapped children." In L. Rowitz (Ed.) (1992). *Mental Retardation in the Year 2000*. New York: Springer-Verlag, p. 95.

Simeonsson, R.J. and McHale, S.M. (1981). "Review; research on handicapped children: sibling relationship." *Child: Care, Health, and Development* 7, 153-171.

Simpson, R.L. (1982). "Future training issues." *Exceptional Education Quarterly* 3:2, 81-88.

Singer, J.D. and Butler, J.A. (1987). "The education of all handicapped children act: schools as agents of social reform." *Harward Educational Review* 57, 125-152.

Smeenge, M., Page, T., Iwata, B., and Ivancic, M. (1980). "Teaching measurement skills to mentally retarded students: training, generalisation and follow-up." *Education and Training of the Mentally Retarded* 15, 224-229.

Sowers, J., Rusch, F.R., Connis, R., and Cummings, L. (1980). "Teaching mentally retarded adults to time manage in a vocational setting." *Journal of Applied Behaviour Analysis* 13, 119-128.

Stainback, S., Stainback, W., and Maurer, S. (1976). "Training teachers for the severely and profoundly handicapped; a new frontier." *Exceptional Children* 42: 4, 203-209.

Stanhope, L. and Bell, R.Q. (1981). "Parents and families." In J.M. Kauffman and D.P. Hallahan (Eds.) (1981). *Handbook of Special Education*. New Jersey; Prentice-Hall, Inc., p. 689.

Steel, R.G.D. and Torrie, J.H. (1980). *Principles and Procedures of Statistics* (2nd edn.) London; McGraw-Hill Book Co.

Steinberg. L.R. (1983). "Facilitation of parent role in programme planning for handicapped children." *Dissertation Abstracts International* (1984), 44: 11, 3358-A.

Stone, K. (1987). "The statementing process, professional power, and parenting interests." In D. Baker and K. Bovair (Eds.) (1989). *Making the Special Schools Ordinary*? Vol.I. London: The Falmer Press, p. 141.

Strickland, B.B. and Turnbull, A.P. (1990). *Developing and Implementing Individualised Education Programmes* (3rd edn.) London: Merrill Publishing Co., pp. 26-193.

Strobino, J.D.S.W. (1984). "Parents' decision about residential placement for their children who are mentally retarded." *Dissertation Abstracts International* 45: 3, 951-A.

Sukumaran, P.S. (1986). *A study of the Family Environment of the Mentally Retarded Children*. Unpublished M. Ed. thesis. University of Kerala, Trivandrum.

Tausig, M. (1985). "Factors in family decision-making about placement for developmentally disabled individuals." *American Journal of Mental Deficiency* 89, 352-361.

Thorne, G.B. (1993). "Parent involvement in the schools: a new paradigm for preservice and inservice education of teachers and administrators." *Dissertation Abstracts International* (1994), 54: 7, 2543-A.

Thressiakutty, A.T. (1994). "Community referenced approach in vocational training and employment." *Update in Mental Retardation.* Secunderabad: NIMH p.66.

Tizard, B. (1977). "Parental Involvement in nursery education." In M. Beveridge and A. Jerrams (1981). "Parental involvement in language development: an evaluaion of a school based parental assistance plan." *The British Journal of Educational Psychology* 51:3, 259-260.

Tomlinson, S. (1981). *Educational Subnormality—A Study in Decision-Making.* London: Routledge and Kegan Paul.

Tomlinson, S. (1982). *A Sociology of Special Education.* London: Routledge and Kegan Paul.

Topping, K. (1986). "Parents as educators." In D. Baker and K. Bovair (Eds.) (1989). *Making the Special Schools Ordinary ?* Vol. I. London: The Falmer Press, p. 139.

Topping, K. and Wolfendale, S. (Eds.) (1985). "Parental involvement in children's reading." In D. Baker and K. Bovair (Eds.) (1989). *Making the Special Schools Ordinary* ? Vol.I. London: The Falmer Press, p. 139.

Townsend, A., Noelker, L., Deimling, G., and Bass, D. (1989). "Longitudinal impact of interhousehold caregiving on adult children's mental health." *Psychology and Aging* 4, 393-401.

Tse, J.W.L. (1991). "Directions in the field of mental retardation in the 1990s: as Asian perspective." *International Social Work* 34: 4, 339-352.

Turnbull, A.P. (1983). "Parent-professional interactions." In J. Yanok and D. Derubertis (1989). "Comparartive study of parental participation in regular and special education programmes." *Exceptional Children* 56: 3, 195.

Turnbull, A.P. and Behr, S.K. (1986). *Positive Contributions that persons with Mental Retardation Make to Their Families.* Paper presented at the Annual Meeting of the American Association on Mental Deficiency, Denver.

Turnbull, A.P. and Turnhull, H.R. III (1982). "Parent involvement in the education of handicapped children: a critque." *Mental Retardation* 20:3, 119.

Turnbull A.P. and Turnbull H.R. (1985). *Stepping Back from Early Intervention. An Ethical Perspective.* Paper presented at the DEC/CEC Early Childhod Conference, Denver.

Turnbull, H.R. and Turnbull, A.P. (1978). "Free appropriate public education: Law and implementation." In M.C. Wang, M.C. Reynolds, and H.J. Walberg (Eds.) (1989). *Handbook of Special Education—Research and Practice* Vol. 3. Oxford: Pergamon Press, p. 295.

Turnbull, K.K. and Hughes, D.L. (1987). "A pragmatic analysis of speech and language IEP conference." In B.B. Strickland and A.P. Turnbull (1990). *Developing and Implementing Individualised Education Programmes* (3rd edn.) London: Merrill Publishing Co., p. 173.

Turner, A.L. (1980). "Therapy with families of a mentally retarded child." *Journal of Marital and Family Therapy* 6, 167-170.

Tymchuk, A.J. (1983). "Interventions with parents of the mentally retarded." In J.L. Matson and J.A. Mulick (Eds.) (1983). *Handbook of Mental Retardation.* New York: Pergamon Press, p. 372.

UNESCO (1995). *Review of the Present Situation in Special Needs Education.* Paris: UNESCO.

US Department of Education (Office of Special Education and Rehabilitation Services (1987). "Ninth Annual Report to Congress on the Implementation of the Education of the Handicapped Act." In B.B. Strickland and A.P. Trunbull (1990). *Developing and Implementing Individualised Education Programmes* (3rd edn.). London: Merrill Publishing Co., p. 173.

Vadasy, P., Fewell, R., Meyer, D., and Schell, G. (1984). "Siblings of handicapped children: a developmental persepctive on family interactions." *Family Relations* 33, 155-167.

Varma, V.K., Verma, S.K., and Kapoor, P. (1992). "Evaluation of a home care programme for the mentally retarded children through training of the mother." *Indian Journal of Medical Research* 96, 29-36.

Vaughan, S. Bos., C.S., Harrell, J.E,. and Lasky, B.A. (1988). "Parent participation in the initial placement/IEP conference ten years after mandated involvement." *Journal of Learning Disabilities* 21, 82-89.

Vincent, L.J., Laten. S., Salisbury, C., Brown. P., and Baumgart, D. (1981). "Family involvement in the educational processes of severely handicapped students: state of the art and directions for the future." In M.C. Wang, M. C. Reynolds, and H.J. Walberg (Eds.) (1987). *Handbook of Special Education—Research and Practice* Vol. I. Oxford: Pergamon Press, pp. 280-286.

Walls, R.T., Sienicki, D.H., and Crist, K. (1981). "Operation training in vocational skills." *American Journal of Mental Deficiency* 85, 357-367.

Wehman, P. (1981). "Competitive employment: new horizons for severely disabled individuals." In N.R. Ellis and N.W. Bray (Eds.) (1986). *International Review of Research in Mental Retardation* Vol. 14. New York: Academic Press, p. 226.

Wehman, P. and Hill, J.W. (1981). "Competitive employment for moderately and severely handicapped individuals." *Exceptional Children* 47, 338-345.

Wehman, P., Hill, M., Goodall, P., Cleveland, P., Brooke, V., and Pentecoste, J. H. Jr. (1982). "Job placement and follow-up of moderately and severely handicapped indiviudals after three years." *Journal of the Association for the Severely Handicapped* 7, 5-16.

Wehman, P. and Schleien, S. (1981). "Leisure programmes for handicapped persons: adaptations techniques, and curriculum," In J. Dattilo and S.J. Schleien (1994). "Understanding lesiure services for individuals with mental retardation." *Mental Retardation* 32: 1, 53-59.

Weigerink, R. and Hocutt, A. (1979). "The policy perspective: congruence between the policy of parent involvement and its implementation." In C.T. Ramey and P.L. Trohanis (Eds.)

(1982). *Finding and Educating High-Risk and Handicapped Infants.* Baltimore: University Park Press, p. 153.

Weinger S. (1992). "Perceptions of siblings of mentally retarded children compared with parental perceptions and severity." *Dissertation Abstracts International* 53: 10, 3677-A.

Wells, M.K. (1994). "The relationship of parent involvement to parent knowledge of legal provisions regarding special education." *Dissertation Abstracts International* 56: 4, 1317-A.

Westmacott, E.V.S. and Cameron, R.J. (1981). "Behaviour can change." In D. Baker and K. Bovair (Eds.) (1989). *Making the Special Schools Ordinary ?* Vol.I. London: The Falmer Press, p. 145.

White, R. and Calhoun, M.L. (1987). "From referral to placement: teachers' perceptions of their responsibilities." *Exceptional Children* 53, 460-468.

Whitman, T.L., Scibak, J.W., and Reid, D.H. (1983). *Behaviour Modification with the Severely and Profoundly Retarded: Research and Application.* New York: Academic Press.

Wikler L. (1981). "Chronic stresses of families of mentally retarded children." *Family Relations* 30, 281-288.

Wikler, L. (1986). "Family stress theory and research on families of children with mental retardation." In J.J. Gallagher and P.M. Vietze (Eds.) *Families of Handicapped Persons: Research, Programmes, and Policy Issues.* Baltimore, MD: Brookes, pp. 167-195.

Wikler, L. and Keenan, M.P. (Eds.) (1987). "Developmental disabilities: no longer a private tragedy." In C.R. Reynolds and L. Mann (Eds.).(1987). *Encyclopedia of Special Education* Vol.2. New York: John Wiley and Sons, pp. 1151-1152.

Wikler, L., Wasow, M., and Hatfield, E. (1981). "Chronic sorrow revisited: parents Vs. professional depiction of the adjustment of parents of mentally retarded children." *American Journal of Orthopsychiatry* 51, 63-70.

Wilgosh, L. (1990). "Issues in education and daily living for families of children with disabilities." In S. Penney and L. Wilgosh (1995). "Parenting a child with special abilities: a qualitative study of parent teacher relationships." *International Journal of Special Education* 10: 2, 2.

Winer, M.E. (1982). "Parental involvement in special education decision-making: access and alienation." *Dissertation abstracts International* 43: 4, 1116-1117-A.

Winton, P. and Turnbull, A.P. (1981). "Parent involvement as viewed by parents of pre-school handicpped children." *Topics in Early Childhood Special Education* 1:3, 11-19.

Wolfendable, S. (1987c). "Primary schools and special needs; policy, planning, and provison." In D. Baker and K. Bovair (Eds.) (1989). *Making the Special Schools Ordinary* ? Vol.1. London: The Falmer press, p. 149.

Wolfensberger, W.A. (1978). "A multi-component advocacy protection scheme." In T.M. Shea and A.M. Bauer (1985). *Parents and Teachers of Exceptional Students—A Handbook for Involvement.* Boston: Allyn and Bacon, Inc., p. 67.

Wright, L.S. (1976). "Chronic grief: The anguish of being an exceptional parent." *The Exceptional Child* 23:3, 160-169.

Yamilkoski, V.J. (1983). "Profesional's perceptions concerning the role of the parent and their own role in involving parents in the IEP process." *Dissertation Abstracts International* 44:5, 1424-A.

Yanok, J. and Derubertis, D. (1989). "Comparative study of parental participation in regular and special education programmes." *Exceptional Children* 56: 3, 195.

Ysseldyke, J.E., Algozzine, B., and Richey, L. (1982). "Judgement under uncertainty; how many children are handicaped ?" *Exceptional Children* 48, 531-534.

Zarit, S., Reever, K., and Bach-Peterson, J. (1980). "Relatives of the impaired elderly: Correlates of feelings of burden." In L. Rowitz (Ed.) (1992). *Mental Retardation in the Year 2000.* New York: Springer-Verlag, p. 94.

Zetlin, A. (1986). "Mentally retarded adults and their siblings." *American Journal of Mental Deficiency* 91, 217-225.

Zigler, E. (1981). "A plea to end the use of the patterning treatment for retarded children." *American Journal of Orthopsychiatry* 51, 388-390.

Index